D0480452

THE GROWTH OF GARDENS

By the same author

Richard Gorer

MULTI-SEASON SHRUBS AND TREES

Thomas Rochford and Richard Gorer

THE ROCHFORD BOOK OF FLOWERING POT PLANTS
THE ROCHFORD BOOK OF HOUSE PLANTS
ROCHFORD'S HOUSE-PLANTS FOR EVERYONE

THE GROWTH OF GARDENS

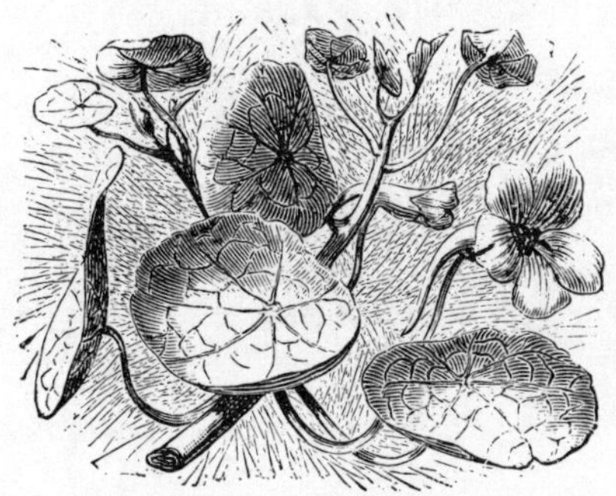

RICHARD GORER

London FABER AND FABER *Boston*

First published in 1978
by Faber and Faber Limited
3 Queen Square London WC1
Photoset in VIP Sabon by
Western Printing Services Ltd, Bristol
and printed in Great Britain by
Redwood Burn Ltd, Trowbridge & Esher

British Library Cataloguing in Publication Data

Gorer, Richard
The growth of gardens.
1. Gardens – History
I. Title
635.9′09 SB451

ISBN 0–571–10757–5

Contents

ACKNOWLEDGEMENTS

I would like to thank the British Museum (Natural History) for permission to quote from the Journals of Allan Cunningham;

Dr Brian Morley of the Botanic Garden, Glasnevin, for information about the sendings of Tweedie and Madden to that garden;

Lady Scott for the loan of the 1909 catalogue of Messrs Forbes of Hawick;

Peter Hunt for the loan of Messrs Gauntlett's catalogue and for many useful articles of information.

My greatest debt of gratitude is owed to John Harvey who not only lent me many items, but who also had the kindness to read through the typescript, which has resulted in a marked diminution of mistakes.

All quotations are transcribed literally, except that, where necessary, botanical names have been altered to agree with contemporary taxonomy. For example, in the quotation on page 130 I have altered the more or less incomprehensible *Hemimeris* to *Alonsoa*.

INTRODUCTION

If in spring you walk around any place where there are gardens, you will be in no way amazed to see forsythia, flowering currant, the purple-leaved *Prunus* 'Pissardii', amelanchier, *Berberis darwinii* and a 'Kanzan' cherry. Now the forsythia comes from China, the flowering currant from western U.S.A., the *Prunus* 'Pissardii' from Iran, the amelanchier from the eastern U.S.A., the berberis from Chile and the cherry from Japan, yet here they all are growing happily in Thames Ditton or in Norwich. This cultivation of exotic plants in gardens has been going on for about 500 years in western Europe and subsequently in North America, but someone has to find the plants in various parts of the globe and get them back to western Europe and there they have to be raised, either by amateur gardeners or by nurserymen, and proved to be suitable for easy cultivation.

One of the purposes of this book is to examine who collected these plants originally and how they were discovered. This, however, is only one aspect of what we should be looking at. The design of gardens depends on a number of factors, such as the amount of land available, the amount of man-power that is available to the owner of the garden, the prevailing taste of the time and, finally, the material available. It can be shown that the design is largely affected by this last consideration. Take, for example, the plants I mentioned in my opening sentence; 200 years ago the only one that anyone could have had in their gardens was the amelanchier, which John Bartram had sent over before 1746. Of the other plants, the first forsythia arrived in cultivation in 1833, although the one in gardens is more likely to be *F. viridissima*, which Fortune brought from China in 1844; *Berberis darwinii* was brought over by William Lobb in 1849. The flowering currant, *Ribes sanguinem*, first arrived in this country in 1820 (or, according to Loudon, 1817) although it was barely in cultivation until David Douglas sent it back in 1826. The prunus was brought back from the Shah's garden by his gardener, M. Pissart, in 1880, while the 'Kanzan' cherry arrived in the early years of this century, although the first of these Japanese cherries was 'Fugenzo', brought over by Sir Harry Veitch from Japan in 1892.

Obviously, if the plants had not been introduced to cultivation people could not have grown them and even a hundred years ago the Japanese cherry and *Prunus* 'Pissardii' were still unknown. Some other introductions are almost more surprising. Although privet hedges have been known since the sixteenth century the privet used was our native *Ligustrum vulgare*. Modern privet hedges are made from the Japanese *L. ovalifolium*, with smaller leaves and a neater habit and this has only been in cultivation since around 1885: another popular hedging plant, *Lonicera nitida*, was brought from China by E. H. Wilson as recently as 1908. So we can see that even the least regarded parts of the garden have been continually changing.

In the case of the plants mentioned at the beginning we were able in the main to say who had introduced the plants to cultivation for the first time, but this is by no means invariably the case, and the facts are often unknown even to people living shortly after the event. J. C. Loudon in his massive *Arboretum et Fruticetum*, which appeared during the eighteen-thirties, when writing of the numerous introductions towards the end of the eighteenth century, commented 'It is somewhat remarkable that of such a number of species introduced ... the names of so few of the introducers should be known; but it must be recollected that the means of introducing were, at this period, principally by packets of seeds sent to the nurserymen by correspondents, or by amateurs; and that, as several years must necessarily elapse between the period of introduction, and that of flowering and naming, the name of the collector who sent the seeds or of the nurseryman who first raised plants from them, is forgotten, or ceases to be of the same interest. The case is different when living plants are brought into the country, and it is, in truth, chiefly of the introducers of such that the names are known.' This is certainly true.

The role of the amateur in plant introductions may be important, but usually the professional has to get in somewhere before the new plants can become widespread. In the early years of the nineteenth century the botanical magazines were full of paintings of South African and South

American bulbous plants that were grown by Mr William Griffin of Lambeth, whose name has been honoured in the amaryllidaceous genus *Griffinia*. He appears to have been enthusiastic and a brilliant cultivator, but he does not seem to have been interested in propagating his plants and very few have been in general cultivation at any time, although many would seem to merit this. It was all right for the anonymous amateur to send his seeds or plants to Kennedy and Lee, or to Loddiges, as they were professional nurserymen who would, if the plants seemed to them to be worthy, not only cultivate, but also propagate the plants.

In the nineteenth century there was a great deal of one-upmanship among the great gardeners. The Duke of Devonshire, with his enthusiastic gardener, Paxton, sent one of his gardeners to India to collect principally the very rare *Amherstia nobilis* and he was highly mortified when Mrs Lawrence of Ealing succeeded in flowering it before he did. However, he was able to get his glory by being the first to flower the huge water-lily, *Victoria amazonica*. None of these plants were suitable subjects for amateurs to grow, but some of the other plants brought back from India with the amherstia by the gardener, John Gibson, such as *Rhododendron formosum* and various orchids, have entered into general distribution, although it is doubtful if the plants descend from Gibson's collecting. No doubt the Duke did distribute some plants to his particular friends and possibly the Horticultural Society (not yet Royal), in which he was interested, may have received some plants, but it seems more likely that the plants now available descend from later collections.

The eighteenth and first half of the nineteenth centuries could show many gardeners who either sent out their own collectors or who took shares in paying a collector's fees in exchange for a share in the proceeds, but it was not until the eighteen-forties that it became financially worthwhile for a nurseryman to send out a collector on his own behalf. There seem to be a couple of exceptions to this in that Kennedy and Lee, together with Sir Joseph Banks, sent David Burton to collect plants in New South Wales, while apparently Francis Henchman, who seems to have been a sort of sleeping partner in the firm of Mackay, sent William Baxter to Australia in 1823–5. Baxter was in Australia again from 1829 to 1832 and the nurseryman Joseph Knight is said to have bought his sendings for £1,500—a quite extraordinarily high sum for those days and one that shows how lucrative the nursery trade must have become. Indeed, during the later eighteen-thirties and into the eighteen-forties James Drummond seems to have made a considerable income in sending to a number of nurserymen seeds from the mainly unexplored and floristically rich Western Australia. After these dates a number of the larger nurserymen sent out collectors, but none so much as the firm of Veitch, whose collectors visited nearly every continent of the globe.

Europe was an exception; presumably it was thought to have been well covered, and nothing appears to have been thought of Western Asia.

It was through the efforts of these systematic collectors that most of the plants we know were introduced to cultivation, although the amateur could (and still can) make his contribution, provided that his seeds were obtained by a professional propagator and not buried in some fortunate recipient's garden. During the eighteenth century most collectors were financed by a syndicate of rich enthusiasts or by the Crown. The Kew collectors, Masson, Kerr, Bowie, Cunningham, Hove, David Nelson, etc., although they received their instructions from Sir Joseph Banks, had their salaries paid from the Privy Purse. It was this fact that made the distribution of surplus plants rather difficult. It was obviously unthinkable that the Crown could engage in commerce and it was scarcely possible for his employees, however distinguished, to give the King's plants away. The only possibility seemed to be exchange and a number of Kew plants were obtained by Kennedy and Lee, presumably in exchange for plants that they had obtained and which Kew had not. Kew also received plants from Loddiges and presumably they, too, were recompensed, but a number of plants that were received by Kew had to be re-collected in later years owing to the inability of the employees to distribute surplus goods or plants.

This became serious from 1815 onwards, when both Banks and Aiton were becoming old and infirm and many of the results of their collections from Brazil, Australia and South Africa were so mismanaged that very few plants were preserved. In his *Records of the Royal Botanic Gardens at Kew* (1880) the erstwhile Curator, John Smith, writes that when he first went to Kew in 1822, he saw the collection of orchids sent back from Brazil by Bowie and Cunningham 'potted in common soil' and left near unshaded glass, with the inevitable result that 'they were in a deplorable state, dead or dying.' We have Cunningham's journal of this expedition, so we know that at least 500 different packets of seed were sent back to Kew, but many of these seem to have come to nought.

It is obviously undesirable that a single institution, even if it is in good hands, should have the sole handling of a collector's sendings, and the modern system whereby an expedition is financed by a number of subscribers, which will include commercial firms, botanical institutions and private individuals, may well ensure that more of the sendings are brought into cultivation, but it would obviously have been asking too much for a nursery firm or a botanical instititution which had financed the expedition not to have required that they had the sole rights. So far as we know this seems to have worked reasonably well, with the sole exception of Kew, in the last years of the first decade and the second decade of the nineteenth century, but of course we do not know how many sendings from the collectors of Veitch, Low, William Bull and others failed to get into cultivation.

It is evident that the gradual introduction of exotic plants into cultivation could, on occasion, effectively alter the design and planting of gardens and it will be one of the objects of this book to chart both the significant introductions and their effect on garden planting and design. There remains, however, one other factor to take into consideration. Let us return to our suburban gardens. In addition to the plants already mentioned, there may well be a magnolia. This will be *Magnolia* x *soulangiana* which has never been found growing wild anywhere. It is, in fact, a hybrid between two Chinese magnolias, *M. denudata* and *M. liliiflora*. Hybrids often have considerable horticultural advantages over the pure species, partly owing to the unusual vigour of many of them, and partly owing to what may well be a concomitant of this, greater floriferousness. This magnolia happened by chance. Monsieur Soulange-Bodin was a keen gardener and grew both the parent species in his garden; an adventurous insect effected cross-pollination, and the original *M.* x *soulangiana* was the result. Such accidental crosses continually happen in gardens, but nowadays most hybrids are created deliberately.

This interest in the crossing of different species started to be generally applied around 1830 and has continued to this day. Generally speaking the true species have more graceful and attractive flowers, or so we think today, but during the nineteenth century (and to a certain extent even nowadays) most gardeners wanted large and bright flowers, and these the hybridist could produce. The result is that in some cases gardeners no longer know what the original species look like. The bedding verbena is the product of four species, none of which are now in general cultivation; the modern petunia is a hybrid between two species, the modern schizanthus a hybrid of perhaps three species; the main parents of the large-flowered clematis are no longer to be found in gardens. In fact, such original species are not to be found even in Botanic Gardens, which, one would have thought, have a duty to preserve such plants in cultivation. This may well prove regrettable.

The recent expedition of Watson, Cheese and Beckett to the Chilean Andes has brought back into cultivation the original schizanthus species, which are seen to have many charms that the hybrids lack (but they are somewhat more difficult to cultivate), and it may well be found that other original, now lost, species would prove equally attractive. This, however, is irrelevant. The point I want to make is that plant introductions can have two results. They can not only provide valuable garden plants, but they can also provide parents for hybrids, which may, in their turn, affect the design of the garden. It is often possible by hybridisation, to get the qualities of tender species transferred to hardy hybrids and, indeed, it was the desire to do this that created the first hardy rhododendron hybrids, which I suppose have changed the outlines of gardens to a greater extent than any other single development in the last two centuries. Thus the influence of plant introductions is twofold. Plants may be introduced that are attractive in themselves or, should they prove somewhat difficult in cultivation, their attractive characters may be preserved by means of hybridisation. Of course a lot of unnecessary hybridisation takes place, but time will eventually winnow the grain from the chaff.

There is one further aspect which may be briefly mentioned. If popular plants are grown in large numbers, variants are almost sure to appear from time to time. In the wild, such plants may be dysgenic and will eventually perish: one thinks particularly of double flowers, where the stamens of pistil have become petaloid. Under cultivation, such plants can be preserved, so that eventually, as a result of continual selection, races can be bred that bear little resemblance to the original wild plants, although no other species has been bred in. The modern sweet pea hybrids and the greenhouse cyclamen can serve as two salient examples for modern taste is tending to turn away from these giant forms. The smaller-flowered, but fragrant *Cyclamen persicum* is regaining the popularity that it had before the giant forms appeared, and the heady perfume of the true *Lathyrus odoratus* may again be experienced in gardens, where previously only the far less scented, but larger flowered and more attractively coloured sweet pea held sway. To sum up, the garden can be embellished by wild plants from around the globe or by the results of hybridisation of these wild plants, or by the results of selective breeding of such plants. Nevertheless, the first essential to produce any of these results is to bring the plants into cultivation, and we may as well start by examining the technique of plant collecting.

CHAPTER I

Plant Collecting

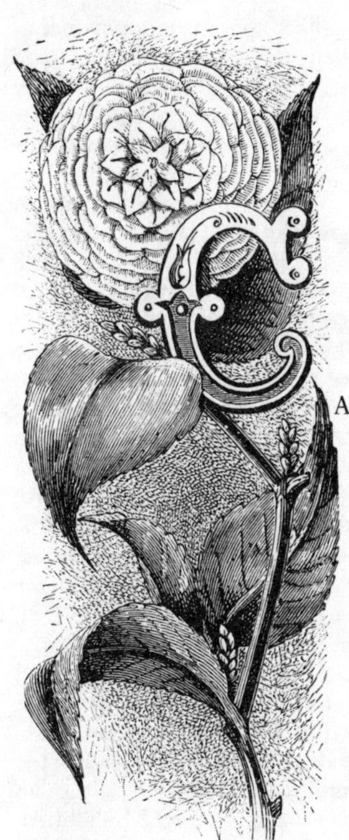

CAESAR divided All Gaul into three parts, and we can do much the same with plant collecting. You have to find the plants, you have to get them back to England, or from whatever country you set out, and they have to be brought successfully into cultivation.

The first operation may prove the easiest. Almost as soon as districts became inhabited by Europeans, the botanist would turn up to list the flora, and the various botanical institutions would receive exsiccata; plants that had been dried and pressed. Indeed, in the nineteenth century, some botanists were enabled to increase their incomes by the sale of botanical specimens. Not that the pay was very rewarding. For example, during the eighteen-fifties Richard Spruce was sending back specimens from central South America, while James Drummond was doing the same from Western Australia. They were paid £2 for each hundred specimens. If you were working nearer to home, say in the Near East or Iran, the pay was only £1 10s or 1½d for each specimen. Admittedly £2 in the eighteen-fifties had considerably more purchasing power than it has today. When Gardner was travelling in Brazil in the eighteen-forties he noted that 'an ox could be purchased for about twenty-five shillings, and a sheep or a goat for four or five; Pedro bought a fowl in fine condition for about 2½d, and eight eggs for a penny.' Even so the rewards were not princely, although they may have helped the botanist, they must have entailed considerable work.

One of the most irritating jobs in plant collecting is the maintenance of the herbarium. Every evening, at a time when all the collector wants to do is to rest, he has to take out his specimens, place them between fresh dry sheets of paper (besides preparing whatever he may have collected during the day's work) and attempt to dry the rest of the paper. Nowadays the collector will start with a good supply of paper, but in pioneering days this in itself could prove a difficulty. Here is James Drummond writing in 1839: 'It is one of the greatest disadvantages of Swan River that two years are necessary for us to send a letter and receive an answer. . . . My stock of brown paper is expended, and till I can receive more from England . . . I must be at a standstill. The article is not to be had for love or money in Swan River and, from this cause, many of my specimens are imperfectly dried.' This lack also limited the amount of seed that he was able to send back and, since a large number of nurserymen had contracted to purchase seeds from him (notably Lucombe Pince & Co. of Exeter and later Veitch from the same city, as well as Hugh Low at Clapton), this shortage of paper must have produced an unexpected problem. Owing to its distance from other countries, Australia must have been particularly bad for the replenishment of what we regard as too common to be worth noticing. Cunningham in his journals often bewails the lack of timber to make packing cases. As for his attempts to get a horse, they seem to have caused considerable unpleasantness between him and Governor Macquarie.

It must also be remembered that during the years when much plant collecting was done, in the late eighteenth and first half of the nineteenth centuries, the provision of food was more difficult than it is today, when tinned and dehydrated foods are easily obtainable. The more so when the collector was exploring unknown and uninhabited regions, although difficulties could exist even in regions that were quite thickly inhabited. In 1815 Bowie and Cunningham were collecting plants for Kew in Brazil, and were making a trip to Sao Paulo from Rio; most of the time they could put up at inns, but on occasion this was not possible and they spent the nights in farm sheds and ate cooked dried beans. At one stage of their journey, one of their servants decamped with the iron pot in which the beans were prepared, leaving them unable to do any further cooking until they arrived at some town where a substitute saucepan could be purchased.

In 1817 Allan Cunningham was a member of a party surveying the interior of Australia. The party was quite large, consisting of two surveyors, two botanists and nine convicts, who would obtain free pardons when they returned. They were moving into unknown and uninhabited territory. They took with them a quantity of flour (some of which fell into a river and was lost) and salt pork in casks of brine, and quite soon ran into difficulties. Fortunately Cunningham recognised in a rhagodia, a member of the *Chenopodiaceae* which was widespread in their journeying, a plant whose leaves would probably be edible, and he says that it proved an excellent substitute for either cabbage or spinach.

One of their difficulties was lack of water. On 17 July 1817 he wrote 'After a diligent search for water, about a quart was found at dusk in a rocky hole'. The next day two people were sent over towards some hills in the hope of finding water and 'they returned with a small quantity, enabling us to distribute to each of us a pint for our breakfast'. Before that, on 21 May, he had noted: 'We had hitherto been tolerably supplied with water, nor was it till this morning that we learned to appreciate the value of good water which, like all other blessings, are only estimated by the loss of them. All the water we could procure, which we brought from distant corrupted holes, was very foul and muddy and filled with Animalculi; to destroy which we boiled and strained the water' and a few days later he states, 'In order to rest our horses, who had by reason of hard labour through an intricate country with little provision and still less water become much debilitated, we remained at this place, where is good grass', and this necessity to rest the horses accounts for a number of stops in the ensuing weeks. On the last day of May appears the following unpleasing entry: 'We had taken the precaution to carry some *dirty* water with us from Mount Aiton, which we served out at 1 pint per man.'

They had firing pieces with them, but seem to have had more success with their dogs, although the diet could not always have been agreeable. They frequently ate kangaroo rats, while on 18 June: 'our dogs killed a native dog, which was *devoured* among us.' On the 29th Cunningham wrote: 'Those unwearied purveyors our dogs provided for us two of the largest emu we have seen in the course of this expedition, standing at least 8 feet. We are not likely to starve, although our flour and pork ration is exceeding scanty. Our fishermen caught only small fish of $3\frac{1}{2}$ and 4 pounds weight.' Indeed, at one time they were reduced to eating parrots, but found the flesh tough and rancid.

Few explorers nowadays are liable to have to live entirely off the country, as was necessary in the days when Australia was *terra incognita* away from the coastline, but people like Kingdon-Ward voyaging in Tibet, where the maps were somewhat dubious, had to reckon on being away for weeks on end from places where food could be obtained. This entails taking stores with you and this, in turn, entails baggage animals and people to look after them. Moreover, as the countries become more inhabited the plant hunter must journey further into the unknown. At a time when there were very few Chilean plants in cultivation, any amateur who went around the environs of his place of business in Chile could send back seeds of plants that were unknown and welcome. New introductions were easy, but as the plants became better known it was necessary to penetrate further into the Andes to discover novelties. Not that novelty is always essential to a successful collection. One of the most gratifying results from Lobb's first journey to Chile in 1840–4 was a great quantity of seed of the monkey puzzle, *Araucaria araucana*. This was not a novelty. A few seeds had been introduced by Archibald Menzies as early as 1797 and a quantity of seed would seem to have been received in 1839, but it would appear that it was Lobb's collection which made the plant eventually common in cultivation. If the person employing the collector was a nurseryman, he would be equally pleased with novelties or with material of plants that might be in cultivation, but which were still uncommon. In the case of the araucaria, no plant would attain fruiting size for about twenty years and since, in any case, seed is rarely set in Great Britain, it is only by importation of seeds that stocks can be kept going.

Some of the early collectors, such as Cunningham, who went into unexplored country, would have no idea what plants they were liable to find, but when the country has been explored, there is usually some record of the vegetation. Exploring parties, such as the one that Cunningham went on, would take a botanist with them and he would arrive back with exsiccata, so that the plants could be identified and the descriptions of new species published. The trouble for the collector might be in seeing collections other than his own. When western China became accessible to collectors, there would be David's collections in Paris and such sendings of Delavay as had been examined; the discoveries of Augustine Henry and A. E. Pratt would be in London, while those of Przewalski and Potanin would be in St Petersburg. It was obviously not easy to get a true survey of so rich and widespread a region and it is surprising that there seems to have been comparatively little overlapping in the naming of the various plants.

These herbaria are a help to the collector in two ways: they can tell him what sorts of plants he is liable to find, and also the region in which the botanist found them. This latter is not invariably helpful. The popular blue poppy, *Meconopsis betonicifolia*, was originally discovered by Delavay at the most eastern extremity of its range, where it was neither particularly thriving nor particularly well-coloured. It was only when Kingdon-Ward found it in Tibet, that its potentialities as a garden plant were revealed. Plants from Delavay's original locality were very weak and unsatisfactory.

Although the collector may have some idea as to what he is liable to find, there is always the chance of some new plant turning up, and in regions which have been only sparingly botanised, such things are almost certain. Whether they will be good ornamental plants in cultivation is another matter. There are a large number of splendid autumn-flowering gentians in the Sino-Himalaya, but only *Gentiana sino-ornata* and *G. farreri* have maintained themselves in cultivation, with *G. veitchiorum* just maintaining a foothold in Scotland; *G. gilvo-striata* and *G. georgei* are just names in the Royal Horticultural Society's *Dictionary*. Indeed, the ability of plants to flourish in alien conditions is a matter of uncertainty. We do not have to go to China or the Himalaya to illustrate this; one of the commonest of European alpines, *Viola calcarata*, is generally unsatisfactory in cultivation. *Anemone baldensis*, another alpine, survives but never flowers satisfactorily. The same thing may happen with plants further afield. Of *Incarvillea lutea* George Forrest wrote: 'Of the countless and beautiful alpines which inhabit the mountains of N.W. Yunnan, few stand out more prominently than *Incarvillea lutea*'. He sent back ample seed, but we read in the *Journeys and Plant Introductions of George Forrest* (R.H.S. 1952): 'In culture it is not in the least difficult to grow. Seeds germinate freely and fine large plants with thick carroty tubers develop, but flowers are produced very rarely indeed. In fact only one record of flowering is known to the writer.'

Kingdon-Ward was not much given to raptures about his plants and this extract from *Plant Hunting on the Edge of the World* (1930) is unusual. 'I ran across the snow bridge and ... had scarcely reached the bank when I stopped in amazement. Was I dreaming? I rubbed my eyes and looked again. No! Just above the edge of the snow a vivid blush pink flower stood out of the grey earth. It was as big as a rose, and of that fresh clear pink seen in "Madam Butterfly." Of course it could not really be a rose ... but what could it be? Yet so fascinating was it to stand there and gaze on this marvel in an aching pain of wonder that I felt no desire to step forward and break the spell ... I can recall several flowers which at first sight have knocked the breath out of me, but only two or three which have taken me by storm as did this one. The sudden vision is like a physical blow, a blow in the pit of the stomach; one can only gasp and stare.... And so it was now. I just stood there transfixed on the snow-cone in a honeymoon of bliss, feasting my eyes on a masterpiece. The vulgar thought—is it new?—did not at the moment occur to me, if only for the reason that I had not the faintest foggiest notion to what genus or even to what family it belonged.... Yet it was with a certain reluctance that I now approached it more nearly, breaking the fragile spell I had woven about the tea rose primula—for a primula I perceived it to be as soon as I realised that the flower was a head of flowers. And *what* a primula! The rosy globe resolved itself into a tight head of flowers, eight in number, borne on a short but sturdy stem. Each flower measured an inch across. Later the saw-edged, ribbon-like, wash-leathery leaves grew up, the stem lengthened until it stood four inches high, and behold! *Primula agleniana* var *thearosa*, the tea-rose primula!'

Obviously any collector who met it would send back seed of so desirable a plant, and there were numerous sendings both from Kingdon-Ward and from Forrest, but the results were very disappointing. 'Most sowings were without result. The late Mr J. C. Williams of Caerhays scattered some seeds in Cornwall broadcast near some beeches and the resultant plants flowered, but as usual they did not persist. Neither did the solitary plant of the variety *alba*, which bloomed for one or two seasons in the Edinburgh rock garden. It died without offspring.' (*Journeys and Plant Introductions of George Forrest*).

The list can be prolonged, particularly with regard to montane plants. A number of different meconopsis have been introduced, but never the fragrant bright blue *M. speciosa*, although seeds have often been received. The scarlet *M. punicea* has germinated and flowered, but has never set seed and so is no longer in cultivation. The same thing happened with Forrest's favourite *Primula spicata*. 'There is no difficulty in raising plants from mature seeds; the trouble is that such plants die after flowering without ripening their capsules.' (*Op. cit.*) It looks as though the necessary insect pollinators were absent, although one would have thought artificial pollination must have been tried, and one wonders if sufficient attention was not given during a period when so many Chinese novelties were flooding in.

Even in the early days politics might limit the activities of the plant collector. Apart from the East India Company's station at Canton, China was closed to most travellers after about 1750 until 1840; an exception was made for a few Jesuit missionaries, but for no one else. Similarly Japan was closed until 1860, although von Siebold was able to circulate somewhat from the Dutch East India Company's base at Deshima, owing to his medical knowledge; most of the earlier Japanese plants reached Europe through his instrumentality. When Sir Joseph Banks and Captain Cook were en route to Tahiti in 1768 and arrived at Rio de Janeiro: 'instead of being received as friends and allies of His Most Faithful Majesty, orders were immediately issued out that every insult possible should be offered to the officers of our ship, whose duty obliged them to land; and as for us (*foutus philosophes*) we were refused to land on any pretense whatsoever, on the peril of being sent to Portugal in irons; a thing I verily believe their absurd Viceroy would have done, had he caught either Dr Solander or myself upon any of our little excursions' (Banks to Count Lauraguais, 1772). Generally the reason for the refusal of permission for plant collectors to proceed was due to xenophobia, although this could scarcely have obtained at Brazil, where it was apparently due to the caprice of the Viceroy d'Azambusio. Nowadays, people tend to think that those who go wandering about the country with trowels, presses and cameras are either prospecting for minerals or engaged in espionage, and there seems little hope in the near future of any further expeditions to western China, Tibet or Burma.

The number of people engaged on an expedition must depend on the nature of the country and the amount of baggage and provisions that have to be taken. In 1815 when travelling from Rio to Sao Paulo, Bowie and Cunningham started off with two negroes and three mules, but found before they had proceeded very far that they required a fourth mule.

For excursions through the Himalaya, Major Madden, writing in 1846, gave some rules, which are perhaps worth reproducing:

1st. Avoid forming a party of more than three, in consequence of the difficulty, increasing in geometrical ratio, of obtaining supplies and porters for a greater number.

2nd. Change the latter daily; one may thus halt at pleasure without expense, when desirable; the rate of payment is only three annas per diem instead of four as near Simla, and the difficulty, often a serious one near the snowy range, is obviated of procuring large supplies and of adjusting the fair rate to be paid for them; a frequent source of angry and interminable discussion ...

3rd. Encumber yourself with the least possible number of servants; but let these be able-bodied, in sound health, and warmly clothed; their falling sick will cause much delay and inconvenience; and on no account start without a small tent for their use.

4th. Let this tent (and your own) be only of such a weight that one strong man can carry it well, even when soaked with rain ...

5th. ... A double wax cloth to keep one's bedding dry is essential, and five times as many pairs of shoes as you would expend at Simla in an equal period. The country-made articles ... will not, particularly during wet weather, stand more than a hard day's work on the rugged paths of the interior; and in the end, the purchase of European shoes will be found to economise cash, space and skin.

6th. Let your cups, jugs, plates and dishes be of metal; with these only may you defy fate and falls; and as for provender to adorn them, an ample supply of tea, sugar, Carr's biscuits, hermetically sealed soup and bouilli, fowls, sliced bread rebaked into everlasting rusks, with a liberal allowance of beer, wine and brandy, the latter precious article insured against damage by being decanted into ... stone bottles.' Madden also notes that if your route is predetermined, 'much trouble and expense will be saved by the establishment of a depot at some convenient spot on the return route.'

Finally Madden recommends taking tobacco, coarse powder and small shot to be given as presents. Later on in his narrative he comments: 'every traveller should carry a small supply [of medicine] to meet the demands which will be almost daily made by patients suffering from liver, spleen, dysentery, and in short all the ills that flesh is heir to, save blue cholera; and if unflinching faith in the skill of the physician be conducive to a cure, the practitioner here should be successful indeed.' If for some reason a tarpaulin to put under one's bedding is not available, Madden notes: 'a very excellent substitute is a thick layer of pine or yew branches.'

Madden evidently travelled fairly lightly and engaged porters from one village to the next. Five years later, Joseph Hooker set out with a vast party. Admittedly it was not only plant collecting that was in question. Hooker was to do a geographical and geological survey and was accompanied by Mr Hodgson, who was studying the fauna. Even so it sounds elaborate.

'My party mustered fifty-six persons, including myself and one personal servant, a Portuguese half-cast, who undertook all offices and spared me the usual train of Hindoo and Mahometan servants. My tent and equipments . . . instruments, bed, clothes, books and papers required a man for each. Seven more carried my papers for drying plants, and other scientific stores. The Nepalese guard had two coolies of their own. My interpreter, the coolie Sirdar (or headman) and my chief plant collector . . . had a man each. Mr Hodgson's bird and animal shooter, collector, and stuffer, for their ammunition and indispensables had four more; there were besides three Lepcha lads to climb trees and change the plant papers . . . and the party was completed by fourteen Bhutan coolies laden with food, consisting chiefly of rice, with ghee, oil, capsicums, salt and flour.' As a contrast to this large caravanserai, we may note that Messrs Ludlow and Sherriff in 1936 had a retinue of only eight, made up of two private servants, two Lepcha collectors, two Bhutanese servants and two cooks and this for a longer expedition, although somewhat less all-embracing in its objects.

Kingdon-Ward seems to have followed the example of Madden and travelled with only a couple of servants; he depended on getting porters from one village to the next and this habit of having only a few permanent members of the staff seems to have been fairly general in India and China. On the other hand, Burbidge in Borneo seems to have had a large retinue and his advice dating from 1877 is also interesting. 'A party of, say, twenty natives will require a clear head to manage it rightly, and it is only by maintaining a system that the thing can be conveniently done.'

Burbidge first deals with health, saying that: 'great care should be taken to put on dry clothes the first thing after a halt is made for the night.' 'All your clothing should be light and if of flannel so much the better', while for the feet he recommends: 'a light pair of English walking boots.' It is advisable to carry a change of clothes in a knapsack as: 'you are then independent of luggage bearers who will often linger miles behind yourself and guides.' 'Three changes of travelling clothes will be sufficient, this gives one suit on, one being washed, and one suit dry and clean. For bedding take a waterproof sheet, a drab rug and a red blanket.' Should the ground be wet: 'a light net hammock becomes useful, a roof to it is readily made with the waterproof sheet.'

'Food is of the utmost importance. Rice, biscuits and oatmeal may form the staple, and tinned soups, Liebig's extract of meat, and dried fish may be added. Chocolate and milk in sealed tins is convenient and refreshing. Tea, coffee, sugar and salt must be packed in well-corked bottles to keep them dry and free from ants.... Be very careful of the water drunk in travelling and use a pocket filter when it is in any way doubtful. I always drank coconut water when procurable, as being pure and harmless, and with a dash of brandy it is extremely refreshing. As to the quantity of food required, two pounds of rice is ample for a man's daily supply. . . .' Cooking should be well understood by all who propose to rough it in a wild land (although most collectors, at least in modern days, seem to take a cook with them), 'two cook-pots are necessary—one large enough to boil a fowl when cut up, and the other for rice.

'Always bathe in the morning. Care must be taken not to frequent alligator-infested streams. Whenever there is any doubt, never enter a stream, but bale up the water and pour it over the body.'

So far as medicine is concerned, Burbidge says: 'The three most useful of all medicines for travellers ... are Cockle's pills, Collis Brown's chlorodyne and Howard's sulphate of quinine.' These and a bottle of brandy must always be taken, together with a roll of sticking plaster, needles, silk thread and a few long bandages. He also recommends carbolic acid to mix with fifteen or twenty parts of oil as a dressing for mosquito bites and small flesh wounds such as scratches. Burbidge also observes that it is as well to be able to set a broken limb.

'There are not many countries wherein it is necessary to carry goods for barter. In the interior of the Malay islands and in the far interior or mountainous districts of other countries, however, it still happens that money is useless'. As a result you must carry goods for barter. 'White or grey shirting and chopper blades are generally acceptable throughout the interior of Borneo', but: 'whatever you take let it be good of its kind, and always remember that necessaries are more valued than beads and other ornaments.' Most importantly: 'All goods for barter should be so packed that any article may be brought out for examination without exposing the remainder. The more goods the natives perceive you to have the higher they will value their own edibles and services.'

Unfortunately few collectors have been so lavish with details as Madden and Burbidge, and we get the impression that most of the collectors were entirely on their own. Alexander Cruckshank was only a part time collector, but in Hooker's *Magazine of Botany* for 1831 he published his journal of a trip from Lima to the mining centre of Pasco in the Andes and for this: 'our party consisted of six individuals, and we had with us three English workmen belonging to the Company (the mines at Pasco), a servant and three muleteers; eight laden mules completed the cavalcade.' Presumably collectors such as William Lobb must have had a muleteer and a porter, although we have no knowledge of this. It does seem, however, to have been the pattern with collectors employed by outside bodies. We know from his narrative that Masson, when travelling around South Africa had two servants, one of whom drove the bullock waggon, while the other seemed to have less specialist duties. Similarly we learn from his journal that in the western U.S.A. David Douglas sometimes travelled alone, but on at least one occasion he engaged an Indian to act as guide and also took with him as a servant a 'Canadian'. On the other hand, when Burchell was making his projected journey from Cape Town to Mozambique, he was forced to turn back, as his native servants were too terrified to continue further north than Botswana.

This pattern of either a large, elaborately-staffed expedition or one consisting of only a few people seems to have persisted to this day. Kingdon-Ward travelled with only a minimum of staff, while Forrest had a large retinue, mainly employed in collecting seeds from places he had previously indicated. Nowadays with mechanical transport largely available, it is possible for a small group to be fairly self-sufficient, and the necessity for guides, cooks, etc., is somewhat less, although they would probably still be found necessary in the more remote parts of Burma, Tibet and China, were such places accessible to collectors.

What all this entails, among other matters, is that plant expeditions are very costly to mount. In 1773 Kew sent Francis Masson to South Africa for three years. He was paid a salary of £100 per year (which, however, he would not receive until he returned, so should he have perished the sum of £300 would have been saved), while the remainder of the expedition cost the Privy Purse £583 *8s 6d*. His six year trip to Madeira, the Canary Islands and the West Indies, cost £1430. It is interesting to note that the fare to Jamaica from London was £40. In 1849 Joseph Hooker's elaborate expedition to Sikkim and the Khasia Hills cost £2,000, of which only £800 was paid by the East India Company, and Hooker himself had to find the balance. E. H. M. Cox told me that his ten-month trip with Farrer to Burma in 1919 cost about£1,400, while the late Frank Ludlow told me that an expedition with Captain Sherriff to Tibet in the 30s cost £3,500.

We do not know what nurserymen such as Veitch and William Bull paid their collectors, but inevitably the cost of the expedition must have been high and if it proved unsuccessful, must have caused much consternation. In *Hortus Veitchii*, the main source of information about the collectors employed by James Veitch, we read for example: 'Carl Kramer

... was sent on a collecting mission to Japan ... but his mission was a failure. He was afterwards sent to Costa Rica and Guatemala for Orchids, but he again sent home little of note. Kramer proved entirely unsuitable for the work he had undertaken and apparently had not that adaptability and resource essential to successful exploration.'

Even a successful collector such as Gustave Wallis had his failures. In 1870 Veitch sent him to the Philippines but: 'The mission proved very expensive, was practically a failure and Wallis had to be recalled.' Finally there was Christopher Mudd who: 'went on an expedition to South Africa in 1877 and great things were expected to result from the undertaking. These expectations, however, were not realised for Mudd, who seemed to have no special aptitude for collecting, and entirely lacked the explorer's instinct, sent home little of horticultural value, and the mission, which was practically a failure, had to be recalled.' Veitch, being a very wealthy firm, was able to ride these contretemps, but such experiences would have been impossible for nurserymen who were less well off. It does also seem to indicate that it must have been profitable to be able to offer new plants and, indeed, they were sold for high prices in much the same way that nowadays new cultivars and hybrids will fetch higher prices than those that are already known to be reliable. Novelty has a great charm for gardeners, and presumably the employers got their profits, otherwise they would not have continued to send out collectors.

Once the collector has selected his district he has to make his collection. Ideally, this would entail a stay of about a year at least, so that plants could be discovered when in flower and later revisited to collect the seed harvest. There may, of course, be snags. Some seeds lose their viability altogether if not sown immediately and it has proved almost impossible to bring any of the *Amethystinae* series of primula into cultivation. Magnolias, also, have seeds with a short life out of soil and this seems to have been recognised early on. We find Miller in his *Gardener's Dictionary* saying that the seeds: 'should be put up in sand and sent over to England as soon as possible, for if they are kept long out of the ground they very rarely grow.' While a few years later Mawe and Abercrombie in the *Universal Gardener and Botanist* say that the seeds of magnolias were 'received annually from America preserved in sand.' In the eighteenth and early nineteenth centuries travelling would take a long time. It took Masson four months to sail from Sheerness to Cape Town, while the period from London to Sydney was about six months. Cunningham left Spithead on 3 October 1814, was delayed until the 29th, and then sailed non-stop to Rio, where he arrived on 28 December. These long journeys would evidently pass through extremes of temperature, with unpredictable effects on any plants or seeds that might be in transit. There were other dangers too. One of the first of the great collectors was the American

John Bartram who was sending plants and seeds back from the U.S.A. from 1736 until 1776, and his main client was the Quaker draper, Peter Collinson. Collinson used to send Bartram paper to make up into seed bags, but it was soon found that once on board ship, vermin of various types, from cockroaches to rats, would eat the bags and the seed. In despair Collinson suggested that the seeds should be put in sand or dry soils and carried in glass bottles and it may have been this, rather than recognition of their short life, which accounted for the magnolia seeds arriving in sand.

Quite apart from the risk of destruction by vermin, it was found also that, as they passed through the varying temperatures that were an inevitable concomitant of a long voyage, the seeds often arrived rotted, and much research was undertaken to devise means by which this might be obviated—mainly by a Dr John Ellis. He seemed to think that the most satisfactory methods were to embed the seeds in wax, which was warmed until it was malleable, but not too hot to damage the seeds. Dripping was regarded as an alternative to wax. With very small seeds Ellis recommended that the capsules should be wrapped in wax paper and that this packet should then be embedded. The great Linnaeus prescribed a highly complicated method in which the seeds were packed in sand in a small glass vessel, which was then placed in a larger one with about 2 inches clearance all round and this intervening space was filled with a mixture of nitre with a small amount of salt and sal ammoniac. 'This saline mass' he wrote, 'which should be rather moist, will always be so cold that the seeds in the inner bottle will never suffer during the voyage from the heat of the air.'

Dr John Livingstone was particularly concerned with the despatch of seeds from China which, at the end of the eighteenth century, meant from the East India Company's depot at Canton. Here the rain was so frequent from April until October that the drying out of the seeds became well-nigh impossible. If they were covered up, they were destroyed by mildew, while if they were not covered up they were attacked and destroyed by insects. With large seeds he recommended putting them in a dish over concentrated sulphuric acid, which would keep the air in the immediate vicinity sufficiently dry. Possibly this might be effective, but it was scarcely practicable for the ordinary collector. Even odder seems his other recommendation that small seeds were best kept in sugar 'or with currants and raisins'. One would have thought that a sure way of ensuring that vermin would be attracted, and yet we find that Nathaniel Wallich, who was responsible for an enormous amount of introductions through the Calcutta Botanic Garden in the early years of the nineteenth century, sent many of his seeds mixed in coarse brown sugar; the first Himalayan rhododendron seeds arrived in this manner, so it seems to have been successful, however improbable it sounds. Wallich also recommended that the paper used for wrapping plants should be impregnated with arsenic to kill off any would-be attackers and this may have been an additional safeguard with his seed packets, or else the seeds and sugar may have been in sealed jars.

The problem has not been entirely solved even today. At one time it was hoped that packing seed with a very short life out of the ground in vacuum flasks might be the answer, but it does not seem to have been. Robert Fortune managed to transmit short-lived seeds in 1849 by sowing them in the Wardian Cases, which had first become well-known in 1833 and which had made the transport of living plants considerably easier. However, although the Wardian case may have been successful when the short-lived seeds were brought to the ship, they would certainly prove impracticable in the high Sino-Himalaya.

Although the transport of seeds had its problems, they were little when compared to the transport of plants. Comparatively few plants can withstand salt spray, and protection from this, while still enabling the plants to receive adequate light, was one of the main problems attached to the importation of living plants; although there was always the additional one of nursing the plants through extremes of temperature. Chinese-cultivated plants such as azaleas, tree peonies and camellias were particularly wanted, but the journey from Canton would go first to the Philippines, through the tropics to South Africa, thence north to St Helena, where a custom arose of taking the plants off the ship to recuperate, before sending them through the tropics to London. Here they were liable to be detained for a long time by the customs, unless a firm line were taken, and the loss was enormous. Livingstone reckoned that only one plant in a thousand arrived safely. If one was a man of authority, such as Sir Joseph Banks, one could probably get the master of the East Indiaman to take a personal interest in the plants under his care. Outstanding among these would seem to have been Edward Cumming, the captain of *Britannia*, who brought back plants for Banks. In 1789 he wrote to say that he had lit a fire in his cabin to keep frost from the guinea grass (*Panicum maximum* or millet). The next year he reported a number of plants from Batavia, which were still in good condition in spite of the long voyage and damage during a hurricane, but suggested that Banks should arrange for them to be collected as soon as the ship berthed. Two years later, writing in April, he again advises speedy collection, as two cases of plants from Canton were being affected by cold. There were other captains who realised that they could make additional money by looking after the plants committed to their care; the names of Rawes, Cuffnell, Dod, Wellbank and Prendergast have all survived in this connection, but others would ignore such freight and give it no special consideration.

The problems involved in transporting plants by sea had been occupying minds since the end of the seventeenth century. Evelyn, the diarist, noted that trees were best preserved in barrels, 'their roots wrapped about with moss; the smaller the plants and trees the better.' He also seems to have anticipated the modern plastic spray. 'Some are of the opinion that plants and roots that come from abroad will be better preserved if they are rubbed over with honey before they are covered with moss, pretending that the honey has a styptic quality to hinder the moisture that is in the plants from perspiring.'[1] The idea was probably sound enough, although honey would certainly have attracted vermin. When the voyage was not too long, it would seem that methods corresponding to those used by sending plants by post nowadays were successful. In 1771 we find John Fothergill writing: 'William Young sends his plants over very safely by wrapping them up in moss and packing them pretty close in a box. They come thus very safe and we lose very few of them. He ties the moss in a ball about the roots, with a piece of pack-thread or matting, and hemp strings, and puts them so close as to prevent them from shaking about in the box. It is surprising how well they keep in this manner.'

Young was sending plants from America, where the crossing was not too long (although with contrary winds it could last up to two months), but such packing would not be possible for longer voyages and for these it was necessary to have the containers on deck for most of the time and yet the plants had to be protected from sea-spray. When the *Bounty* expedition was in preparation, Joseph Banks wrote some detailed instructions, which, one feels, might well have caused a mutiny among the upper echelons rather than among the crew, so firmly did it contradict all the usual rules of naval discipline. Among other things, Banks demanded that: 'the cabin be appropriated to the sole purpose of making a kind of greenhouse and the key of it given to the custody of the gardener; and that in case of cold weather going round the Cape, a stove be provided ... ' The bread fruit trees were to be planted in half tubs and 'as these tubs, which will be very heavy, must be frequently brought upon the deck ... the crew must assist in moving them, as indeed they must assist the gardener on all occasions in which he stands in need of their help.' Moreover, as it would be necessary to wash off any salt which may fall upon the leaves frequently, there must be a large quantity of additional water provided.

In any case, this was a special expedition for transporting plants and what the government could authorise a private collector could not. For such a man Lindley published some directions in 1825. First the plants

[1] The idea of coating cuttings with honey dates back to *Le Menagier de Paris* of 1393.

must be established. 'The idea which seems to exist, that to tear a plant from its native soil, to plant it in fresh earth, to fasten it in a wooden case and put it on board a vessel in the care of some officer, is sufficient, is of all others the most erroneous and has led to the most ruinous consequences.' It was first necessary to establish the plants in their containers. 'With any herbaceous plant this requires only a short space of time, but for such as are ... of hard, woody texture a period, in many instances, of not more than two or three months is absolutely necessary.'

Lindley recommended that the plants be placed in wooden containers, which were less liable to breakage than pots would be, and that the corners should be reinforced with iron binding as the plants were liable to be roughly handled. The plants were then to be put in a wooden container with sloping lids. These containers should ideally be 4 feet long, 20 inches wide and 36 inches high, the first 20 inches being perpendicular, the remaining to be sloped inwards like a greenhouse roof. They would be hinged at this point, so that they could be opened in calm weather and closed when it was stormy and covered with a tarpaulin to exclude any sea spray. Should any plants be touched by spray, they should, said Lindley somewhat optimistically, be immediately sponged with fresh water. This was unlikely to be done unless there was someone present whose business it was to look after the plants, and these were comparatively few. Most collectors packed their plants up and entrusted them to the captain, who, even if willing, could not give much attention to the plants during bad weather. Such an arrangement was far from ideal and we find Banks instructing Menzies, when departing with Vancouver on *Discovery*: 'when you meet with curious or valuable plants which you do not think likely to be propagated from seeds ... you are to dig up proper specimens of them, plant them in the glass frame provided for that purpose and use your utmost endeavours to preserve them alive till your return.'

What was this glass frame? Probably a wooden box with a glass lid, like the modern garden frame. It would not have been hermetically sealed, as the Wardian case was to be, so that the plants would dry out and need attention in various ways. Since Menzies was unable to bring back any live plants we must conclude that it was not a success.

The invention of the Wardian case solved the main problem of how to bring back plants by sea, without them dying en route, although there was always a risk of the cases being smashed up in exceptionally severe weather, but it did not completely solve the problem of getting plants back alive. If you are travelling over rough terrain, especially if you are alone or with only a single helper, you certainly cannot manhandle Wardian cases in the saddle bags of your mule. In mountainous country 10 miles per day is quite good going, so that collectors in places well remote from seaports would have long voyages to make. Thus, for example, it took Joseph Hooker at least a month in 1849 to travel from Darjeeling to Calcutta, and it took nearly as long, in 1836, for John Gibson to travel the 250 miles from Calcutta to the Khasia hills. While there he collected a great number of plants. They were sent back to Calcutta in baskets which could each hold fifty plants. The plants were wrapped individually in moss and the baskets were then filled with more moss, while the plants were supported with sticks: 'so that they may be turned about in any way without being broken.' Fortunately Gibson was dispatching his plants in the rainy season, so that there was little risk of their drying out during the journey back to Calcutta, but in the dry season the matter might have been rather different, and when plants were brought down from the Himalaya, the different temperature zones through which they had to pass made their survival somewhat problematical.

Indeed, with the exception of garden plants, such as roses and azaleas, it was early realised that once he was any distance from the port the collector would have to send back chiefly seeds. There were, however, exceptions. Bulbs and tubers were generally collected, as they could be dried off and sent back when in a dormant state, and orchids had to be sent back as plants, as the technique of growing them from seed was not learned until the mid-nineteenth century. Orchids, fortunately, are extremely tough plants, which can survive extreme desiccation without dying, as most other plants would do under similar conditions, and so orchids could usually be relied upon to arrive in a state where they could soon be brought back to a thriving condition.

On occasions it was essential to bring back plants, where seeds were liable to be too short-lived and we have a vivid description from Richard Spruce of the bringing of Cinchona plants, the source of quinine, from Ecuador to the Peruvian coast and thence to Kew and India. This was in 1859 and 1860 and the plants were growing fairly high in the Andes. Spruce collected seeds, but also took cuttings and layers, so that if the seeds should lose their viability, there would be a reserve of plants. Rooting the cuttings had its problems.

'The mornings were always cool . . . but at seven o'clock or so the sun would often come out blazing hot . . . on these occasions, and on the days of sustained heat, the only means of keeping the plants from withering was to give them abundance of water; and then there was the risk, on the other hand, of their damping off. . . . In a few weeks the cuttings began to root, and then they were attacked by caterpillars. In short, it is impossible to detail here all the obstacles encountered, and which only Mr Cross's unremitting watchfulness enabled him to surmount.' From their Andean base camp Spruce and Cross had to get down to Aguacatal, whence they could travel by raft down the river. Spruce started on 28 September 1860 and arrived at Guayaquil on 6 October, where he purchased a raft and made up the wardian cases. Cross did not arrive until 13 December, having lost a number of plants owing to the oxen running wildly into the jungle, so that some of the baskets were crushed. In spite of this they had 637 rooted cuttings. These were planted in the cases but, 'as we might expect some rough treatment on the descent . . . we did not venture to put on the glasses, but in their stead stretched moistened strips of calico, which seemed to answer admirably. As Mr Cross wished the plants to be firmly established in their new residence before removing them . . . I determined to delay our departure until the last possible moment.' The descent from Aguacatal to Guayaquil was somewhat alarming, but although the plants were damaged and the cases received 'a few slight cracks' no irreparable damage was done. They arrived at Guayaquil on 27 December and two days later a steamer came in which would take the plants to Lima on 2 January, while on the 14th the plants would be transferred to another boat from Lima to Panama. A large number did arrive safely in India.

In much the same way, although this time not with the consent of the authorities, the rubber plant, *Hevea brasiliensis*, was smuggled out of Brazil to Kew and thence to Ceylon and Malaya.

Such matters are, however, somewhat exceptional, although nowadays, when plants can be quickly brought back by aeroplane, the introduction of living plants is less uncommon than it was. A number of Tibetan primulas were brought back to Great Britain from the Tibetan journeys of Ludlow and Sherriff and, in the nineteen-thirties, a great sensation was caused when plants of *Primula sonchifolia* were exhibited, after having been brought back by air from Burma, this being, apparently, the first time that plants had been transported by air, as well as being the first time that the primula had been seen in Great Britain. Air freight is now used to import plants from foreign nurserymen, but it is costly. An alternative method of importing plants was noted by Joseph Hooker in his Himalayan Journals. Ice was imported from America into India and a number of fruit trees in a dormant state were imported frozen into blocks of ice from America to India. These arrived in a perfect condition and started to grow as soon as they were thawed out. However, it was obvious that this would only be successful in ice ships and only with plants that are used to freezing conditions. It would be useless for tropical plants.

Most of the earliest plant collectors spent a year or more in their chosen locality. Masson, for example, spent two years in South Africa on his first expedition, and nine years on his second, but such protracted stays were not so common. Cunningham and Bowie spent less than two years in Brazil and somewhat shorter stays became the rule, although they all tended to exceed twelve months. William Lobb's two South American trips each lasted for three years. It took eight months for Douglas to travel from Britain to Fort Vancouver in Oregon since, the Panama canal not having yet been built, it was necessary to go right round South America. Hence nearly a year of a three-year stay in South America, might be spent in the outgoing and returning passage. When this travelling time could be cut down, the total length of any expedition could also be lessened. Although it was not until 1869 that the Suez canal was opened, it had earlier been found to be more rapid to take one ship to Alexandria and then travel overland to Port Suez and there take another ship, so that the long voyage around Africa could be eliminated. This was less easy in the Americas as the Panama isthmus was so extremely difficult to traverse.

As we have said ideally the collector should spend about a year, at least, in his chosen locality, so that desirable plants can be marked when in flower and later they can be revisited when the seed is ripe. Some collectors would collect plants immediately and plant them at their base camp and await the seed harvest that way, but this entails moving plants in flower and is not usually satisfactory if the expedition is only for a single year. When Masson went on his second trip to South Africa, which lasted for nine years, he was instructed by Banks to construct a garden at the base of Table Mountain, where he could establish his plants and also collect their seeds, and similar 'gardens' have been constructed by other collectors, but it is usually easier to get large quantities by collecting in the wild. Nowadays when expeditions are financed by a number of subscribers, large quantities are necessary, so that every subscriber can get his money's worth. When collectors were sent out by botanic gardens or by nurserymen the quantities could be somewhat smaller.

In the early days of collecting, novelty in itself was a sufficient recommendation and a new chickweed would be received with the same enthusiasm as some more ornamental plant, but when plant collecting became linked with commerce, it was only plants that might be reckoned saleable that were wanted and the collector would become somewhat selective. In some ways this is unfortunate as plants appear to have fashions in much the same way as clothes. It is only recently, for example, that euphorbias have been much regarded as garden ornamentals, so that the number of hardy species of this genus introduced is small and there are doubtless other lacunae. There are many more good eremurus than the handful in cultivation and lathyrus, to take another example, is poorly represented in gardens. A plant as handsome as the eastern Mediterranean *L. digitata* is not to be found in commerce. However, there is obviously nothing to be done about this. Plants from the eastern Mediterranean are easy to come by, but not so from further afield, and there are doubtless still a number of plants that could yet be introduced with advantage.

The actual technique of plant collecting was well adumbrated by Sir Joseph Banks writing to Archibald Menzies before the departure of *Discovery*'s voyage.

'As far as you find yourself able, you are to enumerate all the trees, shrubs, plants, grasses, ferns and mosses you shall meet with in each country you visit by their scientific names as well as those used in the language of the natives, noting particularly the places where each is found, especially those which are new or particularly curious; you are also to dry specimens of all such as you shall judge worthy of being brought home. . . .

'Whenever you meet with ripe seeds of plants, you are carefully to collect them, and, having dried them properly, to put them up in paper packages, writing on the outside or in a corresponding list, such particulars relative to the Soil and Climate where each was found and the mode of culture most likely to succeed with it, as you may think necessary to be communicated to His Majesty's gardeners at Kew....

'When you meet with curious or valuable plants, which you do not think likely to be propagated from seeds ... you are to dig up proper specimens of them, plant them in the glass frame provided for that purpose and use your utmost endeavours to preserve them alive till your return.'

To translate this into modern usage, the collector is to make a herbarium, collect seeds where possible with ample field notes and only bother with plants where seeds are not liable to be successful (or not to be found at the crucial times).

This is still the technique followed nowadays, except that the collections are simply numbered in succession and the field notes are given separately rather than inscribed on the packets. Even the numbering came into existence in Banks's lifetime. Cunningham's journals are full of numbers, although they sometimes seem rather haphazard. The usual method is to begin with one and continue until the expedition is complete in sequence, with herbarium specimens and seeds each in the same list. Thus, for example, should the collector's first plant be a handsome berberis he will label his herbarium specimen 1. By the time he gets round to collecting the seed of the berberis he may have added some 500 items to his collection, so that 501 may be the seeds of 1. This fact will, of course, be noted in the field notes. Some confusion may arise if there are several plants of the berberis present. Ideally, the seeds from each plant should have a separate number, 501, 502 etc. but, in practice, it is probably easier to lump them all together as 501.

Unfortunately most field notes are somewhat inadequate. This is not surprising as the collector has to write them at the end of a tiring day, when the light is fading and all he wants to do is to go to sleep. Sometimes they are later amplified, but even so can be somewhat inadequate. Here is William Bartram describing a plant (about 1776):

'No. 30 is another lovely inhabitant of the Green Savannahs and seems to be of the family No. 24, but still more admirably beautiful. The flowers are produced in vast profusion, very large; some I have seen, when blown, 4 and 5 inches over, of a deep rose colour with a splendid golden star in the midst, raised on a bed of deep crimson. The number of petals are various, from fifteen to twenty or thirty, but never saw any double flowers. It is a capital plant.'

It may well have been a capital plant, but as a field note this is almost useless. We do not know if we are dealing with a woody or a herbaceous plant, nor whether it is annual or perennial. There is no indication as to how it should be cultivated, except for the fact that it grows on the green Savannahs. In point of fact the plant is a biennial, *Sabbatia decandra* of the *Gentianaceae*; presumably sabbatias have been found difficult to grow, as these desirable plants are never seen.

Cunningham rather rarely gives cultural notes in his journals, but on the few occasions that he does they are pertinent. Here he is on the *Proteaceae* of King George's Sound in south-west Australia. This was written on 30 January 1818.

'Before I take my leave of this rich Botanical Repository . . . the submission of a few general remarks on its Soils may not be altogether inutile and unnecessary. The Slopes or easy declivities of the Hills are of a barren, hard, stony, sandy soil very dry and of a reddish colour. On these Hills are elevated level tracts, where the rain from the Slopes, having met with a Lodgement, has form'd damp, heathy, boggy spots, of a black peaty description, in which certain species of plants exist, not occupying a Situation on the dry exposed sides of these Elevated Grounds. The lower flats, just above the Level of the Sea, are either marshy, boggy Grounds, in the vicinity of Lagoons, or subsalt marshes, or arid Downs of very loose Sand.

'The Extensive Family of Proteaceae, whose Genera and species occupy a very considerable portion of the Shores of the Sound have a varied diffusion. *Banksia grandis* is only to be found on the above mentioned dry exposed sides of the Hills, where it flowers and fruits in a limited but healthful state of Luxuriance. *B. attenuata* has been observed on the Shore in a Deeper peaty Soil, forming a Tree of some bulk. *B. marcescens*, *coccinea – quercifolia* grow near the immediate shore in arid dry places, but rarely on the Hills and never in loose sand. Excepting *Dryandra pteridifolia* and *blechnifolia*, the whole of this Genus inhabits dry sterile Hills with *Banksia grandis*. From the nature of the soil (preventing them from expending their saps in useless luxuriance or exuberant growth, but rendering it more concentrated) they are capable of existing and resisting great Droughts and will flourish under them, but appear impatient of Humidity, and from this natural Habit, nothing appears more injurious or pernicious to their Health than much water, and more particularly stagnant water, around their Roots; a circumstance not existing in their natural exposed dry situation. . . . From these few Hints something may perhaps be gather'd, whereby the true Culture of these most interesting plants will be better understood than it may be at present in England; at all Events their native Habit and Soil will be known, whereof little or no Loam forms a component Part. It is a well-known fact that our Pride of New South Wales, *Telopea speciosissima*, so tenacious of Life in its natural sterile shallow Rocky places of Growth, seldom retains it when removed by the Settlers into the richer loamy Soil of their Gardens.'

The style is somewhat prolix but the information is valuable. Unfortunately such detailed information is not very frequent in Cunningham's journals, although much can be inferred from his descriptions of the landscape. On the other hand, the way he arranged his collections seems very peculiar. Here he is in Brazil on 23 August 1815.

'Collected on the way seeds of Bignonia sp. No. 405, seeds of Convolvulus sp.: leaves sagittate and small, with yellow flowers in a stony valley No. 374 . . . seeds of Dolichos sp.; large hairy pods—seeds and specimens of a plant with capsules 5-locular, seed and capsules very prickly, plant dead to the ground, No. 362 . . . capsules (bladder'd, 3-seeded) of a climbing plant common on the Roadsides, allied to Cardiospermum, No. 373.'

Modern collectors number their gatherings consecutively and what Cunningham was doing numbering his plants 405, 374, 362, 373 is anyone's guess. This is not exceptional. He appears to have done it consistently.

So far as I am aware we do not have many of the field notes of the earlier collectors. In Douglas's Journal the notes are there, but very short, such as:

'202. *Silene* sp. perennial; leaves opposite, sessile lanceolate; flowers white; plant glutinous; a low plant a foot to 18 inches high; in small tufts on rocky and gravelly soils near Spokane.' Occasionally he writes slightly more, such as this entry for *Paeonia brownii*: 'perennial; root large and jointed, partly creeping; stem glaucous red; leaves alternate, compoundly lobed, smooth and glaucous; flowers small, petals of the same length as the stamens, centre and the outside deep purple, on the edge and inside bright yellow; a low plant 6 inches to a foot high; in great abundance, in clumps, among low bushes on the sunny side of the mountains, flowering in perfection on the confines of perpetual snow; lower down it is seen in feeble enervated plants, and in the more temperate regions completely disappears.' By and large the notes are perfectly adequate, giving the character of the plant, its dimensions and the conditions under which it was growing, and these are the essentials.

Moreover, even if you write at greater length it is not easy to give much more information. In 1916 the RHS Journal published some of Farrer's field notes, which he had amplified for the occasion. Like all Farrer's writings they are wonderfully readable, but are not over informative in spite of their length.

'*Cotoneaster dammeri* var. *radicans* (F. 148) . . . I have seen it only at one point, in the limestone bottom of the great Siku gorge where, growing and resting and re-rooting as it goes, in almost pure limestone silt, it ramps perfectly tight and flat along the floor, moulding each boulder in its embrace, and developing a carpet many yards across, of refulgently glossy and apparently evergreen rounded foliage, among which grows in September–October a richly scattered profusion of brilliant scarlet fruits like holly berries peppered over a lucent ground willow, with here and there the amber leaves of autumn enhancing the sombre gloss of the carpet's green and the flashing wealth of its bejewelment of berries.' It is certainly nicer to read this than to read: 'prostrate shrub, leaves small, orbicular, glossy green; berries red and conspicuous; in limestone silt, Siku gorge', but the information is the same. Still, one can forgive much for a note like this:

'*Cypripedium bardolphianum*. sp. nov. (F. 139). It is a wee running thing, with pairs of leaves, and stems about 2 inches high, and green-segmented half-open tiny flowers, with a lip of brilliant waxy gold, whelked and warted and bubukled like Bardolph's nose. It careers about occasionally in mossy grass in opener places of the mountain woodland, in such close association with *C. luteum* as often to run in and out of its stems. It has not only the exotic look of a wee Catasetum, but a Catasetum's heavy and cloying exotic scent of aromatics. I noted it only once, in the Siku gorges.'

Incidentally these notes indicate yet one more of the collector's difficulties. Of *Dipelta elegans* Farrer wrote: 'Of this I got two large sackfuls, yet, having husked so many seeds and found them all bad, I hardly dare distribute the rest, for fear there may not prove a single sound kernel in the lot.'

Sometimes the field notes may be confusing. Here is Forrest 10423. 'Rhododendron sp. Shrub of 9–12 feet. Fls? In fruit. In thickets on the mountains in the N.E. of the Yangtze bend. Yunnan. W. China. Alt. 11,000 feet.' And here is Kingdon-Ward's 4486. 'Undershrub of 1–2 feet. Large leafy calyx and scale-clad leaves. On shaded limestone cliffs, Mu-li at 10,000 feet.' Now both these numbers germinated as *Rhododendron ravum*, a dwarf shrub of from 1–4 feet in height. Forrest's note of 9–12 feet suggests that he must have confused this with another plant when writing up his field notes and one wonders how often this can take place. It is also possible to mix up the seeds. Kingdon-Ward's number 5718 was *R. calvescens*, a rare member of the Selense subseries of the Thomsonii series. But at Borde Hill KW 5718 was *R. melinanthum* of the Trichocladum series, while at Tower Court *R. telopeum* of the Campylocarpum subseries of Thomsonii was the result of sowing KW 5718. One cannot help suspecting that labels got confused at Tower Court, since 5718 was collected in Tibet, but *R. melinanthum* is only recorded from Burma.

Indeed, as one of our most distinguished contemporary collectors, Rear-Admiral Paul Furse, has pointed out: 'When collecting bulbs which are not in flower, it is all too easy to mix two species which are growing together, particularly when young, without recognising that there are two until they flower at home. . . . The conscientious collector spreads his bulbs out to dry off any condensation: a gust of wind blows away two labels or a goat eats them, or a shepherd stirs up the bulbs hoping to find some which he would like for his dinner. . . .

'Later on the bulbs are put in a consignment to go home and a charming and courteous Customs official opens the box and some of the bags and confirms their contents and tastes them to make sure that they are not mixed with Cannabis; he puts them back carefully but not always in their own bags.

'When the consignment gets home the distributor is always rushed and overloaded, and the bags of bulb-salad get stirred up and muddled still more. . . . It may be eight or ten years before the first flower appears, while birds and mice and squirrels play 'hunt the label', and admiring visitors pick up the pot, take the label out to read it with reverence or to take a photograph, but forget to replace it equally reverently in the same pot. The grower has to re-write many labels, and this brings as many mistakes as transcribing the Bible.

'The great day comes and No. 732847 (if it has managed to retain its original label throughout the years) flowers in a dozen different gardens. . . . The odd thing is that seven different tulips flower under this number, as well as three colchicums, five alliums and two muscari. Probably the species which the collector put on his notes doesn't appear at all because he guessed wrong.' Allowing for some pardonable exaggeration it is surprising that so few errors appear to result.

A question that does not seem to have even occurred to the earlier plant collectors, is that of conservation, nowadays so frequently mentioned. In the early nineteenth century John Lyon made journeys to the eastern U.S.A., and in his journal we can find many entries like this for 24

September, 1808: 'Got about 300 young plants of Magnolia macrophylla', and since he is the last man known to have seen *Franklinia alatamaha* in the wild, one wonders if its extinction was due to him. In 1850 Joseph Hooker wrote to his father from the Khasia hills: 'What with Jenkins's and Simon's collectors here, twenty or thirty of Falconer's, Lobb's, my friends Raban and Cave, and Inglis's friends, the roads here are becoming stripped like the Penang jungles, and I assure you for miles it sometimes looks as if a gale had strewed the road with rotten branches and Orchideae. Falconer's men sent down 100 baskets the other day.' Yet we find Hooker writing in his Himalayan Journals with reference to *Vanda caerulea*: 'We collected seven men's load of this superb plant . . . but owing to unavoidable accidents and difficulties few specimens reached England alive. A gentleman who sent his gardener with us to be shown the locality was more successful: he sent one man's load to England on commission, and though it arrived in a very poor state, it sold for £300, the individual plants fetching prices varying from £3 to £10. Had all arrived alive, they would have cleared £1,000. An active collector, with the facilities that I possessed, might easily clear from £2,000 to £3,000 in one season by the sale of Khasia orchids.'

Now if Hooker, one of the most distinguished botanists of the day, could write like that, it is scarcely surprising that less learned men were unconcerned at the result of their ravages. At that time, when the raising of epiphytal orchids from seed was extremely difficult, it seemed natural enough to collect orchids in quantity. To this day we cannot raise the seeds of terrestrial orchids satisfactorily, and the populations of the more showy cypripediums were seriously depleted, before there was any legislation to conserve them. One has only to read the list of Roezl's sendings from Mexico and central America to realise the depredations that unthinking collectors could contrive. In 1870 he sent back 10,000 orchids from Panama and Colombia; a few months later 3,000 odontoglossums came from Colombia. A few years later he was despatching eight tons of orchids from Venezuela, later ten tons of various plants from Mexico, finally in 1873, after agreeing to pay the local Indians from 10 to 15 francs for a 100 orchids, Roezl was able to amass 100,000 plants. As Alice Coats says: 'one gets the impression that if parts of Mexico are now desert and devoid of vegetation, it is because Roezl had been there.'

However, while orchidomania was at its height, there were numerous other collectors just as unscrupulous as Roezl, although possibly less successful. Owing to the difficulty of raising orchids from seed there might be some excuse for such extensive collection, but there could be none for the wholesale destruction of many European plants. The white daffodil, *Narcissus alpestris*, was a rare plant of the Pyrenees. During the intensive daffodil breeding craze of the early years of this century the plant was collected to extinction. Fortunately a fresh colony has recently been found, but the risk of extinction was certainly there. Since it is perfectly easy, although somewhat slow to raise narcissus species from seed, there was no need for such extensive collecting. Nor is this an isolated instance. *N. cyclamineus* is now very rare in the wild. No one has ever seen the red form of *Lilium pyrenaicum* in the wild, so it was presumably a single colony extirpated by collectors. Only a year or so ago a firm imported 50,000 *Cyclamen neapolitanum* from Turkey. These turned out not to be *C. neapolitanum*, but the rare and rather delicate *C. mirabile*, which must now be considerably rarer. This, again, is inexcusable. It is perfectly easy to grow cyclamen from seed. Equally inexcusably, the Vésubie valley in the Alpes Maritimes was stripped of every plant of *Lilium pomponium* shortly after the war.

At times collection may help to save plants. The South African government has very strict conservation laws; it is even forbidden to pick wild flowers, but laws seem to fall into abeyance when commercial developments are in question, and several localities for rare ericas have been destroyed to make way for commercial development. Such plants can probably be preserved in cultivation after their sites have been removed and we have a number of plants which are widespread in cultivation and either extinct or very rare in the wild. They include *Pinus radiata, Cupressus macrocarpa, Ginkgo biloba, Metasequoia glyptostroboides, Malus spectabilis* and *Primula sinensis*. Plant collection does not necessarily militate against survival, and in places where the population is small, it may well help to ensure survival. The horse chestnut is scarce in the wild and so in the tropics is the flamboyant, yet both are widespread in cultivation. So long as the natural populations are not diminished, it is probably advantageous to bring plants into cultivation.

CHAPTER II

The Beginnings

THE creation of ornamental gardens indicates a degree of civilisation and a settled economy. If you do not live permanently in one place, if your house is liable to be periodically destroyed by marauding bands, or if you have not sufficient land to keep yourself in food, you will not take the trouble to make a garden for ornament. Decorative plants are a luxury, and this degree of politic and economic security arrived comparatively late in western Europe. Such conditions had obtained long before the Christian era in China and also for a long time in Persia, whence they spread to Turkey about A.D. 1360. It is true that the richer Romans seem to have had pleasaunces, but we have no record of flowers forming any large feature of their villas. Judging from the writings of Pliny the main emphasis was on topiary.

On the other hand, flowers seem to have been preponderant in Chinese gardens, mainly drawn, as one would expect, from such plants as could be found growing wild but, once contact was established with the west via the Silk Road, a few exotics were brought in, of which *Narcissus tazetta* is the best known. The best-known plants to be developed by the Chinese were peonies, both the moutan and the herbaceous *Paeonia albiflora.* Moutans or tree peonies were available in a large number of different colours which, by the time that John Reeves had Chinese plants painted early in the nineteenth century, included a bright yellow (which suggests that *P. lutea* must have been bred into the strain) and a coppery bronze, which would suggest the influence of *P. delavayi*, although neither *P. lutea* nor *P. delavayi* seem to have been in cultivation at the time when Reeves was having his paintings executed. Other plants that were developed by the Chinese over a very long period include the chrysanthemum, which has a very long recorded history, the camellia and the rose. They also cultivated many other local plants and the survival of the ginkgo seems to have been entirely due to the fact that it was planted near their temples; it has never been found convincingly wild in recent times.

The Persian and Turkish gardens also depended largely on local plants. It would seem that anemones were among the earliest to be brought into cultivation, to be followed by tulips, hyacinths and ranunculus, all of which were considerably developed. They also grew the horse chestnut, lilac, both the common and Persian jasmine, syringa (*Philadelphus*) and irises. Along the silk trail a few Indian plants, such as the hollyhock and the balsam, seem to have been accepted by both cultures. We should note also that some plants imported for their medicinal virtues were later to persist as ornamentals. The two hemerocallis, *H. fulva* and *H. flava* were known to Pliny and to Dioscorides, but they were known for their medicinal virtues; they were, however, to persist in cultivation for centuries up to the present day.

With the collapse of the Roman empire and the arrival of the Dark Ages, we are left to conjecture. The general impression is that civilisation took a downward turn and that gardens were entirely a matter of growing food and materia medica. There are one or two indications in poems of the period that this may not be entirely correct, but the Dark Ages remain dark so far as garden history is concerned. With the Renaissance with its cultivated rich people, gardens were to become a status symbol. They were consciously made to reflect the Roman gardens with the emphasis on topiary, waterworks and sculpture and once again there is no indication that flowers played any very large part. Gardening obviously depends very much on climate, and Italy with its mild spring and autumn and hot dry summer was a place where shade and splashing water would be most grateful. Such conditions could not apply to the colder north of Europe. Although by and large flowers were ignored in these early gardens there seem always to have been two exceptions: the lily and the rose. The lily was the Madonna, *L. candidum*, with its pure white flowers and heady perfume, which seems to have had an association with religion since the days of Cretan civilisation; both it and the rose are depicted in the frescoes of Knossos. Probably the heavy perfume was one reason for its popularity, as it would overmaster the more pungent smells of the congregation at a period when soap was a luxury and washing a difficult accomplishment. The popularity of the rose is less easy to explain, but I suppose it is possible that individual worshippers might have carried one to smell privily when the effluvium of unwashed humanity became overwhelming.

With the onset of the fifteenth century and Paracelsus's promulgation of the Doctrine of Signatures, a number of ornamentals were grown for their medicinal qualities. The Doctrine of Signatures stated that every plant had some medical virtue and that this could be discovered by observation. Thus the swollen root of the colchicum suggested the appearance of someone with gout, so that it might be presumed that a decoction would benefit that complaint; the blotched leaves of lungwort, (*Pulmonaria)* resembled diseased lungs, so it might be regarded as a specific for tuberculosis. Such plants would be cultivated in the gardens of monasteries and other places where medicines might be made and so a large number of plants, both local and exotic, were brought into cultivation.

At some stage during this period it would seem that the flower garden made its appearance. When we reach the Fromond list of plants, which dates in its present form from 1500, but which probably existed considerably earlier, we find among other lists of plants and vegetables a list of Plants for Savour and Beauty and a list of plants for an arbour. It is not possible to identify all these plants, but it is noteworthy that most of the plants for savour and beauty are perfumed or aromatic. They include the gylloflower gentyl, which is probably the clove carnation, sweet marjoram, basil, French lavender, philypendula (probably meadow sweet, *Filipendula*), poppy royal, germander (*Teucrium* spp.), Jerusalem cowslips (*Pulmonaria*), vervein, dill, and some unidentifiable plants. Of these only the poppy would lack perfume. For the arbour one grew vines, roses, lilies, dewberries, almonds, bay trees, gourds, peaches, pines, the Roman peony, rose campion, carthamnus, columbine and hellebore (which could be either *Helleborus* or *Veratrum*). Even as early as this there were a large number of plants that were not native to the British Isles being cultivated.

There is reason to suppose that the first great influx of exotics into Europe came from the Moors in Spain, who brought to that country many of the plants that the Persians had been long growing. These included jasmine, the musk rose, the double yellow Persian rose and the Persian lilac, all of which were to get into more northern gardens.

Indeed it would seem to be the Spaniards who first brought plants from the New World, among these earliest introductions being the French and African marigolds, the marvel of Peru, the nasturtium (*Tropaeolum minus*), the tuberose, the passion flower and the Indian shot, *Canna indica*. It was not only the potato and tobacco that they brought back.

By the time we reach the sixteenth century we are on slightly firmer ground. The Turkish plants were introduced to western gardens, many through that enterprising ambassador of the Holy Roman Empire, Ghiselin de Busbecq, who seems to have been responsible for the first florist's forms of the anemone, ranunculus, tulip and hyacinth to reach the west, as well as such plants as *Iris susiana* and the crown imperial (*Fritillaria imperialis*). It was not long before there arose a trade between Turkish nurserymen and western Europe, although the Turks had a bad reputation for selling goods under false descriptions, most notably supplying single Ranunculus when doubles had been paid for. Although relations between Spain and England were bad, a very large number of Spanish plants had got into cultivation. It cannot be coincidence that *Iris xiphioides* has always been known as the English iris and we know that Clusius, who had botanised in Spain, did not see *Scilla peruviana* until he visited Bristol. It would seem that it was in England and the Low Countries towards the end of the sixteenth century that floriculture was first seriously undertaken and that an interest in growing plants from foreign sources became widespread.

One must be careful not to generalise too far, but the actual material available to garden designers earlier had not been large. The Tudor Knot Garden was made up of elaborate geometric designs that would be outlined in dwarf box, or germander, or marjoram, while later santolina would be much used. Unfortunately there were very few plants that could be inserted within these outlines and the choice seems to have been either coloured earths or examples of topiary. Colour seems to have been lacking from these gardens which required the bedding plants that were to be developed in the nineteenth century to make their full effect.

I suppose our key document for the sixteenth century garden is Bacon's famous essay, published in 1625, but probably written at the end of the sixteenth century. In this he lists all the plants that could be got to flower in the various months, so that one could have perpetual spring. The list is not very large and it is clear that once June was past there were very few flowering plants available. Bacon lists the plants as they flower and for July he could only list: 'Gillyflowers of all varieties; musk roses; the lime tree in blossom', while in August the only flower he mentions is: 'Monkshoods of all colours'; in September only: 'poppies of all colours', which sounds a bit dubious, while in October he could advise only: 'roses cut or removed to come late' and hollyhocks. The roses would be the autumn damask, which flowered in the autumn if pruned in a certain way.

Apart from a single feature, to which we must give some attention in a minute, it would seem that the bulk of Bacon's garden consisted of lawns and tall hedges, which would be agreeably shaped behind trellis. Bacon scorned the geometric knots: 'As for the making of knots or figures with divers coloured earths ... they be but toys: you may see as good sights many times in tarts.' Nor did Bacon care for elaborate topiary. 'I ... do not like images cut out in juniper or other garden stuff, they be for children.' Nevertheless, the garden did contain flowers and here the emphasis was as much on fragrance as on floral beauty and Bacon had a lot to say about this.

'Roses damask and red are fast flowers of their smells; so that you may walk by a whole row of them and find nothing of their sweetness; yea, though it be in a morning's dew. Bays likewise yield no smell as they grow. Rosemary little; nor sweet marjoram. That which above all yields the sweetest smell in the air is the violet; specially the double white violet which comes twice a year; about the middle of April and about Bartholomew tide. Next to that is the musk rose. Then the strawberry leaves dying, which yields a most excellent cordial smell. Then the flower of the vines; it is a little dust like the dust of a bent, which grows among the cluster in the first coming forth. Then sweet-briar. Then wall-flowers which are very delightful to be set under a parlour or low chamber window. Then pinks and gillyflowers, specially the matted pink and clove gillyflower. Then the flowers of the lime tree. Then the honeysuckles, so they be somewhat far off. Of bean flowers I speak not, because they are field flowers. But those which perfume the air most delightfully, not passed by as the rest, but being trodden upon and crushed are three: that is burnet, wild thyme and water mint. Therefore you are to set whole alleys of them, to have the pleasure when you walk or tread.'

Evidently perfuming the air was a major preoccupation with Bacon and the ornamental features of the flowers were rather secondary, except in the furthest portion of the garden, which Bacon termed the heath and which later horticultural writers would call the wilderness. 'For the heath . . .' Bacon wrote, 'I wish it to be framed as much as may be to a natural wilderness'. Here suddenly, published in 1625 but probably written around the fifteen-nineties, is the germ of the 'English Garden', which would not emerge in its own right until the middle of the eighteenth century, but which, it would seem, must have been a feature of many gardens before. It is true that only Bacon mentions this feature for some time, but there is no reason to suppose that he was not referring to a traditional design. In the next century you will find the great French garden designers planting a grove or bosquet, which would seem to be a formalised version of Bacon's heath.

As the seventeenth century started the number of introduced plants increased. From North America the French had brought back *Lilium canadense* and the acacia, *Robinia pseudoacacia*, and the number of American plants would be increased considerably as the century advanced, so that when Parkinson published his *Paradisus* in 1629 there are quite a number of plants from outside Europe, which were, presumably, available to many gardeners. The fact that there was a public to purchase the *Paradisus* and that there were nurserymen to import and propagate such plants does suggest that gardening had become a popular diversion by the sixteen-twenties. Among the plants that Parkinson lists are, from North America, *Lilium canadense,* the evening primrose (*Oenothera biennis*), *Lobelia cardinalis*, *Asclepias syriaca* and *A. variegata*, *Passiflora incarnata*, *Thuja occidentalis*, and *Zephyranthes atamasco*. From South and Central America had come *Sprekelia formosissima,* the Jacobaean lily, the nasturtium, *Tropaeolum minus,* French and African marigolds, marvel of Peru, *Convolvulus major* (*Pharbitis purpurea* and *P. hederacea,*) three datura or thorn apples (as well as a fourth species from India), *Canna indica,* the tomato, which was grown for ornament only in those days, and the prickly pear (*Opuntia ficus-indica*)as well as the tuberose. From Asia, besides the Turkish florist's flowers, came *Iris persica* and *I. susiana,* balsam, cockscomb, love-lies-bleeding and the ornamental leaved *Amaranthus gangeticus tricolor, Lamium orvala,* the hollyhock, *Jasminum officinale, Syringa persica, Rosa moschata* and *Hibiscus syriacus.* There was even a South African bulb, which Parkinson called the African marine hyacinth, which would seem to have been *Haemanthus coccineus.* Parkinson did not succeed in keeping this last rarity alive.

The number of North American importations increased considerably in the succeeding years, partly, it would seem, owing to the activities of the younger John Tradescant, who visited Virginia at least twice and possibly three times and brought back plants and seeds. He and his father had what was to all intents a botanic garden at Lambeth and catalogues of this garden in 1634 and in 1656 have survived. The last catalogue contains 1600 names, some of which are cultivars; they had, for example, twenty different named anemones and thirty tulips and a lot are plants that we should now consider weeds, but even so there is an impressive display of ornamentals. Perhaps the most important were some North American goldenrods and Michaelmas daisies, which would prolong the floral display to the late summer and autumn. There were also many trees and shrubs, which included the deciduous cypress, liquidambar, *Acer rubrum, Campsis radicans,* the stag's horn sumach, the Virginia creeper, the western plane, possibly *Gleditsia triacanthos, Juglans cinerea* and two other 'walnuts', which could be either *Juglans* or *Carya,* the bladder nut, *Staphylea trifolia,* the witch hazel, *Hamamelis virginiana,* a couple of vines and a hawthorn, as well as the first perennial lupin, *Lupinus perennis* and the plant named after the Tradescants, *Tradescantia virginiana*, although they probably did not introduce this plant, which Parkinson had in 1629.

In 1659 Sir Thomas Hanmer wrote his Garden Book, which, however, has only been published in this century. One interesting feature of the plants that he lists, are sixty cultivars of the Spanish iris. So far as I know this is the first mention of this plant being developed and it seems to have been an isolated instance. In the mid-eighteenth century Miller only mentions two or three variants, while towards the end of the eighteenth century Mawe and Abercrombie list about thirteen English and Spanish iris and it is not until we get to the eighteen-thirties that we find long lists of named Spanish iris again. Tradescant had possessed one South African plant, a night-scented geranium, which is thought to have been *Pelargonium triste*, and Hanmer had another which sounds like an antholyza. He called it a gladiolus and said that it had: 'a very great netted bulbous root and light red towards scarlet flowers growing on both sides of the stalk.' By the end of the seventeenth century, as we shall see in Chapter IV, a large number of South African plants had been received in cultivation. Among other plants that Hanmer possessed was the red Virginian lily. This sounds like *Lilium superbum*, the sort of plant that one would think that any collector would bring back, although it does not seem to have entered into general cultivation before the seventeen-thirties. Among other exotic plants that Hanmer had in 1659 was the cedar of Lebanon. This must have been a very recent introduction and one would like to know how it got into cultivation. The first collector who we know visited the Near East was Sir George Wheler in the sixteen-seventies. It is true both that there was a considerable trade with Aleppo and Alexandretta and that most of the cedars grow in Turkey rather than in Lebanon, so it might well be through the Turkish nurserymen that this plant arrived. When William Lucas published his catalogue in 1677 he was able to offer plants, so they must have been well established in cultivation by that date.

The presence of this catalogue is of more interest in determining the sort of plants that the ordinary keen gardener could grow than are the lists of great plantsmen such as Tradescant and Hanmer, who may have obtained plants that were in very short supply, and it is sad that there are very few catalogues available between 1677 and 1750, so we should perhaps look at this list in some detail, if we wish to gain an idea as to the sort of plants that the enthusiast could obtain towards the end of the seventeenth century. The list starts with seeds and it is amusing to note that *Tropaeolum minus* had left the flower garden and was being grown as a salad herb. The flower seeds include the carnation, the pink, the 'mountain pink', double columbine and Virginian columbine (*Aquilegia canadensis*), various larkspurs, *Tagetes, Antirrhinum,* candytuft, sweet scabious and 'Spanish scabious', London pride, *Capsicum, Specularia, Omphalodes linifolia,* French honeysuckle (*Hedysarum coronarium*,) *Lychnis chalcedonica* and *L. coronaria*, balsam, marvel of Peru, sweet sultan, red valerian and Greek valerian, which was the *Polemonium*, the sunflower, Canterbury bells, *Adonis aestivalis*, foxtail grass, *Digitalis ferruginea, Nigella*, the Roman nettle, *Verbascum blattaria*, various love-lies-bleeding, including the green-flowered form, prince's feather, the tomato, the thorn apple (*Datura stramonium*), double opium poppies, hollyhocks, *Silene armeria, Galega officinalis*, aconite, *Ipomoe purpurea* (syn. *Convolvulus major*) and *Convolvulus minor*, cornflowers, globe thistle, annual lupins, scarlet runner beans, at that time grown solely for ornament like the tomato, everlasting pea, various *Medicago* spp. which were grown for their oddly shaped capsules and known as 'Snails, Caterpillars, Horns and Hedgehogs', Auricula, Polyanthus and primrose and two sensitive *Mimosa* species. Staying with flowers, among the roots you could purchase were Ranunculus, anemones and tulips, *Iris persica, I. susiana* and *I. pumila*, crown imperials in various colours and with double flowers, 'Lilies of all sorts', which is a little vague, *Dictamnus, Hepatica,* crocus, *Narcissus*, hyacinths, which included the feather hyacinth, *Muscari comosum monstrosum*, and *Scilla peruviana*, jonquils, peonies which were 'Black, Red, Purple and Striped', fritillaries of all sorts, *Veratrum album* and *V. nigrum*, *Helleborus niger*, *Colchicum*, gladiolus of all sorts and a spring and an autumn flowering cyclamen.

One would dearly like to know what the black peony was.

The trees and shrub list starts off with a number of tender subjects, such as oranges, lemons, pomegranate, myrtles and oleander. We also find here our old friend the Christmas cherry, *Solanum capsicastrum*. Among more amenable subjects are the two phillyreas, the variegated *Rhamnus alaternus*, one of the prides of the seventeenth-century gardener, *Medicago arborea, Cytisus sessilifolius,* various forms of holly, the arbutus, *Paliurus spina-christi,* the olive, the cedar of Lebanon and the Bermuda cedar and one called *Cedrus sempervirens*, which might be *Thuja occidentalis, Vitex agnus-castus*, Judas tree, both the eastern and the western plane, the tragacanth, the horse chestnut and the sweet chestnut, various jasmines which would include *Syringa persica,* and *Cistus* of all sorts. The plant known as *Marum syriacum*, which seems to have been *Teucrium marum*, but might have been an *Origanum* species was very popular in the seventeenth and eighteenth centuries, presumably on account of its aromatic qualities. Miller noted that it had: 'a piercing grateful scent, so quick as to cause sneezing'. It is also very attractive to cats and was later known as cat thyme as well as the Syrian marum and, according to Abercrombie, as mastick.

To return to Lucas he also supplied *Yucca gloriosa, Hibiscus syriacus* and variegated forms of *Solanum dulcamara* and *Lonicera periclymenum.* There were also various trees of which he could provide seeds, but not apparently plants. These included the cypress, a number of pines and firs, *Pyracantha, Laurustinus,* mezereon, *Prunus laurocerasus,* the bay, *Juniperus communis*, the yew, the evergreen oak, the cork oak, lime *Colutea arborescens*, almonds, Spanish broom and both the common and the alpine laburnum. Apparently Lucas had none of the Michaelmas daisies, eupatoriums and goldenrods that had come from the Americas. They were in cultivation, but not yet in commerce.

It will be observed that most of the common trees have not been listed by Lucas, but for an account of them we can turn to *The English Gardener*, published in 1670 and written by Leonard Meager. Here he lists the 'Trees fit to plant by Out-walk sides, or otherwise.' The main subjects here are ash, beech, birch, chestnut, elm, hornbeam, lime, oak, black and white poplars, service, sycamore, walnut, willow and a number of conifers. Willows were only to be planted in damp situations. These were the trees used to form avenues, which had become popular as the influence of Le Nôtre spread from France. However, owing to the climate, there was an essential difference between the French and English gardens. The French summer tends to be more reliable than the British, so that perambulation was not necessary in France. It was regarded as satisfactory to have a great vista from which most of the garden would be visible and you enjoyed your garden sitting down rather than walking round, although you could move from one vista to another. The so-called goose foot or *patte d'oie*, a sort of central area whence avenues radiated in all directions, was satisfactory enough with very large acreages, but it was not a feature that the owners of rather small gardens could imitate. In England, even in the larger gardens, it would seem as though flowers were quite a feature, although one would not guess this from most of the contemporary descriptions. In his *Gardens of Epicurus*, Sir William Temple describes the best garden he ever knew, the one at Moor Park, as he first knew it: 'about thirty years ago'. Since the book was published in 1685 this would seem to place it about 1655. The house at Moor Park was situated at the top of a hill and in front was: 'a terrace gravel walk; 300 paces long and proportionately broad and there was also a border set with standard Bay trees,' at large distances, which have the beauty of orange trees out of flower and fruit. 'From this terrace three staircases, one at each end and the third in the centre, descended to a second terrace, which was 'a very large parterre'. This was, in fact, a knot garden, the beds divided by gravel walks and the whole was adorned with two fountains and eight statues. At either end of this second terrace were summer houses, while the sides of the parterre are ranged with two large cloisters, which are paved with stone . . . roofed with lead and enclosed in trellis work.' Temple noted that the south-facing cloister was covered with vines and would in his day have been used as an orangery, while the other would in 1685 have held myrtles and other tender evergreens. From this second terrace you had two staircases, one at each end, which led you to a wilderness of fruit trees with grass paths, which suggests a straightforward orchard. However, the base of the terrace between the two flights of steps had been excavated to form a grotto 'embellished with figures of shell rockwork, fountains and water-works'. Temple notes that there were very few evergreens, but that this was compensated for in the second garden behind the house, which was entirely composed of evergreens 'very wild, shady and adorned with rough rockwork and fountains'. The rockwork in those days would be composed of blocks of rock cemented together to form grottoes and suchlike baroque fancies, but they do not seem to have contemplated planting saxatile plants among them.

Moor Park in the sixteen fifties, although apparently destitute of flowering plants, still showed some affinities with the Jacobaean gardens, but this was soon to vanish. The very wild, shady garden soon turned into the bosquet always designed as Mawe and Abercrombie wrote, 'with the greatest uniformity, the ground being divided by walks into many squares and angles, all corresponding, and all the walks straight, and the principal ones leading to some common centre ... with all the quarters or divisions surrounded with close hedges.' It would seem, in fact, as though the Victorian shrubbery descends directly from the baroque bosquet. However, where the choice of plants was limited interest had to be created by other ways, so the hedges were formed into 'pilasters, arcades or arches, porticoes, galleries, amphitheatres ... likewise regular arbors having the sides formed into arcades and sometimes the top vaulted.' Moreover, these hedges were sometimes very large, sometimes 'to 30 or 40 feet high; sometimes trained perfectly close from the very bottom to the top, others open below a considerable way and formed into regular arches etc., all of which sometimes appeared magnificent ... but were troublesome and expensive to keep in order.' In the midst of all this artificiality there was also something much like the Broad Walk in Regent's Park. Mawe and Abercrombie are, so far as I know, the only writers to mention this grand walk 'extended in a straight line immediately in front of the mansion, having each side verged either with a regular straight border ... furnished with a variety of flowers etc., sometimes having a verge of grass three or four feet wide, then a border embellished as above with various plants; this main walk being sometimes intersected by others at regular distances, so as sometimes to divide the space immediately in front of the house into ... equal squares, some of which were sometimes formed into parterres, sometimes only naked grass plots.'

The baroque garden was not only very expensive to maintain, but it became tedious. Mawe and Abercrombie noted that 'with the same thing often prevailing in almost every part ... even gardens of very considerable extent afforded very little variety and the perpetual show of stiff formality ... became at last in a manner disgusting and unentertaining in the general appearance to persons of taste and observation'. Still with very limited materials to work with, it was not easy to break away from the set mould. Although numerous plants were brought into cultivation during the seventeenth and early eighteenth centuries they took time to become widespread and for their real worth to be appreciated. The cedar of Lebanon may have arrived about 1650, but it would take many years before its potentialities would be realised. Other trees such as the horse chestnut or the weeping willow would show their charms earlier and it is significant that the first rebellion against the formal garden came at a time when more exotic flowering plants and shrubs were getting into circulation. By the mid-eighteenth century the formal bosquet had become almost a woodland garden as we can learn from this description by Philip Miller. 'There may be planted next the walks and openings, Roses, Honeysuckles, Spiraee frutex (*Spiraea salicifolia*) and other kinds of low flowering shrubs . . . and at the foot of them, near the sides of the walks may be planted Primroses, Violets, Daffodils and many other sorts of wood flowers to appear as in a natural wood. Behind these should be planted Syringas, Cytisuses, Althaea frutex (*Hibiscus syriacus*), Mezereons and other flowering shrubs of middle growth, which may be backed by other shrubs of a large growth.'

'As in a natural wood.' The words presage the spirit that was to animate the gardens of the eighteenth and early nineteenth centuries. When suitable plants appeared in the nineteenth century we will see a return to the geometric garden and the embroidered parterre, but for the next century the emphasis will be on nature.

CHAPTER III

North America

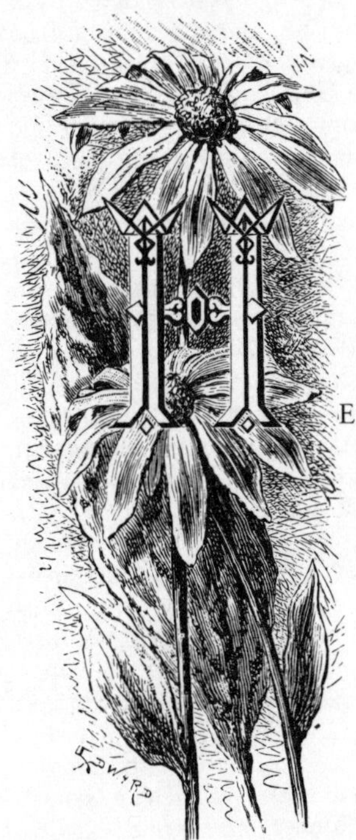

HENRY Compton was Bishop of London from 1675 until 1713. During much of this time he was an active politician and, as this was a period when revolutionary activities were prevalent, he frequently found himself out of favour. During such periods he discreetly laid low and cultivated the garden at Fulham Palace. The result, as Sir William Watson informed the Royal Society in 1751, was that he 'planted a greater variety of curious exotic plants and trees than had at that time been collected in any garden in England.... By means of a large correspondence with the principal botanists of Europe and America, he introduced into England a great number of plants, but more especially trees, which had never been seen here before and described by no author'. Watson goes on to praise the generosity with which he distributed seeds and plants and allowed botanists to visit his garden. Among Compton's duties was the appointment of missionaries and in 1685 he sent a keen botanist, the Rev. John Banister, to Virginia. Banister sent back seeds, possibly plants, and botanical specimens. Many of his specimens were described by John Ray in his *Historia Plantarum* and their elucidation provides some odd problems. A plant is described, for example, as the smaller yellow anchusa. This sounds easy enough to identify, but we then learn that it is called Puccoon by the Indians. This means that the plant is the bloodroot, *Sanguinaria canadensis*, which is not an anchusa, nor is it yellow. Banister's interest in botany cost him his life; in 1692 he fell from a cliff while in pursuit of his hobby.

One rather tends to assume that all the new North American plants in the Bishop's garden were supplied by Banister, but this may not be accurate. One of the plants was *Picea glauca*, which is very northern in its distribution, not getting further south than New York. Did Banister get up to Maine and similar places or did Compton have more than one correspondent? We just do not know. There is a surprising piece of information about one of his sendings in Miller's *Dictionary*. He says that most of the seedlings raised from his sending of the hop tree, *Ptelea trifoliata*, were killed in a very severe winter. Normally this would prove quite frost-resistant and it might seem that he must have sent seed from the more southerly part of the plant's range. Probably his most significant and attractive sending was the swamp bay, *Magnolia virginiana*, the first magnolia to arrive in cultivation. Since this has fragrant flowers all through the summer it must have eventually proved a delightful newcomer to the garden and was the first arrival of a type of gardening that would eventually be known as the American Garden, which was to be composed of various ericaceous shrubs and magnolias.

Banister also sent back a number of other woody subjects, which included the scarlet oak, the box maple, *Acer negundo*, the liquidambar, one of the North American hawthorns that were lumped by Linnaeus as *Crataegus coccinea*, a name that is now fairly meaningless, *Cornus amomum*, which used to be prized for its very pale blue fruits, *Gleditsia triacanthos*, which had probably already been introduced by the younger Tradescant, the first North American spiraea, which is now called *Physocarpus opulifolius*, probably *Rubus odoratus*, an ornamental raspberry, and a number of conifers. Of these both *Picea glauca* (syn. *P. alba*) and *P. mariana* have persisted in cultivation. *Pinus taeda* has always proved unsatisfactory in the British Isles and so nowadays does the balsam fir, *Abies balsamea*. This does not seem always to have been the case as plants of it were offered for forestry work during the eighteenth century and in the opening years of the next century. Banister also sent back a number of herbaceous plants, which included *Dodecatheon meadia*, a plant that every collector sent back from Tradescant onwards, but one which it seemed very hard to preserve for long in cultivation and it was not until the middle of the eighteenth century that it was sufficiently established to appear in commercial catalogues. Gardeners were more successful with other Banister sendings such as the cone flower, *Echinacea purpurea*, or with *Rudbeckia triloba, Mertensia virginica* and *Rhexia virginica*. He also sent back a number of hemp agrimonies, *Eupatorium* spp., which are practically never seen in gardens nowadays, but which were at one time very popular.

As we shall be seeing, most plant collecting in the eighteenth century had official backing, but this always seems to have been lacking in the case of North America, where plant collecting was either due to a syndicate financing a collector or to private enterprise on the part of nurserymen.

Our next collector was financed by a syndicate of four keen botanist-gardeners, William Sherard, whose famous garden at Eltham was catalogued by Dillenius, Dr Hans Sloane, whose collections were to form the nucleus of the British Museum, Dr Richard Mead and the Duke of Chandos, who were both keen gardeners. The man they fixed on was Mark Catesby, who was later to produce that exquisite book, the *Natural History of Carolina*. Catesby was to make two collecting trips between 1722 and 1725 and, although most of his time was spent in Carolina, he also visited the Bahamas, from where he brought back the jacaranda. The majority of the plants accredited to him in *Hortus Kewensis* have dropped out of cultivation, but even so there are still a number of useful plants. Perhaps that most frequently seen is *Catalpa bignonioides*, which Catesby not only introduced to his patrons but also to the inhabitants of Charleston, who planted it around their town, with the result that fresh seed was always available and the tree soon became popular. At this time there lived in Virginia John Clayton, a keen and enthusiastic botanist who furnished the Dutch botanist Gronovius with sufficient specimens for him to publish in 1732 a *Flora Virginica*. It was he who furnished Catesby with *Stewartia malachodendron*, a very attractive tree with open white flowers with a conspicuous boss of purple stamens, which is still cultivated with enthusiasm by those who can succeed with it; it is by no means easy of cultivation. Catesby also brought the first wisteria into cultivation; this was *W. frutescens*, now supplanted by the showier Asian species, but probably well worth a reintroduction since it flowers in June and July when the Asian wisterias are over. To Catesby we also owe our first sight of the spice tree, *Calycanthus floridus* and a couple of the North American roses: *Rosa carolina* and *R. foliolosa*. Among herbaceous plants he is credited with *Lilium superbum*, although it may well have been grown previously by Sir Thomas Hanmer, *Liatris squarrosa* and *L. spicata*, still popular herbaceous subjects, *Canna glauca*, one of the parents of the modern hybrid cannas and that most popular of phlox, *P. paniculata*. Many of these plants were obtained by the nurseryman, Robert Furber, and so soon got into commerce and general distribution.

So far plants collected in America had had a somewhat limited distribution. This was soon to be changed through the activities of Peter Collinson, the Quaker cloth-merchant and plantsman. In 1728 we find him writing: 'Hitherto the laudable design of improving and cultivating exotic trees in this country meets with a number of discouragements too tedious to enumerate except one, which I think is hereditary to America, that is—great promise but slender performance.' This was soon to change. Writing thirty-eight years later, in 1766, Collinson explained that 'at last some more artful than the rest contrived to get rid of my importunities by recommending a person whose business it should be to gather seeds and send over plants. Accordingly John Bartram was recommended to me as a very proper person, being a native of Pennsylvania with numerous family. The profits arising from gathering seed would enable him to support it. At first it was not thought that sending over would prove a trade, but, with the demand, the price was fixed at £5 5*s* 0*d* a box.'

John Bartram (1699–1777) had settled in Philadelphia in 1728, where he had a farm. Ther are several stories as to how his interest in wild flowers was awakened, but it seems fairly clear that he was originally self-taught, although later he picked up some elementary botany. On the other hand, he seems to have been notably observant and indefatigable. He started serious collecting about 1734 and continued for over thirty years until his sight began to fail. During this time he is said to have introduced over 200 plants to British gardens and these introductions were made in large quantities, so that the plants became generally available. When Bartram started he had only three subscribers: Collinson, Philip Miller and Lord Petre, a very keen gardener who was unfortunately to die young in 1742. As time went on the number of subscribers increased to sixty-one. The three original subscribers paid Bartram £10 0*s* 0*d* per year and it was only when the number grew that the five guinea subscription came into force. For this each subscriber received seeds of 105 different shrubs and trees; at least this is what is shown in the sole list of a sending which survives. This included 4 pines, the hemlock, 2 magnolias, 6 maples, 3 birches, 12 oaks, 4 hickories, *Rhododendron maximum*, 2 kalmias, 4 sumachs, 3 or 4 crataegus, 2 walnuts, 6 viburnums and a couple of spiraeas, besides a large number of other shrubs and trees. By no means all these plants were previously unknown, but hitherto they had been rare in cultivation. In addition Collinson received herbaceous and bulbous subjects and he would give the seeds to the nurserymen James Gordon and Christopher Gray to raise, allowing them to keep the surplus. Gordon had been Lord Petre's head gardener before setting up on his own and for long he was the only nurseryman who was able to raise the various ericaceous plants, such as azaleas and kalmias from seed, so that he was able to have a monopoly of these for some time. *Rhododendron maximum* was the first large rhododendron seen in cultivation and one of the first of Bartram's sendings. It seems curious that it was introduced some twenty-five years before the now omnipresent *R. ponticum*. Of the American azaleas, the swamp honeysuckle, *Rhododendron viscosum*, first flowered in Britain in 1732 according to Catesby, so, if he is correct, there must have been a sending before

Bartram's, but Bartram is certainly responsible for the introduction of *R. nudiflorum*, which was eventually available in a number of colour forms. Of magnolias, Bartram certainly introduced *M. acuminata* and *M. tripetala*; it is not clear whether he can be credited with *M. grandiflora*. This is said to have arrived in 1734, so it is possible, but it seems somewhat unlikely. Collinson's son was very interested in hardy orchids and obtained a number from Bartram, including three cypripediums, *Goodyera pubescens, Liparis liliifolia* and *Spiranthes cernua*. It is to Bartram that we owe *Kalmia latifolia* and *K. angustifolia*, the scarlet bergamot (*Monarda didyma*), *Lilium catesbaei* and *L. philadelphicum*, the Dutchman's pipe (*Aristolochia macrophylla*), *Hydrangea arborescens*, the white cedar, *Chamaecyparis thyoides* and many other plants, which have now vanished from our gardens.

During his thirty years' wanderings Bartram visited most of the inhabited parts of the United States. We can get some idea as to what travelling conditions were like from his journal of 1765 which has survived and been published. Bartram's spelling and orthography was somewhat eccentric and I have modernised them here.

'August 29. Set out for Georgia and parted with my friends Lamboll and Dr Garden. Rode over exceeding flat rich ground full of bushes and pretty good timber; as large hickory, white oak, oak of our common sort, willow oak, beech, elm, linden, hornbeam, liquidambar, chinquapin, poplor, catalpa, pine, mulberry, fartle berry, bay, white berry cornus, aralia spinosa, all jumbled promiscuously together. Dined at Cooper's at the first bridge then over Rantowle's bridge, after which we missed our right road and took the left, which led us much too near the salts and sometimes took over much tolerable piney soil, until towards night, when we began to look for a house; one of which we rode to, having the appearance of a gentleman's house. But he would not let us stay upon any terms, but directed us to the next plantation. He said it was about a mile off, but we found it above two miles. But he too would not let us stay although it was then just dark. He directed us to the next neighbour . . . he ordered his negro to put us on the way. He led us a great way round a deep branch, then over a brooked dam, but the water was so deep that the horses almost swam and our feet and legs were wet. When we came to the house, which made a good appearance, the master was as ill-natured as the others; he told us he could not entertain us, for he entertained no travellers. We told him that we had travelled a great way and were very weary and that our horses were quite tired and could go no further and must lay us down in the field. After a good while he consented we should stay, but we must lie in a little old hut, little better than a hog stye, being the worst outhouse he had . . . we found a candle stuck in an old bottle for a candle stick and some hominy and two horn spoons to eat it with. We pulled off our wet clothes and hung them up to dry and lay down among the rats, weevils, grubs and mosquitoes to refresh ourselves after a tedious ride.' This was Southern hospitality in the seventeen-sixties, but evidently Bartram thought it sufficiently bad to comment.

On this trip Bartram was accompanied by his son William, who was later to explore Georgia and Florida for Dr Fothergill. It was on this expedition that *Franklinia alatamaha* was first discovered. The plant is only known from this one locality and soon became extinct in the wild. The last recorded sighting, as we shall see, was in 1803. It has persisted in cultivation, although it is unsatisfactory in the U.K. as it needs a hot dry summer to ripen its wood. It has large white flowers in August and September and the leaves colour brilliantly in the autumn, so it is very ornamental. The Bartrams were there in October, at which time it is quite possible that the seeds would have been ripe. According to Aiton the plant was introduced to Kew by William Malcolm in 1774. Malcolm had an extremely fine nursery and may well have received seeds from Collinson, as one of the plants credited to him by Aiton, *Paeonia tenuifolia*, had originally been obtained by Collinson. It is possible therefore that this introduction came from seeds sent by Bartram in 1766. In his *Travels* William Bartram wrote, 'This very curious tree was first taken notice of about ten or twelve years ago, at this place when I attended my father on a botanical excursion; but, it being then late in the autumn, we could form no opinion to what class or tribe it belonged.' It would seem, therefore, as though it were 1775 or later that William revisited the site. Even so his remarks are slightly ambiguous. 'I employed myself during the spring and fore part of the summer in revisiting the several districts in Georgia ... collecting ... and shipping them off to England. In the course of these excursions I had the opportunity of observing the new flowering shrub resembling the Gordonia in perfect bloom as well as bearing ripe fruit.' Now the franklinia does not flower in the 'fore part of the summer'; no doubt the capsules hang for some time on the tree.

When writing in about 1775 William stated; 'at this place there are two or three acres of ground where it grows plentifully.' When the nurseryman John Lyon, visited the site in 1803 on 1 June he noted 'here there is not more than six or eight full-grown trees of it, which does not spread over more than half an acre of ground.' The diminution of the wild population in twenty-five years or so is marked. It does seem as though there is something about Georgian plants that predisposes them towards extinction. Recently it was found that the attractive ericaceous *Elliottia racemosa* was ceasing to set seed either in the wild or in cultivation and only in the last few years has a method of vegetative propagation been discovered, so perhaps this plant, like the franklinia, will survive only in cultivation.

In 1761 William Young, a protegé of that dubious character but knowledgeable gardener John Hill, arrived in the Southern states and was appointed Queen's Botanist (John Bartram was King's Botanist). He introduced very few novelties, but his plants, as we have seen, were very carefully packed and arrived in good condition. Although he sent plants to various subscribers, he also hired a plot of ground in which to grow and sell his plants. He also seems to have sent a large number to Vilmorin in Paris, who in 1783 listed 173 woody and 145 herbaceous American plants that Young could supply. By this time he seems to have established a nursery in Philadelphia.

The desire to make money from the direct sale of collected plants and from the raising of American plants from seed animated the next two collectors, John Fraser (1752–1811) and John Lyon, who died in 1814. Fraser made his first expedition in 1784, possibly financed in part by the elder Aiton and by the founder of the Linnaean Society, Sir James Smith. He would appear to have been in a loose partnership with Frank Thoburn, with whom he had a tedious and inconclusive lawsuit. Thoburn claimed, according to Loudon, that many of the plants had arrived dead and those that survived were of little value. Apparently undiscouraged by this failure, Fraser crossed a second time to Charleston to make further collections in 1785. While collecting plants he also assisted Thomas Walter in his *Flora of Carolina*. Indeed he was able to add a further 420 species to the 640 that Walter had already collected, which is an extremely large proportion. Fraser also met and went on excursions with the French collector, André Michaux. Fraser remained in America until 1788, when he returned to England, but had to sell his collections immediately to provide sufficient funds for him to survive. He also had brought a new grass, *Agrostis perennis*, which he had hopes would prove of the greatest agricultural value, but which seems to have proved disappointing. After two further collecting trips Fraser opened a nursery at Sloane Square. This seems to have been started about 1786, although it does not seem to have become fully operational until some six to nine years later. In 1796 Fraser established a profitable connection with the Russian court, being appointed botanical collector to the Czar and Czarina. Unfortunately after Czar Paul's assassination his successor repudiated the appointment and Fraser was unable to obtain his arrears of salary. In the meantime he continued to make collecting trips, being now accompanied by his son also called John. In 1800 on his return home he visited Cuba, where he met the great Humboldt and his botanist companion Bonpland. Humboldt seems to have been impressed by the younger Fraser and invited him to accompany them on their forthcoming trip to Mexico, but the younger Fraser declined. It would seem it was from Humboldt that they received the scarlet dahlia, which they introduced from this expedition, which had included visits to Kentucky and Tennessee. It was young John who took the plants back to England, as well as two cases of Humboldt's while his father returned for further collecting, returning to England in 1802. He remained in Europe for five years, vainly trying to get money from the Russian court, returning to the States in 1807 and remaining until 1810. It was on this last trip that he discovered *Rhododendron catawbiense*, a plant of great frost resistance and the principal parents for the hardy hybrid rhododendrons that were to be bred in increasing numbers as the century progressed.

As his last trip was coming to an end Fraser had the misfortune to fall from his horse and break several ribs. This was in a district where no medical aid was available and it was a very ill man who returned to England. When he returned to England, according to Loudon, 'frequent disappointments, ill-treatment and other circumstances all tended to break down one of the most indefatigable and perservering men that ever embarked in the cause of botany and natural science'. He died in 1811. His son made a further collecting trip to America. He left the Sloane Square nursery in 1817 and opened a nursery at Ramsgate; the Sloane Square nursery remained open under his brother James Fraser until 1827.

In the *Companion to the Botanical Magazine* of 1836 Sir William Hooker wrote a memoir of Fraser and listed his introductions, although the list would not seem to be entirely accurate. According to Hooker, Fraser's 'skilful method of packing enabled him to transmit, unimpaired, many living plants to which the hazard of a long sea voyage had always previously proved fatal'.

Among the plants that he introduced that have persisted in general cultivation are *Aesculus parviflora, Elaeagnus commutata, Camassia fraseri, Hydrangea quercifolia, Magnolia fraseri, M. macrophylla* and *M. pyramidata*, five oenotheras, *Phlox stolonifera, Rosa carolina, Stewartia ovata*, a number of *Vaccinium* species and *Zenobia speciosa*. The most important for gardens of his introductions were the azaleas, *Rhododendron calendulaceum* and *R. canescens* and the afore-mentioned *R. catawbiense*. It seems strange that *R. calendulaceum*, which supplies the fiery orange colour to the modern azalea hybrids, had not been introduced before, as the Bartrams certainly mention it. Indeed many of Fraser's introductions had previously been noted by William Bartram on his travels, which took place between 1773 and 1777, and he appears to have observed very many plants that were subsequently diagnosed by other botanists. He is, however, credited by Aiton with the introduction of *Hydrangea quercifolia*, which Hooker gave to Fraser, and he certainly was the first to collect *Magnolia fraseri, M. macrophylla* and *M. pyramidata* and many other of the shrubs introduced by Fraser and by Lyon.

John Lyon remains unknown until he appears as the successor to Pursh in looking after William Hamilton's famous garden at 'The Woodlands' in Philadelphia. He is first known there in 1796 and he remained until 1802, having made a couple of collecting trips on his employer's behalf. In 1802 he started on a collecting trip which was to last two years. He seems to have acted with more thoroughness than many collectors, arranging for the nursery firm of Landreth at Philadelphia to look after his plants and also establishing temporary depots in the gardens of his acquaintances. His journals have survived, but are not very informative about his travels, although we have seen his impressions of the franklinia. Only once does he seem to have expressed any real interest in a flower, when he wrote of *Schizandra coccinea*: 'The anthers of this most beautiful flower are like five golden stars set in a crimson field.' Among other hazards Lyon was bitten by a mad dog and poisoned by *Rhus pumila*, which incapacitated him for more than a month. Although he intended to visit London in 1804 Lyon was delayed for a year and did not arrive until 1805, where he rented a nursery for a time and then put the remainder of his plants up for auction. The actual expedition had cost £252 *9s 0d* while his passage to England and his expenses there (which included the sum of £39 0*s* 0*d* for a year's board) came to £312 0*s* 0*d* which made his outlay £564 9*s* 0*d*. From the sale of plants and seeds at the nursery he got £728 9*s* 9*d* while he realised a further £759 0*s* 0*d* from the auction, giving him a net profit of £923 9*d* 0*d*. This sounds quite impressive, but it only works out at a little over £300 per year, which is not princely.

In 1807 he started on a further collecting trip, which was to continue for four years. This proved to be less rewarding. His expenses in America over the four years were £284 17*s* 0*d*, which indicates a low cost of living. His total expenditure for the four years, which include his stay in America, his passage to and from England and his expenses in England came in all to £668 8*s* 9*d*. His plants realised £1281 15*s* 6*d* giving him what he termed the 'neat amount' of £613 6*s* 9*d*, a little over £150 per year. In 1814 he left on a third expedition, but contracted typhoid, which proved fatal, and he died in that year.

Most of his introductions are much the same as Fraser's, but he brought back such large quantities that the plants got widely disseminated. He seems to have been the first to introduce the allspice, *Calycanthus fertilis*, the attractive but rather unsatisfactory snowdrop tree, *Halesia diptera* and some attractive herbaceous subjects, most notably *Dicentra eximia*, which has been a standby in gardens ever since its introduction, the attractive *Jeffersonia diphylla, Coreopsis major, Trillium erectum, Iris fulva* and *Chelone lyonii*.

It will have been noted that Lyon was able to leave his plants to be tended at the nursery of Messrs Landreth and by the first decade of the nineteenth century there were quite a few nurseries, which not only had a local trade, but also an export line to Europe. Among these firms was the nursery established by Michaux, Landreth, Buist and the Bartram's garden at Kingsessing in Philadelphia. A catalogue dated 1825 for this last firm, which we know, from Loudon, supplied Messrs Loddiges, has survived. This lists some 460 shrubs and trees, about 600 herbaceous subjects and such items as ferns, grasses and even mosses (18 spp). Prices were generally low, the only really expensive items being the *Mahonia aquifolium*, still a rare introduction from the unexplored western part of the continent, and another recently discovered shrub, *Maclura aurantiaca*. These cost 5 dollars a plant. A double form of *Rhododendron nudiflorum* cost 2 dollars. Some of the rarer shrubs cost a dollar apiece, but *Gordonia lasianthus* could be got for 50 cents and the franklinia for half that figure.

Among the herbaceous plants there were only two items that cost as much as a dollar: the aquatic *Thalia dealbata*, which is interesting as being the only member of the *Marantaceae* to be hardy in the U.K., but which is not outstandingly attractive, and a now uncultivated composite, *Grindelia squarrosa*, which had been discovered comparatively recently by Messrs Bradbury and Nuttall in 1811.

From the point of view of decorating the garden the many late flowering American herbaceous subjects were of the greatest importance. Among these Kingsessing listed 13 asclepias, 21 asters (Michaelmas daisies), 10 hemp agrimonies (*Eupatorium*), 9 coreopsis, 6 liatris, 12 oenotheras, 13 phlox and 14 solidagos. The earlier seed and plant lists contained comparatively few plants that flowered after July and these Americans made a great impact originally.

With so many nurserymen specialising in native plants, there was less incitement for collectors to visit the U.S.A. unless there was a chance to reach districts that had been hitherto unexplored. This occurred in 1811 when, independently, John Bradbury, who was collecting for the Liverpool Botanic Garden and Thomas Nuttall, who was a free-lance botanist collecting plants to defray his expenses, joined the Astoria expedition up the Missouri as far as the present town of Campbell. Although a number of oenotheras and some composites were introduced from this trip the only plant to have survived in cultivation is the golden currant, *Ribes odoratum* (syn. *R. aureum*), with its attractive perfume and golden flowers in early spring.

Finally we should mention the disastrous expedition of Thomas Drummond, who was financed by a syndicate of private growers and by Botanic Gardens such as Glasgow and Edinburgh to collect plants in Texas. He left in 1832, but it was not until 1834 that he was able to get well into Texas and he died on his way home in 1835. He sent back a large number of attractive plants, such as *Eustoma russellianum* (syn. *Lisianthus russellianus*), but the majority of his sendings require cool greenhouse conditions and few have persisted in cultivation with the exception of the charming plant that bears his name, *Phlox drummondii*.

The impact of all these American plants on British gardens was considerable and is now rather hard to envisage. For long there existed what were termed American Gardens. These were shrubberies mainly planted with azaleas and other ericaceous shrubs, while above would tower the various American magnolias. Nowadays the true rhododendron species have been replaced by modern hybrids, the magnolias have been replaced by the showier Asiatic species and probably the only original denizen of the American garden which may still be found in the modern woodland or rhododendron garden will be the calico bush, *Kalmia latifolia* and perhaps the sorrel tree, *Oxydendrum arboreum*. Actually the name American Garden persisted until the end of the nineteenth century, even when few of the occupants would be American and the association of rhododendrons, ericaceous shrubs and magnolias still persists to this day.

A number of American trees were also used as specimens or in small groups, most notably some of the oaks with brilliant autumn colour, such as the scarlet oak, the handsome flowering catalpa, the very attractive deciduous cypress, *Taxodium distichum*.

Also towards the end of the eighteenth century many American trees were employed in forestry work. In 1775 the Yorkshire firm of Telfords offered for forestry work the Carolina ash, the red Virginian cedar (*Juniperus virginiana*) the white cedar (*Chamaecyparis thyoides*), the deciduous cypress, *Abies balsamea, Picea glauca* and *P. mariana*, the hemlock spruce, the scarlet oak, Lord Weymouth's pine (*Pinus strobus*), the western plane and three different poplars. Few of these would be considered nowadays and both the balsam fir and the western plane are remarkably unsatisfactory plants in cultivation at the present time.

In spite of all the plants that have since been brought into cultivation the influence of these early introductions still persists. We may no longer see the true azaleas, but their pollen has helped to create those that we do see, while our herbacous borders still depend to a very large extent on American plants.

CHAPTER IV *South Africa*

IN much the same way as the British and the French had been sending back plants from North America, the Dutch had been bringing back plants from their colony at the Cape of Good Hope. Even in 1629 Parkinson had *Haemanthus coccineus*, although we learn that he lost it in the winter, and by the end of the seventeenth century there were a number of South Africans in cultivation. Once William III arrived the number introduced to British gardens became quite considerable and included *Agapanthus*, both the parents of our scarlet geranium, *Pelargonium zonale* and *P. inquinans,* as well as a number of other ornamental species. Also, since their transport was so easy, a large number of *Mesembryanthemum* spp. got into cultivation and readers of eighteenth-century botanic books may have been puzzled by references to *Anemone sperma*. This was *Arctotis aspera*, the first of many that were brought into cultivation between 1710 and 1760. In the Badminton records are drawings of three South African plants by Henrietta London (daughter of the nurseryman George London) dated about 1705. These are not easily identifiable, but seem to include a nemesia, a heliophila and some succulent plant. Presumably the nemesia and heliophila were lost, but their presence does show that there was an early interest in South African plants.

There is also the strange story of the Guernsey lily. This is said to have been *Nerine sarniensis*, which occurred on Jersey after a ship from Japan had been wrecked off the coast in 1650. Doubt has been cast on this story, the more especially as the nerine seems to have been known earlier in Paris. Both stories can be reconciled. There survives a list from the early eighteenth century of the plants that flowered in the garden of Henry Wise, the partner of George London. In August he had in flower the narcissus of Japan and in September the Guernsey lily. If the bulbs really did come from Japan they would be a species of *Lycoris,* which does flower considerably earlier than the nerine, but is not dissimilar in appearance. If both were grown in the Channel Islands, the names could eventually get confused and the original Japan narcissus become the Guernsey lily. It certainly looks from Wise's list as though there were two autumn flowering bulbs of this type.

The trouble with these plants is that they were not hardy in most parts of the British Isles or, indeed, in Holland and had to be overwintered indoors, although no great heat was needed, so, until greenhouses became more general, there was no impetus for the commercial growers to interest themselves in South African plants. One exception was the red hot poker, *Kniphofia uvaria*, which seems to have got quite rapidly into general cultivation.

Joseph Banks had travelled with Captain Cook on his voyage on *Endeavour* from 1768 to 1771 and on this voyage they had visited South Africa. Banks became friendly with George III and persuaded him to take over Princess Augusta's garden at Kew, which had become neglected since the owner's death in 1772. Banks had a vision of Kew becoming a great botanical clearing house, where all the plants of the world could be grown and exchanged with other botanical institutions. It was Banks who masterminded the plan to bring bread fruit from Tahiti to the West Indies, a voyage which caused the famous mutiny on *Bounty*, although a later voyage on *Providence* was successful and it was Banks's vision which sustained the Hookers in their actions, such as bringing the quinine tree to India and the rubber tree to Malaya. Although Banks was a keen botanist and had an enormous herbarium it was plants that he required, not botanical specimens, and for this it was necessary to send out collectors. In 1772 the first, and in many ways the most successful, of the Kew collectors was sent out. This was Francis Masson, whose first expedition lasted from 1772 to 1775 and who revisited the Cape between 1786 and 1795.

By a curious coincidence the Swedish Botanist Thunberg was present at the Cape at the same time, mainly to learn Dutch in preparation for his voyage to Japan with the Dutch East India Company, but also to collect plants and specimens for various Dutch scientific institutions, and the two of them travelled together in 1773 and 1774. It is from Thunberg that we learn that Masson had a large strong wagon pulled by oxen and driven by a European, while in addition Masson had a saddle horse and was attended by four Hottentots. The interior was very sparsely inhabited, but they usually managed to find a farm at which to spend the night, although mostly the conditions were very primitive. Here is Masson describing a 'miserable cottage' not more than a hundred miles from Cape Town. 'The hut had only one room, but our host gave us a corner to sleep in, which was detached by a hanging of reed mats, where he and his wife also slept; and in the other end lay a number of Hottentots promiscuously together.' Nearly forty years later in 1811 a later collector, William Burchell, gives a more detailed but equally dismal picture.

'The situation of the house was bleak and exposed, and exhibited but little display of art or cultivation around it.... One large room, having a mud floor, constituted the principal part of the house; and a single glazed window showed, by its broken panes, proof of the scarcity of glass. At one end were the bedrooms, and a door through the back wall opened into the kitchen. Hanging from the rafters of the thatched roof was seen a heterogeneous assemblage of domestic utensils and stores. The other end was filled by a very deep and wide fire-place, exactly resembling that of an English farmhouse and a large iron cauldron of boiling soap was standing over the fire. A small window near the fireplace was, at this season, kept constantly closed with a wooden shutter, in order to keep out the cold wind, as it had neither sash nor glass. Against the wall under the glazed window stood a small table partly occupied by a little old-fashioned coffee urn, an article in continual employ. On each side of this table two homely chairs were stationed with their backs close to the wall: in these sat the master and mistress. A few chairs and benches, with the large family dining table, were ranged in order round the room. On a shelf lay a variety of articles, with a large Bible and other books.'

The description could apply to almost any pioneering homestead at almost any period and does convey the arduous life that the Boer farmers endured. Also in the late eighteenth and early nineteenth centuries there were dangerous animals around. When Masson and Thunberg were crossing the Great Karoo they were directed by a fellow traveller who said: 'he would tie a piece of white cloth on a branch of a tree where he knew there was water; but desired us not to go to these places without fire-arms, as there was commonly a lion lurking near them, who, knowing that all the animals must come there to drink, he seldom failed to seize his prey.' Later they met again with this obliging gentleman: 'who had taken his lodging on a bare eminence without a bush to shelter him; though at some distance there was a small bush of mimosa trees along the banks of a river, which was then dry, which we thought much preferable ... but he told us it was much more dangerous on account of wild beasts; and there often fell such sudden showers in the mountains that people who had camped by the rivers had, with their waggons and oxen, been carried away in the night while they lay asleep.' Generally these botanists thought that the flora amply compensated for their hardships: 'we thought our labour and difficulties largely repaid by the number of rare plants we found here' is a sentiment that Masson often expresses. There were, not unnaturally, disappointments. At one time they climbed 'one of the highest mountains in this part of Africa, whose top is covered with snow for the greatest part of the year. Here we expected to find plants that might endure the severity of our climate, but when we arrived at the top we found nothing but a few grasses.'

The number of plants that Masson was able to introduce to Kew was enormous, although few of his plants remain in cultivation now. The great wealth of South African heathers was unknown before Masson's visit and he was able to introduce no fewer than eighty-six different species. The nineteenth century made a speciality of South African heaths and many nurserymen, most notably Rollisson of Tooting, specialised largely in these and created many hybrids. Since they could be had in flower in every month of the year and required only enough heat to keep out frost and dry the atmosphere, they were popular with amateurs and it is not altogether clear why they should now have practically vanished from cultivation. Two winter flowering plants, *Erica nivalis* and *E. hyemalis* still make an appearance for the Christmas trade, while the attractive *E. canaliculata* grows in sheltered situations in Cornwall. All the other delightful species and hybrids seem to have vanished from cultivation as though they had never been in our greenhouses at all. The same can be said of the proteas and their relatives which Masson also brought into cultivation. A couple of leucadendrons had been known previously, but the true proteas with their fantastic but beautiful flower heads had not been seen before. Being somewhat bulky they never became as popular as the ericas, but most respectable nurserymen offered them in the first half of the nineteenth century. Later they tended to disappear from commerce. The same would seem to apply to the forty-nine different species of oxalis which Masson introduced. Kew grew no less than fifty-eight South African oxalis, the only one of which we see nowadays is the infamous Bermuda buttercup, *O. pes-caprae*, which Miller had grown before Masson's expedition and which has now become a pernicious weed in much of Europe; moreover it has done this without ever setting a seed in the continent. These were popular for quite a long time, especially as house plants, as they were very easy to grow and required only enough heat to keep the frost away.

Kew was not a publicly owned garden as it is nowadays, but the private possession of George III, and so the plants brought back by the various Kew collectors were the private property of the monarch. It was unthinkable that the crown could engage in commerce and it was not easy for his servants to give gifts of the royal possessions. It was, however, considered reasonable to exchange plants, so that if a nurseryman could present a novelty to Kew he could be recompensed by the present of a new plant. George Lee of the famous Vineyard nursery obtained a large number of new plants through various correspondents and it was Lee and Kennedy who obtained many Kew plants and so introduced them to commerce, but a very large number of the new plants were never distributed and the nurserymen or private plantsmen found that they had to send out collectors themselves. Of these collectors the most successful seems to have been James Niven, who was sent out by a wealthy plantsman, George Hibbert, to collect from 1798 to 1803. On his return he was immediately re-engaged by a syndicate headed by Lee and Kennedy, but including the Empress Josephine, to whom John Kennedy was an adviser. The fact that France and Britain were at war was regarded as irrelevant so far as scientific work was concerned. Unfortunately Britain was engaged at the time in conquering the Cape colony and also in fighting various Kaffir wars and since Niven not only spoke Dutch but had also learned the 'Caffre tongue' he was forcibly enrolled in the army as a scout, which must have considerably interfered with any plant collecting. In spite of these drawbacks there are a large number of plants introduced by Niven, including an additional thirty species of *Erica*. These plants got at once into commerce. Niven returned to England in 1812 and died fifteen years later.

It is possible that William Rollisson, who was later to found a nursery that specialised in Cape Heaths, travelled to collect these at the start of his career. *Hortus Kewensis* credits him with the introduction of fifteen species between 1796 and 1800 and if he did not collect them himself it is not clear how he could have obtained them.

Although the number of new plants introduced by W. J. Burchell between 1811 and 1815 was not particularly large, his *Travels* give by far the most vivid picture of conditions at the Cape at the turn of the century. He was, naturally, responsible for some novelties of which the first lithops was notable. Here is his description: 'On picking up from the stony ground what was supposed to be a curiously shaped pebble it proved to be a plant and an additional new species to the numerous tribe of Mesembryanthemum.' Indeed Burchell was particularly good with the desert flora. 'The incomplete list which a botanist would form from travelling but once over the dry plains of Africa may be well exemplified by the collection made between Klaarwater and the Kloof settlement in the preceding month of September as compared with that which was made during January. At that time only six numbers were added to my catalogue, but at this fifty-eight.' Moreover the desert flora was so evanescent. On 15 January 1812 he had noted a plain covered with *Nerine lucida*. Ten days later he returned, but 'I now looked in vain for that rosy wild flower garden which decorated these plains ... it had totally disappeared and so astonishingly and almost incredibly rapid is the progress of vegetation in these regions with respect to bulbous flowers, that in the space of ten days the beautiful lilies then observed just coming into bloom, had completed their flowering and ripened the seed; the flower stems were dried up, had parted from the roots and were nearly all dried away.'

When Burchell returned to England he had with him bulbs of 276 species, including crinums and brunsvigias, and seeds of some 2000 species. He grew these in his father's garden and they were offered for sale. Dean Herbert, who was writing a monograph on the *Amaryllidaceae* looked through his herbarium and noted a fan of leaves, which Burchell thought was an agapanthus. Herbert was sure it was something else and after obtaining its locality from Burchell instructed a Mr Tate, of whom nothing is known, to obtain the plant and send it to him. It turned out to be *Clivia nobilis*, which Herbert was thus able to obtain before it was introduced to Kew by our next collector.

This was James Bowie, the last of the collectors sent out from Kew by Banks and Aiton. Originally he and Allan Cunningham had gone to Brazil in 1814. This joint expedition ended in 1816 and Cunningham went to Australia, while Bowie went to South Africa, where he remained until 1823. He seems to have added to the number of succulents in cultivation, he introduced the clivia in quantity and he also sent over the first of the large-flowered streptocarpus, *S. rexii*. Banks had died in 1820 and even previous to that time the garden had been running down. Very few of the plants and seeds sent by Cunningham and Bowie from Brazil had survived and Bowie found the atmosphere depressing. He resigned in 1827 and returned to South Africa as a free-lance collector. This seems to have been a failure and he was often in want. When he was in England his behaviour seems to have left something to be desired, although it must be noted that the rather slanderous remarks were published long after this period. John Smith, curator of Kew, wrote in the *Gardener's Chronicle* in the 1870s: 'He spent his evenings in public houses, telling stories of his encounters with buffaloes etc.' Smith at least had known Bowie, but in 1889 a writer in the *Journal of Botany* had expanded Smith's mild remarks into saying that Bowie spent his time 'among the free and easy companions of the bar parlours, recounting apocryphal stories of his Brazilian and Cape travels, largely illustrated with big snake and wildebeeste adventures.' This is surely just libel. How could the writer have known whether the tales were apocryphal or not?

Bowie may well have introduced two of the gladiolus species which were parents to the first large-flowered hybrids. *G. psittacinus* was introduced in 1830 and Bowie is the only collector who we know was in South Africa at that time, although it could well have been sent back by an amateur. *G. oppositiflorus* was collected in Madagascar about 1823 according to Dean Herbert, but since the plant is only known from South Africa, Herbert must be wrong. If, however, the date of 1823 is correct, then again Bowie is the most likely introducer. Unfortunately neither the *Hortus Britannicus* of Loudon, nor the book of the same title by Sweet, mentioned *G. oppositiflorus* at all. If Herbert is correct the first large-flowered hybrid gladiolus, known as *gandavensis*, was raised in 1842 by crossing *psittacinus* with *oppositiflorus*. However, other authorities give the parentage of *gandavensis* as being the same as *brenchleyensis*, namely *psittacinus* x *cardinalis*. Indeed the parentage of this first large-flowered hybrid is far from clear. Paxton says that one parent was the plant known as *pudibundus*, which was a hybrid between *cardinalis* and *blandus*. Probably most of the early records have been lost. 'Colvillii' is said to be *G. cardinalis* x *G. tristis*, but the early illustrations of 'colvillii' do not look at all like our modern plants of the same name, which one would expect to be *cardinalis* x *blandus*.

Although the florist's gladiolus would seem to be the main surviving feature of all these collectors' work, it is comparatively modern and by no means all its parents are South African.

Indeed it is chiefly the bulbous plants of South Africa that have survived in much cultivation; such plants as sparaxis, ixia, babiana, crocosmia and freesia remain in cultivation, although more often as garden hybrids than as the wild species. The shrubs that used to grace the amateur's greenhouse are only rarely to be seen in the larger botanic gardens and they never appear to have got into cultivation in such places as the Mediterranean where they might have thrived out of doors. The one South African genus that is found in many places is what used to be known as mesembryanthemum. It at least, has persisted wherever it can be grown.

CHAPTER V

China I

HE flowers and the gardens of China both seem to have had an attraction for western nations since the late seventeenth century. In 1685 in his *Gardens of Epicurus*, we find Sir William Temple writing of the planting of trees in avenues or other straight lines. 'The Chineses scorn this way of planting and say a boy that can tell a hundred may plant walks of trees in straight lines and over against one another, and to what length and extent he pleases.' Precisely how Sir William knew what the 'Chineses' thought is not clear and he may have been adumbrating the same line as was to be followed by Sir William Chambers in 1774 (in his *Dissertation on Oriental Gardening*), namely that of giving his own opinions and attributing them to the Chinese. In 1752 the work of the Jesuit Pere J. D. d'Attiret, which gave first-hand descriptions of Chinese Gardens, was translated into English and seems to have made an immediate impression. In 1757 in *Eden*, that dubious character but fine gardener 'Sir' John Hill noted that rather Gothic scenes were particularly appreciated by the Chinese. 'There are in Nature, Objects of Disgust and Horror, which yet may be introduced happily; burnt Hills and blasted Heaths and barren Rocks and the wild waste of Commons afford a contrast.... These objects therefore will be sure to please, but they must be introduced with a sparing hand ... they are the Discords in the Musick of Gardening.' He went on to say, with reference to the Chinese: 'Let us learn from them that the sudden transition from Agreeable to horrid and from gay to gloomy is pleasing; but let us correct the untutored Wildness of their Imaginations by forming nothing beyond the laws of Nature.' What travellers had to say struck a responsive note in British garden designers and their descriptions of the various plants, many of which were depicted on the porcelain that was becoming so popular, caused considerable interest in their garden products. However, there were great difficulties in obtaining Chinese plants, one physical, the other political.

In order to get from China to Britain you first sailed to Java, thence to Cape Town, then to St Helena and through the tropics a second time to Britain. The journey was long, taking several months, and passed through a number of trying climatic conditions, which made the preservation of plants a risky business. Since, as we shall see, many of the most desirable plants were what the west would have termed florists' varieties, it was not practicable to send back seeds, which would evidently have travelled much more easily, although seeds of some wild plants were sent back by the Jesuits.

Since 1755 foreigners were not permitted to travel in China at all; the sole exception being made in favour of some Jesuit priests who were scientific advisers to the court at Pekin and allowed a certain amount of freedom of movement. Otherwise foreign traders were confined to the island of Macao and allowed in Canton only when the merchant fleet was in port. In the late eighteenth century Canton had a renowned complex of nursery gardens, known as Fa-Tee, and many plants could be obtained from this source, if they could be brought back alive.

As early as 1713 Thomas Fairchild is said to have grown the annual *Dianthus chinensis* and in 1739 Lord Petre obtained the first camellia. This was placed in the hottest greenhouse—it was for long assumed that any foreign plant required great heat—and not surprisingly died, but not before his gardener James Gordon, who subsequently opened a famous nursery, had taken cuttings which survived. Lord Petre's plant was the single red wild *Camellia japonica*, but subsequently it would seem to have sported and produced some double flowers and Gordon was able to offer a double red and a double red with white stripes. It is reported that camellias were first offered commercially in 1745, yet Miller fails to mention the plant at all in his famous *Gardener's Dictionary*.

Most of the Jesuits were Frenchmen and sent seeds to Bernard de Jussieu in Paris, which seems to have been a mistake. When d'Incarville's herbarium was re-examined in the eighteen-nineties it was found to contain many packets of seed that had never been sown. In 1728 Jussieu had received seeds of the China aster (*Callistephus chinensis*), but most of the sendings came from d'Incarville, who was at Pekin between 1740 and

1757. Fortunately he was also sending seeds to Peter Collinson in Britain and to Dr Gmelin at St Petersburg. Collinson was also getting seeds from a Père Héberstein. From these sources were received the tree of heaven (*Ailanthus altissima*), the golden rain tree (*Koelreuteria paniculata*) the paper mulberry (*Broussonetia papyrifera*) as well as *Cedrela sinensis*, *Thuja orientalis, Sophora japonica, Caragana sinica* and *Albizia julibrissin.* Collinson also got some unidentified plants including a belamcanda.

Once this source ceased, and we seem to have no further records of plants being sent back after 1757, the importation of plants depended on the employees of the East India Company, which had the monopoly of the Chinese trade. In 1770 Benjamin Torin sent a collection of plants to Kew, which included *Daphne odora*, that popular house plant *Saxifraga sarmentosa (stolonifera)* and, rather surprisingly, a purple-leaved form of *Cordyline terminalis*, which was known as *Dracaena ferrea*. In 1782 John Duncan, a friend of Banks was appointed resident sergeon and he was later to be succeeded by his brother Alexander, so that there were Duncans at Macao from 1782 to 1796, frequently sending plants back to Banks, but with variable results. However, the first yulan, *Magnolia denudata*, arrived in 1789, the same year as saw the first successful importation of a tree peony. In 1788 the first hydrangea, which still survives under the cultivar name of 'Sir Joseph Banks' was received, while in 1796 came the first japonica, *Chaenomeles speciosa*.

In the meantime Dr Fothergill had been obtaining Chinese plants from unknown sources, although since he had many sea captains among his acquaintance, one assumes that it was mainly from this source. Among the plants still in general circulation, he obtained in 1774 *Lychnis coronata* and *Malus spectabilis*.

In William Malcolm's catalogue of 1771 *Rosa chinensis* was offered for sale and it is baffling that *Hortus Kewensis* gives 1789 as its introductory date. Not only did it maintain its position in the Malcolm catalogue, but it is also mentioned as being available in Abercrombie's *Gardener's Daily Assistant* of 1786. One assumes that this China rose was the pale pink plant that is still known as the 'monthly rose' and found occasionally in gardens to this day. Miller is said to have had this in 1752, but it is not mentioned in his *Dictionary*.

An amateur of Chinese plants in the late eighteenth century was Gilbert Slater, who acquired a deep crimson form of the China rose in 1789. This was quite a new colour in roses, but unfortunately has proved to be a triploid and so was not of much use in the later breeding programme that the rose was to experience in the nineteenth century. It seems curious that this plant was originally grown in the greenhouse. Gilbert's brother John Slater appears to have obtained a double white camellia and another double striped form. In 1793 Gilbert sent James Main on a trip to Canton to collect plants for his garden. Main's Journal of the trip was published in 1836 (in *Paxton's Botanical Register*) and this describes graphically the great difficulty that would be experienced by people trying to bring plants back from China. It is clear that the majority of plants must have perished on the journey, although the matter was complicated by Gilbert Slater's death just prior to Main's return. From our point of view one of the most interesting observations made by Main is his statement that while in Canton he would purchase few camellias, as he thought that those that were being bred in England were superior to any he saw in China. We have always assumed that serious breeding of camellias in Europe started with Alfred Chandler in 1819 and one would like to know much more about these superior varieties that Main mentions.

In 1803 William Kerr was sent out, either by Kew or by Banks himself, or by the two in partnership, to Canton and Macao, where he resided for eight years, making a voyage to the Philippines during this time and finally being made superintendent of a botanic garden in Ceylon, where he died in 1814. Kerr not only sent plants to Britain, but also to the Calcutta Botanic Garden, where many survived to arrive later in Britain. The resident surgeon at Macao, Dr Livingstone, who gave much thought to the transport of plants from China to Europe, did not think Kerr was very satisfactory and suggested that he was inadequately paid, so that he could not maintain sufficient status and so lost face. Whether this is the origin of the story that appeared in the *Chinese Repository of Canton* for 1834 (twenty years after Kerr's death, so dubiously valid) that after three or four years of great and exemplary activity Kerr 'became greatly changed. He was then unable to prosecute his work in consequence of some bad habits he had contracted, as unfortunate as they were new to him.' This sounds as though he had become an opium addict. The report is somewhat suspect as he would scarcely have been entrusted with his Ceylon appointment if his behaviour had been so unsatisfactory and it may well be another example of libelling plant collectors after their death, as we have already seen in the case of Bowie. At first many of his sendings were lost *en route* and Banks suggested it might be advantageous to employ a Chinese gardener to accompany the plants back. Accordingly a certain A-Hey was engaged, although it is not clear whether the plants that were transmitted under his supervision arrived in any better condition. Still during his long stay Kerr succeeded in introducing a number of plants and we know that he sent back at least 238 parcels of seed, quite apart from living plants and bulbs. A yellow shrub known as *Corchorus japonicus* was renamed in his honour *Kerria japonica*. Presumably Kerr sent back further exemplars of Chinese plants that had previously been introduced, but among the new plants were the tiger lily, *Lilium tigrinum* and another lily which is now *L. brownii colchesteri*, but which was known at that time as *L. japonicum*. He also sent a magnolia which appears in *Hortus Kewensis* as *Magnolia tomentosa*, which Loudon says is a synonym for *M. kobus*. If this is correct the plant must eventually have been lost as we have no record of this Japanese plant in cultivation until the late 1860s. He introduced a camellia, which could have been either the Japanese *C. sasanqua* or the similar native Chinese *C. oleifera*. Among other hardy plants were three conifers, *Cunninghamia lanceolata, Juniperus chinensis* and *Podocarpus macrophyllus*, the double yellow Banksian rose, the variety of *Lonicera japonica*, now known as *repens*, the attractive *Pieris japonica* (the Fa-Tee gardens seem to have specialised in Japanese plants), the large-flowered fragrant *Pittosporum tobira*, so popular around the Mediterranean, the sacred bamboo, *Nandina domestica*, the Chinese hawthorn, *Photinia glabra*, the only hardy begonia, *B. evansiana*, the orchid *Bletilla striata* (syn. *Bletia hyacinthina*) and that tiny water-lily, *Nymphaea pygmaea*. Since most of these got fairly rapidly into the catalogues of the early nineteenth century it would seem that at least some of Kerr's sendings were Banks's personal property. It would seem that occasionally nurserymen obtained plants from China and it is possible that they could send out a collector or come to some financial arrangement with an East Indiaman captain. Thus the firm of Thomas Barr and Brookes of Balls Pond Road seem to have obtained the first form of a Japanese cherry to be received in Europe and it is not clear how they obtained this.

After 1812 there was some improvement in the number of Chinese plants that arrived in England. This was due to the presence in Macao of John Reeves. He was employed as the tea inspector, but he was extremely interested in Chinese plants and introduced the valuable innovation of establishing them in pots of good soil for a year before transporting them. Previously they had been taken direct from the nurseries to the ships. Tree peonies, for example, which were only imported into Canton for a single season, would have their roots wrapped round with hard clay, which set like concrete during the journey to Europe. When well established in pots they had a better chance of survival, although the climate of Macao was far too warm for them. Reeves also interested various East India captains in the financial rewards that could accrue from bringing back plants, although some had already found this out. The names of Captain Wellbank of *Cuffnels* and Captain Rawes of *Warren Hastings* have survived for their especial skill in bringing plants back alive and 'Captain Rawes' is now the cultivar name of the fine semi-double *Camellia reticulata* he brought back in 1820. Reeves was also interested in obtaining Chinese wild flowers, but seems to have had little success. He did obtain a honeysuckle, looking remarkably like *Lonicera tragophylla*, which he sent to the London Horticultural Society in 1816, the same year as he sent *Wisteria sinensis*, which he had persuaded a Chinese merchant, Consequa, to grow. A second plant came in 1818. This was the famous year when Reeves returned on leave to England, leaving with 100 plants and arriving with 90 still in good condition; a feat that was rightly regarded as remarkable. This second wisteria was planted in the famous Chiswick garden of the Society and twenty years later was 11 feet high but 160 feet wide and attracted a considerable crowd when it was in flower. Since then it has become one of the most popular of all garden plants, so the debt that gardeners owe to Reeves is considerable.

Before the general use of the Wardian Case the loss of Chinese plants was enormous, but once they did arrive safely they seem to have been rapidly propagated and entered quite soon into commerce. The catalogue of a provincial nursery, Messrs Miller and Sweet of Bristol, for 1808 includes thirty plants from China or Japan, while eighteen years later they had forty-four, not including cultivars of such plants as the China rose, the chrysanthemum and the camellia. These with some other Chinese plants became a popular source of breeding as the nineteenth century progressed and it would seem that here would be a proper place to consider their development.

(I) THE CHRYSANTHEMUM

According to Jacob Breyn six different chrysanthemums were received in Holland in 1688, but the plants did not survive after flowering. The curious thing about this story is that only Breyn seems to have seen these plants and, even if they had been grown in a hot greenhouse under the most unsuitable conditions, it would seem unlikely that they would all have died. In 1764 Philip Miller presented specimens of *Matricaria indica* to the Apothecaries' Company. This would seem to be the yellow daisy *Chrysanthemum indicum*, thought to be a principal parent of the modern chrysanthemum, but the matter is not clear. Miller says that the plant was a biennial and that the seed was ripe during the summer, which scarcely suggests a chrysanthemum and the plant does not appear to have persisted in cultivation. We are, however, fairly sure that the first chrysanthemums of the type we know today to be received into cultivation were obtained by M. Blancard in 1789 at Marseilles. Three colour forms were received, but only a crimson-purple survived. According to Henry Phillips, in his entertaining *Flora Historica*, this chrysanthemum, which became known as the Old Purple, did not reach Britain before 1795, when 'it was sold at a high price by the nurserymen in the neighbourhood of our metropolis.' It also produced a bud sport, which had crimson and white florets, and this was propagated. Sir Abram and Lady Amelia

Hume at Wormeleybury had a passion for Chinese plants and the ability to interest East Indiamen captains in their transport and between 1798 and 1808 they obtained seven new varieties of chrysanthemum in colours described as lilac-pink, buff, Spanish brown, yellow and white. Some of these had quilled petals, others had broad ones. In 1820 Joseph Sabine, their Secretary, read a paper about the chrysanthemum to the Horticultural Society and was able to describe only twelve cultivars. In 1821 this society sent John Potts to Canton to collect plants from the nurseries and he obtained as many as forty different sorts, but unfortunately they had to be jettisoned during a storm on the return voyage. Even so Phillips, whose book was published in 1824, was able to write 'we already possess about thirty varieties of this ornamental plant.' In 1824 indeed a second Horticultural Society collector, John Damper Parks, did bring back thirty different cultivars from Canton. When Robert Sweet published his *Hortus Britannicus* in 1830 he listed forty-four different cultivars. Moreover we learn from Phillips that in 1824 the plant not only adorned 'the parterres of the opulent', but was sufficiently cheap to ornament 'the casements of the cottagers'. According to Phillips some had 'florets half tubular and half ligulate, whilst others which expand with petals perfectly flat bear a resemblance to the shape of a China aster; and others, with tubular florets in the centre and rays of plain ones in the circumference, give the seducing form of a beautiful ranunculus. Some of the kinds have their florets so disposed in the calyx as to form a kind of tassel when half expanded, and when fully open they remind us of a French powder puff.' One gets the impression that the flowers were rather more attractive and different in shape in the early nineteenth century than they are nowadays. Their culture also, was rather different. According to Phillips cuttings were not taken before early May. Once rooted they were put into small pots which were plunged into the open border. About the end of August they were moved into larger pots and liberally fed with liquid manure. They were put into a cool house before the frosts came. In this way 'a single stem rises from the pot and at the height of four or five inches branches off into two three or more flowering stems from one to two feet long.' These stems were disbudded to give larger flowers. Phillips says also that the plants are hardy enough to grow outside in a sheltered situation, but must not be left for more than two years in the same situation. After 1830 more cultivars were bred and imported, but there was little change before the introduction of the ragged Japanese chrysanthemums by Robert Fortune in 1860 and the breeding of early flowering chrysanthemums for outdoor planting at the end of the 1870s.

(II) THE PEONY

The Chinese peony, *Paeonia albiflora*, arrived in commerce not from China, originally, but from Siberia, whence Peter Pallas sent plants and seeds which were received in England in 1784. From this sending both a white and a pink form were received. These would appear to have been single flowered and it is not clear how many of the other early cultivars were single. Only two are actually described as double. 'Whitleyi' which is still in commerce was received from China in 1808 according to Sweet. It was evidently sold by Reginald Whitley who had a nursery at Brompton in partnership with Peter Brames. Any list of early Chinese plants will contain the name of Hume and 'Humei'; a double red was obtained in 1810 by them. These are the only two that the contemporary catalogues describe as double, but various other forms in pale pink, deep pink, blush and white were either bred or obtained from China, including a dark red 'Fragrans' so named from its perfume. From this somewhat meagre selection nurserymen were able to increase the number of cultivars so that by 1868 the Belgian firm of Van Houtte was able to offer no less than fifty-eight named sorts.

(III) THE TREE PEONY

Although the nurserymen in Canton sold moutans, the climate was far too warm for their cultivation. They were brought in from nurseries around Shanghai and sold as pot plants that would flower and would then be thrown away. As a result the plants were in very poor soil and often deficient in roots. This meant that they were not easily transported alive to Europe. Nevertheless the same year, 1789, that saw the chrysanthemum established in Europe also saw the first moutan. This was obtained by Sir Joseph Banks and was crimson in colour, but not particularly large. In 1794 he obtained a rather larger-flowered pink variety. In 1806 the Humes obtained 'Papaveracea'. This sounds very like the wild form that was introduced by Joseph Rock in the nineteen-thirties; the flower was large, single and white with a crimson blotch in the centre. Possibly the Humes had obtained a grafted plant on which the scion had died and the stock survived. The Hume's plant became a great sight for gardeners, carrying over 100 blooms at a time. In 1817 the Humes obtained a large double pink; a pale pink sort was brought back by Captain Rawes in 1820, and a double white and a double pale pink arrived prior to 1832. The varieties were intercrossed, usually with 'Papaveracea' as the seed parent and forms with fimbriated petals and with variegated colours were produced. The Earl of Mount Norris at Arley was particularly interested in raising hybrids. His first hybrids flowered about 1831, so we may assume that the first crosses were made about 1825. At first the plants were extremely expensive as they were not easy to propagate—indeed they are not cheap plants nowadays—and they were originally treated as greenhouse plants. As they became commoner it was found that they would survive outside. The number of forms remained fairly constant until Robert Fortune brought back a large number of new cultivars from China in 1844 (see Chapter XII). This created a new interest in the plants and by 1874 Van Houtte was offering the fantastic number of 247 different named tree peonies. Obviously the differences between many of them must have been minimal and the number was soon reduced. Towards the end of the century two other suffruticose peonies were discovered in China, the yellow *Paeonia lutea* and the maroon *P. delavayi*. *P. lutea* was crossed with cultivars of *P. suffruticosa* to give yellow or yellowish tree peonies; *P. delavayi* seems either to have been ignored or none of its crosses have proved satisfactory. At the present time large numbers of semi-double sorts are being imported from Japan.

(IV) THE AZALEA

The Indian azalea, *Rhododendron simsii*, was greatly admired by all who saw it at Canton, but it proved easily the most difficult plant to bring back alive. As late as 1833 Loudon, in his *Gardener's Magazine*, reported on what was regarded as a particularly successful shipment. 'The Chinese Azaleas lately purchased by Mr Knight from Mr M'Gillivray of the East India Company's *Orwell* are as follows: of the variegated azaleas nine plants were shipped at Canton, two of which are now alive ... of the double red azalea six plants were shipped and one plant is now alive in England. Of the red azalea, lighter colour, four were shipped and two survived the voyage in good health; of the large-flowered azalea six plants were shipped and two are now in health'. Loudon goes on to say that 'of the variegated sorts Mr Reeves says that he has shipped at least 500 plants, not one of which ever reached England in a living state.' Captain M'Gillivray and his officers had also purchased some plants on their own account as a speculation, but although they would have taken special pains, not one plant survived the voyage. These were by no means the first azaleas to be received. As early as 1808 or 1809 a scarlet flowered azalea had become established. In 1819 a white, which was probably *Rhododendron mucronatum* (syn. *R. ledifolium*) was received, as was also a double purple cultivar of *R. simsii*. There are also two questionable records. Loudon says that an orange cultivar was received in 1822 and Sweet mentions a double yellow in 1826. Neither colour is known nowadays in any cultivar or hybrid of *R. simsii* and it would seem more likely that they were forms of *R. japonicum* (syn *R. molle*). Loudon also mentions a red and white 'Variegata' in 1824 and a later one in 1832, which is presumably the one referred to in the quotation above. From this rather meagre selection breeding was soon started. 'Smithii', a lilac-coloured plant, appeared in 1826, the pink 'Speciosa' in 1830 and the crimson 'Rawsonii' in 1833. Smith of Norbiton, a noted breeder of rhododendrons, also crossed the indicas with large-leaved hardy species and hybrids, but we do not know about these. Presumably other cultivars were imported from time to time, but the bulk of modern indicas seem to have been bred from a small number of cultivars and many of the most popular varieties are the result of bud-sports. That means that only a small portion of a plant would bear flowers that differed from the bulk of the plant and vegetative propagation from this portion would bring new cultivars into cultivation. Indeed 'Vervaneana' and 'Perle de Noisy', two of the most popular cultivars even nowadays, originated as bud sports. Since about 1860 the breeding of azaleas has become almost a Belgian monopoly, but in 1843 the scarlet 'Apollo' was raised in England and is still in cultivation.

(V) THE ROSE

The late Dr Hurst in the RHS *Journal* for 1941 gave a clear outline of the development of the modern rose from what he termed the four stud Chinas, but unfortunately since his day this clear outline has become somewhat blurred. He appears to have thought that the first remontant China roses were not received before 1789, whereas, as we have seen, they had been in commerce since the seventeen-seventies—probably the pale pink monthly rose of gardens nowadays. In 1809 the Humes obtained the first tea rose, a hybrid between *Rosa chinensis* and *R. gigantea*. In 1821 a cream-coloured China rose, known as 'flavescens' was in cultivation while according to Sweet, a straw-coloured form arrived in 1823. Whether this is the same as Loudon's 'Flavescens' is not clear. In 1824 the Horticultural Society's collector, J. D. Parks, brought back 'Parks's Yellow', which does seem to have been a true yellow. By 1830 Sweet was listing 14 varieties of *R. chinensis* and 21 garden hybrids. The varieties included a purple-flowered form and a very pale pink, known as 'Subalba'. Among the hybrids was one termed 'Moonshine' which sounds as though it were more or less white. Since Sweet lists in all 1237 different garden hybrids, it is clear that the *chinensis* were not being bred particularly intensively. The ever-flowering quality of the China rose is due to a recessive gene, so that if the plant is crossed with a single flowering species the offspring will also be single flowering. If, however, seeds from this offspring are sown, a proportion of approximately a quarter of these seedlings will be remontant. Before this was known, which was to all intents and purposes before the twentieth century, breeding had to be done on an empirical basis and the first two races of remontant roses did not arise in Europe at all, but in America, where *R. chinensis* and *R. moschata* were crossed in 1802. The date sounds suspiciously early for a planned hybridisation. The resultant hybrid was known as 'Champney's Pink Cluster'. Seeds of this were sown by a local nurseryman, Philippe Noisette, and he sent his most successful seedling, a remontant pink climber, to his brother Louis who had a nursery in Paris. In this way the noisette rose came into commerce in 1819.

There seems to have been some semblance of scientific method in the noisette rose; there was none in the next race of remontant roses, the Bourbons. According to a fairly contemporary account: 'In the Isle of Bourbon the inhabitants generally enclose their land with hedges made of two rows of roses; one row of the common China rose, the other of the red Four Seasons.' This latter was the autumn damask, a rose that flowered twice a year. 'M. Perichon ... in planting one of these hedges found among his young plants one very different from the others in shoots and foliage.' This turned out to be the original Bourbon rose and there seems little doubt as to its parentage as it is maintained that no other roses were grown in the island. In 1817 a M. Bréon arrived in the island, propagated the original plants and sent material to a French nurseryman, a M. Jacques, who introduced it to commerce in 1822. The other principal parent of the modern rose was the tea rose, a hybrid, as we now know, of *R. chinensis* and *R. gigantea*, which seems to have arisen in China, although it is not clear whether the crosses were deliberate or fortuitous. Hume's Blush and Parks's Yellow were early importations and all the original tea roses were Chinese imports. It was *R. gigantea* which gave the typical long thin centre, and also presumably its distinctive perfume, to the tea rose. *R. gigantea* is, like *R. chinensis*, a vigorous rambling rose and it seems safe to assume that at some moment, a similar recessive gene emerged which suppressed the production of long climbing stems and encouraged the continuous production of flowering shoots. In the eighteen-thirties one often finds reference to Hybrid Chinas. These roses were the result of crossing the various forms of *R. chinensis* with other garden roses. They would not, themselves, be remontant, but their offspring might well be and if crossed with remontant roses most of the offspring would produce flowers throughout the year. Unfortunately most of these hybrid Chinas seem to have been sterile and we only know of four: 'Malton', 'Brennus', 'Athalie, and 'General Allard' that were used in subsequent breeding. So, by the eighteen-thirties, the rose breeder had five strains with which to work: *R. chinensis* forms, the tea rose, *R. odorata*, which was somewhat tender in England, the Noisettes, the

Bourbons and Hybrid Chinas. The Hybrid Chinas when crossed with remontant roses or when crossed among themselves gave rise to the race known as Hybrid Perpetuals, and these when crossed with tea roses gave us the Hybrid Tea rose, which is still the most popular race, although it has since had the yellow and bicolor *R. foetida* bred in to give the Pernet roses with their shades of yellow and orange and their tendency to disease. Crossed with polyantha roses, which arose from a dwarf mutation of *R. multiflora*, we have got the Floribunda rose.

Rosa multiflora itself, from which so many Rambler roses were bred in the last century, is another Chinese plant first received in cultivation about 1804, and subsequently other forms were imported mainly with flowers that were pink in colour and either single or double, but there was also a white. Loudon says that the Boursault rose, which has the advantage of having no thorns, was a multiflora hybrid, although most writers of the day thought that it was based on the alpine rose, *R. pendulina*, which seems improbable on cytological grounds.

As the century advanced there was a tendency to cross the remontant varieties with the various ramblers and the parentage of the various garden roses became so involved that it is probably not possible nowadays to sort out all the strains that have entered into the modern rose, although the main outline seems reasonably clear.

CHAPTER VI

Australia and New Zealand

EVEN though Australia had only recently been discovered this virtually unknown continent was the next region to be the object of plant collectors; but there were good reasons for this. In the first place Banks, who had made very extensive collections of herbarium material in 1770, had an almost proprietary interest in Australia. It was he who suggested that it should be settled and later, when North America was no longer available, it was he, among others, who saw the continent as a good dumping ground for criminals. Even so Sydney was not founded before 1788 and yet some Australian plants had already been received in cultivation. In 1774 Commander Tobias Furneaux had brought back seed of *Eucalyptus obliqua* from Tasmania and two years later David Nelson, who was attached to Cook's last voyage of 1776 as botanist-gardener, collected a number of seeds, including the still popular *Acacia armata*. By 1788 Kennedy and Lee were offering five Australian plants, including a banksia. In 1789 Kew sent out George Austin and James Smith to the Sydney region. Nothing is known of their activities, but they were presumably responsible for the large number of Australian plants attributed to Banks in *Hortus Kewensis*. In 1790 Kennedy and Lee retained David Burton, nominally Superintendent of convicts at Paramatta, to send back plants and seeds and he is accredited with the introduction of the pretty *Boronia pinnata*. Unfortunately he died in an accident after being out there only six months.

In 1800 George Caley arrived at Sydney. Most of the plant collectors of whom we have any knowledge seem to have been fairly amiable characters, but this could not be claimed for Caley. He was self-opinionated and would take offence at the merest trifle. He was financed privately by Banks, who observed that 'had he been born a gentleman he would long ago have been shot in a duel' and it says much for Banks's kindness and discernment that he tolerated Caley's intemperate letters and perceived the dedicated botanist beneath the prickly and unpleasing exterior.

We must bear in mind that, apart from the settlement at Sydney and a few farms in the vicinity, Australia was a huge question mark. Even its coastal outline was imperfectly surveyed and nothing was known of the interior. Indeed Caley often visited the Blue Mountains in a vain attempt to find a pass through them into the mysterious hinterland. The one point on which all agreed was that the continent was very empty. The aborigines were shy and were rarely to be seen and there is a tale that when some unnamed person accompanied Caley on one of his collecting trips he reported that the only living thing they had seen were two crows and he believed they had lost their way. Apart from plants in the vicinity of the settlement it was also possible to voyage on the surveying ships that were plotting the coast line. In 1801 Caley was on the *Lady Nelson*, which was engaged in surveying the southern coastline. In 1802 Captain Flinders arrived on *Investigator* to survey the whole coastline. He was accompanied by the great botanist, Robert Brown, then at the start of his distinguished career, and a Kew gardener Peter Good, who had already conveyed a collection of plants from India to the Royal Garden and who is credited with ninety-three introductions in *Hortus Kewensis*. His journal has survived and is in course of publication. Unfortunately he died at Sydney in 1803 and it was Brown who brought back his collection. Caley left Australia in 1810 and we know of no further collector until the arrival of the last of the Kew collectors Allan Cunningham in 1816. He had come from Brazil after his joint expedition with James Bowie. Cunningham seems to have been somewhat more knowledgeable than the majority of the Kew collectors and is, indeed, said to have been among those engaged in the preparation of *Hortus Kewensis*. Scarcely had he arrived in Australia than he was engaged to take part in a voyage of exploration into the interior. It should be emphasised that travel in Australia was quite different from that elsewhere in the world. In other places either the land had been settled for some time or at least the natives had fixed abodes, so that there was a rudimentary network of paths and roads. In Australia there was Sydney and the hinterland, Bathurst on the other side of the Blue Mountains was founded in 1815 and Brisbane was to be settled in 1825. Otherwise the country was uninhabited. Tasmania had a settlement at Hobart but here too the interior was uninhabited and little known of the west coast.

The expedition that Cunningham joined was intended to follow the Lachlan River to where it was supposed to join the Macquarie and then follow this river to its supposed estuary on the south coast. With the benefit of hindsight we know that they were consistently moving in the wrong direction away from the Macquarie. The journey would seem to have been particularly unpleasant, although Cunningham continued botanising under all circumstances. It is not easy to find a short extract from his Journal to give the impression that a longer passage would, but perhaps this will give some idea. '*June 29th. Saturday* . . . Cloudy. We continued our Journey on a true westerly course, determining if possible to make the River, altho' from present appearance we could scarcely expect it, but rather be inclined to suspect that we are not far from the spot when the River ceases altogether, or where from the miserable depression of the Country, its Banks being too low to contain it, a general dispersion and inundation commences.

'Having cross'd an extensive grassy woody swamp, with occasional scrubby spots, we arrived at a large expanse of open Country . . . crossing this flat we came to the Banks of the River, which are much higher than could have been reasonably expected. The Channel is in some places very shoaly and narrow and block'd up with drifted decayed Timber. Its inclination being considerably southerly of West, we changed our Course and crossed the Plain in that direction.

'The loose hollow nature of these Plains was very oppressive & heavy for our Horses & in some measure fatiguing to ourselves. The animals frequently sank under their loads up to their knees in its poor sour soil, which produces a plant of the triandrous genus *Arthrotriche* with remarkable undulated leaves. I likewise gathered specimens of *Xerotes* with long radical leaves which are convex and plain. . . . The scrub afforded me a new Acacia with linear round and sulcated leaves in pod. We had travelled several miles on its Banks & had advanced almost 11 miles, when Mr Oxley proposed to halt in a dry situation about 2 o'clock. We now see the fallacy of forming any Ideas respecting this stream; all our Conjectures yesterday are totally overthrown by the observations of this day. We have (by a little perseverance) pass'd the swamps that oblig'd us to turn back yesterday & have now before us, to all appearances, a considerable Journey, if we are determined to see the termination of this Stream. The Bank on which we encamped is very high & of a red sandy marl & the soil of the flats very rich (being the deposition of Floods) and producing abundance of a sp. of Anthericum before noticed. The opposite Bank, which is much lower, has been lately Flooded & the whole Country has been inundated at no very distant Period. The Timber evidently diminishes in size and the Banks are cloathed with *Acacia stenophylla*. I gather seeds of an Aster, an herbaceous plant with blue radiated flowers and Achyranthes from the Swamps. Nos 39 and 128 Seed List....

'Those unwearied Purveyors, our Dogs, provided for us 2 of the largest Emu we have seen in the course of this Expedition, standing at least 8 feet. We are not likely to starve, altho' our Flour and Pork ration is exceedingly scanty. Our Fishermen caught only small Fish of 3½ and 4 lb weight.'

On this journey Cunningham had the company of 'C. Fraser, a private of the 46th Regiment, who had been sent as one of our party in order to form a separate collection of seeds and specimens for Earl Bathurst.... Fraser had been before on these hills in his pursuit of Flora (to which he is very much attracted).'

Charles Fraser soon ceased to be a private and became Colonial Botanist. Cunningham had to send all his collections to Kew, while Fraser was able to distribute his findings more widely. Contemporary writers say that he was very generous with plants and seeds, so he may well have supplied these to various nurseries and we know that he sent both seeds and specimens to the Botanic Gardens at Liverpool, Glasgow and Edinburgh and they would sell surplus stock to local nurserymen. Cunningham himself not only collected around the inhabited settlements, but also led voyages of exploration himself and discovered the fine grazing district known as the Darling Downs, as well as an easy access to it through the mountains. Cunningham also travelled with Captain King in *Mermaid* and later in *Bathurst* on surveying trips around the coastline, during which time he collected assiduously. It is to one of these trips that we owe the introduction of the first eucryphia (then known as carpodontos) to cultivation. This was *E. lucida* from Tasmania. In 1831 Cunningham was brought back to Kew and at the end of the year Fraser died.

During this period the rather shadowy figure of William Baxter was collecting plants for the firm of Low and Mackay of Clapton. He had previously been the gardener to the Comte de Vandes who had a famous garden at Bayswater, from whence the early numbers of the Botanical Magazine got so many of their illustrations. (By a tiresome example of synchroniticity, there was another William Baxter flourishing at the time as curator of the Oxford Botanic Garden.) Baxter's trip was apparently financed by a Francis Henchman, whose connection with Mackay is not easy to establish. There would appear to have been two expeditions made by Baxter; the first lasting from 1823 to 1825 and the second from 1829 to 1832. Apparently in 1832 his contract was completed, but he stayed on in Australia at least until 1836 sending back seeds to Joseph Knight, who ran the famous Exotic Nurseries at Chelsea. Before this Knight is said to have paid £1500 0*s* 0*d* for the seeds from Baxter's final sending to Mackay. The sum sounds impossibly high, but it was reported without much comment by Loudon and it at least indicates the financial reward that could be expected from new plants by nurserymen. It might, however, entail a long wait. Among Baxter's first sendings in 1823 were seeds of *Dryandra pteridifolia* and the first seedlings flowered twelve years later in 1835. No doubt many amateurs would purchase unflowered seedlings of a new plant, but it would seem that financing plant expeditions must have been a chancy business. Baxter collected most of the new proteaceous shrubs that Brown described in the Supplement to his *Prodromus*, which appeared in 1830, and he seems to have reached many places on the south coast of Australia—Lucky Bay, Cape Arid, King George's Sound—which were not yet settled. How did he get there? The only explanation that occurs to me is that, with the pressing need for timber, boats would go out with woodcutters to areas where there were forests and safe anchorage and that Baxter managed to get passage on such boats. So far as I know, no one seems to have asked before how Baxter got to such remote and uninhabited places.

When Cunningham got back to Kew he was disenchanted at the way that so many of his plants had been lost through mismanagement and a failure to follow his instructions. After the death of his brother Richard, who had been appointed to Fraser's position, Cunningham returned to Australia in 1837 as Colonial Botanist, but found the duties distasteful and resigned. He then freelanced, sending material in particular to Messrs Loddiges and made a voyage to New Zealand, but he had contracted tuberculosis and died in 1839.

By this time most of the plants from eastern Australia had been introduced, but western Australia was still unknown apart from visits by Leschenault and later Fraser, but in 1829 it was decided to start a settlement there and the towns of Perth and Fremantle were founded and Sir John Stirling was appointed governor. James Drummond, a curator at the Botanic Garden at Cork, was sent out to lay out a botanic garden at Perth. The wild flowers of this part of Australia were so spectacular that they were being collected with enthusiasm; some plants are even attributed to the Governor himself. The first systematic collecting was organised by Captain James Mangles, whose brother Robert Mangles was a noted plantsman. In 1839 it was stated that Captain Mangles 'has been assiduously engaged for the last eight years in introducing seeds from that most interesting portion of the globe, the Swan River colony. . . . Immediately on receiving packets of seeds, with a liberality which entitles Captain Mangles to the thanks of every botanist in this country, they are distributed gratuitously to the principal nurserymen and other plant establishments belonging to the nobility and gentry.' Mangles's principal supplier would seem to have been a Mrs Georgiana Molloy. James Drummond is also said to have supplied him with material, which Mangles claimed was unsatisfactory. This seems surprising as from 1837 onwards Drummond, whose position had been abolished and who had been presented with a 3000 acre farm as compensation, decided to augment his income by sending back seeds and specimens and obtained contracts with Hugh Low at Clapton, Lucombe Pince of Exeter, Robert Veitch also at Exeter and probably other nurserymen. He supplied specimens to Sir W. J. Hooker at Kew and seeds to Baron Hügel of Vienna. Hooker published many of his letters from 1839 to 1861. He was over fifty when he started collecting and continued until he was seventy-seven years old and the number of good plants he introduced into cultivation was considerable. His letters are full of acute observations and descriptions of conditions in western Australia when it was barely inhabited. For example take this information as to the very restricted habitats of some plants. 'I feel sure that this colony contains twice as many plants as I have yet discovered. In Dr Lindley's "Observations on Swan River Botany" he mentions that Dryandras abound; but though I was always on the look-out for this genus and for Banksia, I spent seven years at Swan River before finding seven Dryandras. Now I have gathered upwards of forty species, but a third of that number are entirely confined to one locality, and of the remaining two-thirds, only two or three species are generally distributed over the country, even where there is the same soil and situation to be found. The way in which plants seem to be restricted to certain spots is one of the remarkable features of this country.... When we consider the great number of species known to grow in only one spot, and these spots exhibiting no very remarkable conditions of land, aspect etc., it is impossible to calculate the amount of novelty which might reward the researches of a naturalist who should traverse the country in various directions.'

For a long time prior to 1914 Australian plants were eagerly cultivated in cool greenhouses. They were never found to be particularly easy, but they had the advantage of requiring little heat. Indeed even nowadays the RHS *Dictionary* describes one of Drummond's introductions, *Leschenaultia biloba* as 'perhaps the most beautiful hard-wooded shrub in cultivation', although one would like to know where it is now cultivated. Still, although the impact of Australian plants on British gardens has been slight, owing to the climate, the effect on gardens and street planting elsewhere has been considerable. It would seem quite possible that the blue gum, *Eucalyptus globulus*, is the most widespread tree in cultivation. You will find it in the Mediterranean, in California, in Argentina, in Ethiopia. It is used to plant around swamps to help with their drainage; it is used in arid regions, because it will endure long periods of drought. It has also the advantage of growing very rapidly. Eucalyptus oil has the reputation of being of considerable medical benefit. After the eucalyptus various species of acacia have also been planted wherever the climate is suitable and at one time the mimosa, *Acacia dealbata*, was extensively grown in southern France for the cut flower trade.

During the nineteenth century there was a rage for 'improving' plants by hybridisation, but few Australian plants were found to be susceptible to 'improvement'. Hybrids were made of various *Epacris* species and also of correas, which were known as Australian fuchsias, but most genera seem to have resisted hybridisation, which may in part account for the disappearance of many Australian plants from cultivation earlier than might have been expected. On the other hand chorozemas, which are rarely seen nowadays, were extremely popular subjects for early spring decoration.

Many more New Zealand plants have been found to be hardy out of doors in Britain, but we know remarkably little as to the introducers of these plants. Allan Cunningham visited North Island in 1826 and sent back collections to Kew and he visited New Zealand again in 1838, whence he sent seeds to Loddiges. In 1833 Richard Cunningham had visited New Zealand, but we have no record as to what, if anything, he introduced. He discovered *Hebe speciosa*, of which great things were expected, but this does not seem to have been introduced before 1842. Loudon records the introduction of *Veronica speciosa* from Tasmania in 1835, but this could scarcely be our plant. The modern hybrid hebes, which are so popular in littoral gardens in Britain, are mainly derived from *H. speciosa, H. elliptica*, which Dr Fothergill had got from the Falkland Islands as early as 1776, and *H. salicifolia*, which seems to have arrived about the middle of the nineteenth century. The hoherias are popular shrubs with their late flowers, but we seem to have no record as to who brought them into cultivation or when. Only *H. glabrata* has an introductory date (1871). It would seem that the introduction of New Zealand plants owes less to professional collectors and more to keen amateurs than the flora of any other country.

CHAPTER VII

Western North America

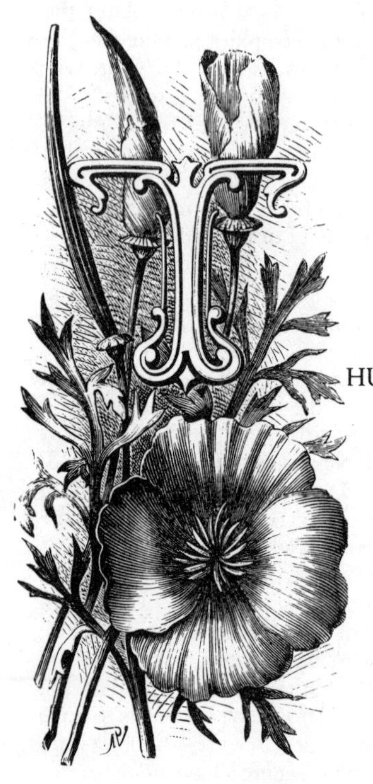

THUS far we have been able to follow the various facets of plant exploration in chronological order, but now the lines become somewhat blurred and the eighteen-twenties see the almost simultaneous exploration of the Pacific seaboard of North America, of temperate South America and of the Himalaya so that the order in which we consider them becomes somewhat arbitrary.

It might seem odd that, with so much of the eastern United States being botanised, the western seaboard should have remained so unknown, but a look at the map will show that it is by no means easily accessible from Europe. It could, it is true, be easily approached from Siberia and there were various Russian settlements, more particularly in Alaska, whence plants occasionally filtered back to the Botanic Garden at St Petersburg. In the eighteen-forties there was considerable rapport between Sir William Hooker at Kew and Dr Fischer at St Petersburg and there was some exchange of plants. At that time a Mr Tschernich was collecting on the island of Ross, while Baron Wrangel sent plants back from the settlement at Port Bodega. Whether these or others were responsible for some earlier importations is by no means clear.

The surgeon on Vancouver's voyage in *Discovery*, Archibald Menzies, was a friend of Banks and had received from him strict instructions as to the collection of seeds and botanical specimens and when he returned in

1794 he was able to introduce quite a number of Californian plants which included the ever popular *Dicentra formosa, Mimulus glutinosus*, which seems to have been lost later as it had to be re-introduced, the yellow *Brodiaea* (*Calliprora*) *ixioides* and two further perennial lupins, *Lupinus nootkatensis* and *L. arboreus*. He also amassed a valuable herbarium which proved useful to later collectors, although his exploration of the land was necessarily restricted.

In 1804 the expedition of Lewis and Clark made the first overland crossing of the continent from the Atlantic to the Pacific and they too returned with a herbarium, which was entrusted to Pursh and published in his *Flora Americae Septentrionalis* and they also brought back some seeds including the Oregon grape, *Mahonia aquifolium*, which has always been popular and, when first introduced, cost £30 0*s* 0*d* a plant and the snowberry, *Symphoricarpos racemosus*.

In the same year, 1804, the London (later the Royal) Horticultural Society was formed and during the eighteen-twenties they started to send out people to collect plants. They were not collectors in the sense that Bartram or Cunningham had been, but were given berths on some ship that would accept them and collected plants at all ports of call. Thus in 1821 George Don visited West Africa, Brazil and the West Indies and in the same year John Forbes was on a ship, the *Leven*, which visited Brazil and eastern Africa, where Forbes unfortunately died, while in 1824 James McRae, sailed *Blonde* to Brazil, Chile, Peru and Hawaii. Many plants were received from all these expeditions and so the Society decided to finance a proper expedition and the man they decided to test out was David Douglas. He had been born at Scone in 1794 and had started work as a gardener's boy at the age of eleven. By the time he was eighteen he had got a well-paid position and used his increased salary to return to school to extend his education. In 1820 he obtained a post at the Glasgow Botanic Garden, where he became associated with William Hooker and assisted him in the preparation of the *Flora Scotica*, and it was Hooker who recommended him to the Horticultural Society. He was first sent on a trial trip to New York in 1823, mainly to collect locally raised fruit trees, and he fulfilled his tasks so well that they decided to entrust him with an expedition to western North America.

At this time the land was very sparsely inhabited. Most of the settlements were trading posts of the Hudson Bay Company, who had already established a range of trading posts across the continent, but mainly in the north. California was nominally a province of Mexico and was more uninhabited than can easily now be imagined. In addition it took a tremendous time to reach the country. The Panama Canal was not even a project and it took Douglas from 25 July 1824 to April 1825 just to travel from Liverpool to Fort Vancouver, although it is true that they had waited a fortnight at Rio and had made stops at Madeira, the Azores, Juan Fernandez and the Galapagos on the way. The rounding of Cape Horn seems to have been comparatively easy, but they met such dreadful storms just before their arrival that they were not able to land until 9 April, although they had expected to anchor a week earlier.

With one exception Douglas had every quality necessary to be a great plant collector. He was energetic, observant, enthusiastic and indefatigable and his only fault was that he was unlucky. Time and time again his collections were destroyed by floods or inclement weather. In 1825 he damaged his leg by falling and a rusty nail penetrated his knee. This festered and left him immobile for a fortnight. This was Douglas's reaction.

'From what I have seen in the country and what I have been enabled to do, there is still much to be done; after a careful consideration as to the propriety of remaining for a season longer than instructed to do, I have resolved not to leave for another year to come. . . .' and he went on to offer to work this further season without remuneration 'if I get only wherewith to purchase a little clothing.'

Although floods and his accident had reduced his 1825 collections, it was by no means a complete loss, but his 1826 collections were larger and more successful. Of course he underwent the annoyances that all collectors have to endure. Thus on 16 June 1826, 'Last night I was much annoyed by a herd of rats, which devoured every particle of seed I had collected, cut a bundle of dry plants almost right through and carried off my razor and soap-brush.' The weather was often a sore trial. 'The facts plainly thus: all hungry and no means of cooking a little of our stock; travelled thirty-three miles; drenched and bleached with rain and sleet, chilled with a piercing north wind, and then, to finish the day, experienced the cooling discomfortless consolation of lying down wet without supper or fire.' Douglas shows his humanity by adding, 'On such occasions I am liable to become fretful.'

By and large Douglas got on well with the Indians, although he does not seem to have liked them. 'The natives are inquisitive in the extreme, treacherous and will pillage and murder when they can do it with impunity. Most of the tribes on the coast (the Chenooks, Cladsaps, Clikitats and Killimucks) . . are, on the whole, not unfriendly. Some of them are by no means deficient of ability.' He appears somewhat surprised that 'they are much prejudiced in favour of their own way of living'.

It is not easy nowadays to envisage how extremely sparsely populated the west was at this time. The Hudson Bay Company had trading posts right across Canada, but they were far apart. California was under the control of Mexico and there were farmers in the south, but further north it was mainly a question of Catholic missionaries hoping to convert the Indians.

There were also trappers who obtained the furs, which made it worth while for the Hudson Bay Company to maintain its trading posts, and there were the native Indians, who seem to have been unmoved by any European visitors. There were no reliable maps. Indeed when Douglas made his second expedition, one of his remits was to make a map of the Columbia River. None of this seems to have worried Douglas in the slightest. 'On my journeys I have a tent where it can be carried, which rarely can be done; sometimes I sleep in one, sometimes under a canoe turned upside down, but most commonly under the shade of a pine tree without anything. In England people shudder at the idea of sleeping with a window open.... I confess at first, although I always stood it well and never felt any bad effects from it, it was looked on by me with a sort of dread. Now I am well accustomed to it.'

Douglas's Journal is full of interesting comments, such as this one on the uses of *Camassia esculenta*. 'When warm they taste much like a baked pear. It is not improbable that a very palatable beverage might be made from them. Lewis observes that when eaten in a large quantity they occasion bowel complaints. This I am not aware of, but assuredly they produce flatulence: when in the Indian hut I was almost blown out by strength of the wind'.

Douglas spent 1826 in making collections of seeds and also amassing a vast amount of herbarium material for W. J. Hooker. In 1827 he was to return home, and decided to cross Canada on foot, following the route of the Hudson Bay Express. He crossed the Rockies, having to travel at that date mainly over snow, and it took him from 28 April until 3 May. He learned also that there was another botanist in the district. This was Thomas Drummond, of whose expedition to Texas we have already written. He was attached to Sir John Franklin's Arctic expedition, but was sent to botanise in the Rockies. He did introduce a number of desirable but extremely difficult plants, such as *Rhododendron albiflorum*, the yellow-flowered *Dryas drummondii* and two dwarf polemoniums, *P. lanatum* and *P. pulcherrimum*. These have always been plants for specialist growers only. Drummond and Douglas met briefly on 3 June 1827 at the staging post known as Carlton House. On 28 August Douglas at last arrived at York Factory, whence he was to sail for England. After a final bit of bad luck, when the boat in which he had visited his ship was dismasted and carried 60 miles out to sea in a storm, Douglas finally landed in England on 11 October.

Of the seeds that Douglas brought back 210 species were raised at the Horticultural Society's garden at Chiswick. Eighty of these the Society decided were 'botanical curiosities' only and were not cultivated further. Seeds of the remaining 130 species were distributed to the members and soon got into general commerce.

In one of his letters to Hooker, Douglas remarked that Hooker must think that Douglas manufactured pines at pleasure and the number of new conifers that he introduced has had the largest effect not so much on gardens as on forestry. *Pseudotsuga menziesii* is always known as the Douglas fir and now covers hundreds of acres of forest land. Another popular forest tree is the sitka spruce, *Picea sitchensis*. In point of fact the successful introduction of this was to await Douglas's second expedition as 'all the seeds of this truly magnificent tree were lost and could not be replaced.' Other conifers from this first trip included *Abies amabilis, A. procera* (syn. *A. nobilis*) and the large-coned *Pinus ponderosa*. Among broad-leaved trees were two maples, the enormous-leaved *Acer macrophyllum* and the red-flowered *A. circinatum*, and the very attractive, seldom-seen, madrona, *Arbutus menziesii*.

There was no question as to the most popular shrub that he introduced; this was the flowering currant, *Ribes sanguineum*. But did he introduce it? In his *Hortus Britannicus* Loudon says it was first introduced in 1817, although later he seems to contradict himself and give 1826 as the introductory date. Sweet also wrote a *Hortus Britannicus* (both volumes appeared in 1830, which must have caused great confusion) and he gives 1820 as the date that *R. sanguineum* was introduced. Since Douglas's plant soon became immensely popular it seems unlikely that there had previously been any significant introduction and it is possible that Sweet and Loudon had confused the plant with the fuchsia-like *Ribes speciosum*, of which Douglas brought back ample material, but of which some seeds had previously been brought back by a ship's surgeon, Alexander Collie. I suppose it is possible that the plants had been temporarily confused. In any case it was only after Douglas's plant began to flower that the plant became immediately popular and widespread in gardens. Douglas himself thought very highly of a yellow-flowered rosaceous shrub, *Purshia tridentata*, but gardeners have never agreed with him. On the other hand *Garrya elliptica* has always been popular with its long green catkins in late winter. The blue-grey waxy-stemmed *Rubus leucodermis* had a long season of popularity, although nowadays it is replaced by rather more brilliant and less invasive Chinese species and the flowering *R. spectabilis* is still to be found in large gardens, although it does spread prodigiously. *Gaultheria shallon* is only nowadays to be found in game preserves, but was remarkably popular on its introduction.

Among herbaceous plants *Lupinus polyphyllus* has proved the most persistent; it is now the parent of all our modern lupins, but at the time it was just one among many. One would like to know what happened to a plant he wished to have called *Lupinus turneri*, which had leaves 'densely covered with silky-white hairs', while the flowers were 'very large, bright golden yellow ... this extremely handsome plant, certainly the finest of the genus .. at the distance of a few miles appears much like Broom on the wild and beautiful heaths of England; 18 inches to 2½ feet high, often producing a spike of perfect blossoms, a foot to 15 inches.' It sounds a marvellous plant. Where is it? Douglas also sent back seeds of various penstemons, the only American peony, *Paeonia brownii*, the first calochortus and the first brodiaea to be brought into cultivation, as well as *Camassia esculenta* and *Fritillaria pudica*.

Although on his return Douglas was honoured and lionised, he soon became bored and irritable and asked the Society to send him back to study the flowers of California. The Society was in its usual state of near-insolvency and was rather unwilling, but when the Colonial Office offered to pay Douglas to survey and map the Columbia river they agreed and Douglas set sail in October 1829. We know much less about this second expedition as all Douglas's journals were destroyed in a disastrous shipwreck on the Fraser river in 1833. We know that on his voyage out he visited Hawaii in the Sandwich Islands and was fascinated by their vegetation. He arrived in June 1830 at the mouth of the Columbia, where he had to stay for some time owing to an epidemic and tribal wars in the interior. Eventually all these troubles were overcome and Douglas sent back a collection of seeds. Towards the end of 1830 Douglas went to Monterey, where he was confined for a long time waiting for permission from the Mexican authorities to go further south. This permission was not received until April 1831. He then travelled south to Santa Barbara, stopping on the way at the various Catholic missions. He returned to Monterey in June and then went inland up the Sacramento river, hoping to find his way to the valley of the Umptqua, which he had visited from the north on his first visit. He was unsuccessful in this and forced to turn back. He spent most of 1832 in and around Monterey waiting for one of the Hudson Bay Company's ships, which, however, never arrived, so he left on another ship to Hawaii and sent back further collections to the Society. In Hawaii he learned that Joseph Sabine, the Secretary to the Horticultural Society and the man to whom he owed his appointment, had been forced to resign. Sabine had been an extremely active member of the Society, had written several important papers on crocus and on various Chinese plants and had been the instigator of the famous garden at Chiswick. During his secretaryship the importance of the Society had greatly increased. In order to get things done efficiently his behaviour was extremely dictatorial and he made many enemies. When it was found that one of his assistants had been embezzling the Society's money the subsequent outcry enabled his enemies to compel him to resign. Douglas had always found Sabine very helpful and on learning of his resignation he immediately offered his own.

Still he agreed to continue collecting, sharing his collections between the Society and W. J. Hooker.

In the autumn of 1832 Douglas returned to the Columbia and the following spring he made a voyage into the Olympic Mountains in Oregon. Later in the same year he started on an expedition that would have taken him to Alaska, whence he was promised passage to Russia and a chance of returning to Britain across Asia and Europe. This seems to have been ill-starred from its inception. Douglas's letters to Hooker speak of 'a series of disasters' without specifying what they were. Douglas decided to give up the attempt and started back to the Columbia. On 13 June, when descending the Fraser river, his canoe was dashed to pieces on some rocks and all his collections, specimens, journals and personal possessions were lost. It was a crippling blow. After this disaster, which had been aggravated earlier by failing eyesight, Douglas tried to restore some of his losses by visiting the Cascade Mountains, where he attempted to climb Mount Hood. As autumn approached he again went to Hawaii, where he spent what was left of his life. He climbed two volcanoes in January and in July his body was found in a pit-trap made to catch the savage wild cattle which had bred from those left by Vancouver. He fell in and was trampled to death by a bull which had already been trapped. He was only thirty-six.

The results of this second trip had, perhaps, greater impact on gardens than his first splendid expedition. It was also of great importance to forestry with the introduction of the Monterey pine, *Pinus radiata*, as well as the successful introduction, this time, of the Sitka spruce. The Monterey pine is confined in the wild to a small area on the peninsula, but it has proved very quick-growing in many parts of the world and is one of the more important subjects for forestry. Indeed the number of cultivated plants is many times that of the wild population, which has never looked particularly healthy. A plant that needs wall protection in Great Britain, but which flowers over a very long period, is the tree poppy, *Dendromecon rigida*. He failed to bring back the other tree poppy, *Romneya coulteri*, although in 1831 he was in company with its discoverer Thomas Coulter. In fact this splendid plant does not seem to have got into cultivation before 1875. It has always seemed odd that Douglas should have failed to introduce any ceanothus, which, with their vivid blue flowers, are among the most attractive of Californian shrubs. We learn, however, from Loudon's *Arboretum* that Douglas did send back seeds of two species, which, one imagines, failed to germinate.

The plants which made the quickest impact and which attracted the greatest attention were the various Californian annuals: eschscholzia, gilia, nemophila, clarkia, godetia and phacelia are the best-known, but there were also the brilliant magenta *Calandrinia menziesii* and the sand verbena, *Abronia mellifera*, which is now regarded as a difficult plant, but now as downingia, were popular for some time as was a yellow daisy, long popular although probably unobtainable now; *Limnanthes douglasii* is popular with bee-keepers. Two plants known then as clintonia, but now as downingia, were popular for some time as was a yellow daisy, *Madia elegans. Platystemon californicus*, a poppy relative, was yet another attractive annual. These all got quite rapidly into commerce. In 1835 the firm of Warner and Warner had the calandrinia, both clarkias, a downingia, three gilias, madia and some godetias. Three years later the firm of John Kernan had clarkias with white and with double flowers, two collinsias, both the eschscholzias, two phacelias, three nemophilas, unspecified numbers of godetia and gilia, the limnanthes and the platystemon. Since many had only been introduced about six years previously they soon made their impact.

This is an important factor to consider about plant introductions. Nowadays we think of Douglas's most important contributions as being various conifers, but it would take many years for this to become apparent. Even after ten years the Douglas fir is still a very slender plant, but annuals make an immediate impact, herbaceous subjects take somewhat longer and shrubs need, usually, a minimum of five years before they flower for the first time. Although he did not always succeed in introducing all the desirable plants he found, Douglas seems to have missed comparatively little and the next collector, Hartweg, was instructed to obtain plants that had featured in Douglas's sendings, but which he had not introduced. There is, however, one very odd blind spot. Douglas spent a lot of time around Fort Vancouver. In 1834 Thomas Nuttall arrived at the Fort and one of the first plants he found was the large-flowered *Cornus nuttallii*. It seems odd that Douglas should have missed so outstanding a plant; possibly he thought it was a form of the eastern *C. florida*, already well-known in gardens, but it seems unlikely. Nuttall introduced the shrub and that was about all he did introduce, although he sent the shrubby *Mimulus glutinosus*, which had previously been introduced in the last century by Menzies, but presumably had been lost in the interval.

In 1838 R. B. Hinds, the surgeon on the survey ship *Sulphur,* introduced *Ceanothus thyrsiflorus* to cultivation. This was the first of the blue-flowered ceanothus from California to come into cultivation and aroused considerable interest. There were also various individual residents sending seeds back to England. Thus about 1840 Dr Tolmie sent seeds of *Spiraea douglasii* to the Glasgow Botanic Gardens where it flowered five years later, and in the early eighteen-forties Kew received *Sequoia sempervirens* from St Petersburg. It was not, however, until 1846 that a fresh professional collector arrived. This was Theodor Hartweg, who was employed, like Douglas, by the Horticultural Society.

He had already undertaken expeditions between 1836 and 1841 to Mexico, Guatemala and the northern Andes and had made various valuable introductions. His instructions in California were to introduce two plants that Douglas had failed to introduce: *Chrysolepis (Castanopsis) chrysophylla* and the Californian fuchsia, *Zauschneria californica*. Hartweg always seemed to arrive in places just as political upheavals were taking place and no sooner had he landed at Monterey when the United States fleet also arrived to take the district from Mexico, so that for most of 1846 Hartweg was confined to the Monterey region. Hartweg's original instructions had been to spend a year in California and the next year in northern Mexico, but he wrote: 'I resolved not to proceed to northern Mexico, where, during the war with the United States my peaceful occupation might be disturbed and my personal safety endangered, but to remain another season in California.... Now, although the country is apparently quiet, it is difficult to foretell how long it may last.... I therefore came to the conclusion of visiting the Sacramento valley, where the settlers are all foreigners and where I need not be under any apprehensions of disturbances.' Hartweg found that the seasons came and went with great rapidity. 'By the end of April the prairies in the Sacramento valley assumed a different aspect; two weeks ago they were a carpet of flowers, which have now disappeared, and a yellow sickly tinge pervades the whole.... Being now aware of the rapidity of Californian vegetation I lost no time in collecting such seeds as were worth taking and returned to my headquarters at the beginning of May. Most kinds had, during the fortnight since I first saw them in flower, ripened their seeds and it was with difficulty I found a few grains of the beautiful little *Leptosiphon aureus (Gilia lutea)* and similar plants, which between their taller neighbours had become almost invisible.' Towards the end of his season Hartweg discovered the attractively coned *Abies bracteata*. He went to the trouble of cutting some trees down, which sounds extravagant, but 'I found to my regret that the cones were but half-grown and had been frost-bitten... I was thus precluded all hope of introducing this remarkable Fir into Europe.'

The list of Hartweg's Californian plants is very long and made up to a large extent of unfamiliar names of plants that have failed to persist in cultivation. Even so a number of attractive plants remain. His name is associated with the rapid-growing, but rather frost-tender Monterey cypress, *Cupressus macrocarpa*, which had originally been introduced in 1838, possibly by the same R. B. Hinds who had brought over the first ceanothus. We know he brought over other Californian seeds, but their identity is not given. In any case it was only after Hartweg that the plant became generally available. Hartweg also introduced another cypress, *C. goveniana*. He also introduced three or four pines which are curious, but not often seen. He was successful in bringing back both the chrysolepis and the zauschneria and he also brought back a female garrya. Since all Douglas's plants had been males, it had hitherto proved impossible to raise further seeds in Great Britain; this now became possible. That early-flowering plum relative *Osmaronia cerasiformis* is not common in gardens, but it still remains in commerce. He also brought back two more limnanthes, *L. alba* and *L. rosea*, but neither seem to have obtained the popularity of *L. douglasii*. Probably the most important of his sendings were the various ceanothus species, *CC. cuneatus, dentatus, papillosus, integerrimus* and *rigidus*. Although they require wall protection in most parts of the U.K. they have remained popular garden subjects ever since.

The Monterey cypress was valued for its extreme rapidity of growth, but exceptionally severe winters were liable to damage it or even to cause its death. In the year 1888 it was unintentionally hybridised with the very hardy *Chamaecyparis nootkatensis* and this hybrid, known as x *Cupressocyparis leylandii* or the Leyland Cypress, grows even more rapidly than the Monterey cypress itself, but is as hardy as the chamaecyparis and is now the first choice whenever a rapid evergreen screen is required.

By the end of the eighteen-forties the value of many of Douglas's conifers to forestry was becoming apparent and it was thought that many other valuable trees might be awaiting collection in western America. A number of Scottish landowners, with interests in forestry, formed the Oregon Association and decided to send out a collector. The man they chose was John Jeffrey of Perth who sailed for Canada in 1850 in his twenty-fourth year. He did not arrive at the Rockies until April 1851 and for the remainder of that year he explored what is now British Columbia. In October he sent back the result of his first year's work. In spring 1852 he was on Vancouver Island, later he went to Oregon and into the Cascade mountains. He spent the winter in Vancouver Island. In 1853 he made his way through Oregon into California, arriving at San Francisco in October. His 1853 sendings were small and it is thought that he may have been unwell. His contract expired in 1853, but a member of the Association, William Murray, expected to be in San Francisco early in 1854 and was instructed to interview Jeffrey with a view to extending his contract. Jeffrey failed to arrive and nothing was subsequently heard either from or about him. There were various rumours, but nothing has ever been known for certain.

Owing to the fact that the records of the Hudson Bay Company have been preserved we have an unusually accurate list of Jeffrey's sendings, although we have no knowledge as to how they fared on arrival. He seems to have been the first to find any of the western American lilies, sending back *Lilium bolanderi* and *L. washingtonianum*, neither of which have proved at all easy of cultivation. He is also reported to have sent back *Camassia leichtlinii*, both seeds and bulbs, although only six of the latter arrived in good condition. Since the nurseryman Max Leichtlin after whom the plant is named was only twenty years old in 1851, it would seem that the plant must have originally just been considered an outstanding form of *C. esculenta*. He also introduced a number of other ornamental plants: *Dodecatheon jeffreyi* was named in his honour and among his other sendings were *Delphinium nudicaule* with scarlet flowers, *Lewisia rediviva*, apparently the first of the genus to get into cultivation, the attractive and easy *Polemonium carneum* and the rather intractable *Silene hookeri* and *Viola douglasii*.

It was, however, timber trees that were his chief concern and he did fairly well. His main work lay in conifers, but he did introduce the oak relative *Lithocarpus densiflorus* and two evergreen oaks, the maul oak, *Quercus chrysolepis*, and another which it is suggested was *Q. englemannii*, which has not persisted in cultivation, and it would seem that none of the maul oaks survived for long. Here is a field note of a new species that he discovered and introduced. (Incidentally where I put *Tsuga*, which is the genus now recognised, Jeffrey wrote *Abies*.)

'Found on the Mount Baker range of mountains. This species makes its appearance at the point where *Tsuga canadensis* disappears; that is at an elevation of about 5000 feet above the sea; from that point it is found to the margin of perpetual snow. Along the lower part of its range it is a noble looking tree, rising to the height of 150 feet and 13½ feet in circumference. As it ascends the mountain it gets gradually smaller, till at last it dwindles into a shrub of not more than 4 feet high. . . . The soil on which this tree was growing most luxuriant was red loam, very stony and moist. If this tree proves undescribed I hope it will be known under the name of *Tsuga pattoniana*.'

Jeffrey's wish was ignored and the plant is well-known under the name of *T. mertensiana*. It was one of three new species that Jeffrey discovered, the others being *T. heterophylla* and a natural hybrid between the two, *T. jeffreyi*. These are all good trees, although the hybrid is, somewhat unusually, less vigorous than either of its parents. A plant that has proved superb in gardens is that lovely columnar shrub *Calocedrus (Libocedrus) decurrens*, although it cannot have proved of much use to foresters. *Thuja plicata* was sent back both by Jeffrey and by our next collector William Lobb and it is impossible to say who was first, nor is the matter of much importance. The same can be said of *Abies concolor lowiana* and possibly of *A. magnifica*. Jeffrey was certainly first with *Cupressus macnabiana*, which is rather a large shrub than a tree, but which has proved remarkably hardy, and some pines which have never been much cultivated.

Our next collector, William Lobb, arrived in California before Jeffrey and continued to visit it until his death in 1863. He had been employed by the firm of Robert Veitch since 1840 and is the first example of a nurseryman consistently employing a collector for many seasons. As we have seen the Clapton nursery, belonging first to Mackay and later to Hugh Low, had sent Baxter to Australia and later they sent John Henchman to collect orchids in Venezuela, so they were probably the pioneers in the commercial employment of plant collectors, but it was the firm of Veitch that made its name in this field and their list of collectors starts in 1840 with William Lobb and ends in 1910 with Purdom, who later accompanied Farrer to Kansu.

Lobb first arrived in California in 1849, the year of the Gold Rush and not a good time, one would have thought, for botanising, particularly in the interior. Lobb went south to San Diego and here he was able to obtain seed of *Abies bracteata*; the tree that Hartweg had tried so hard to bring back. Although Lobb is credited with a very large number of excellent introductions we have very few writings from him, so it is perhaps worthwhile reproducing his remarks about this attractive but difficult tree.

'This beautiful and singular tree forms here the most conspicuous ornament of the arborescent vegetation. On the western slopes towards the sea it occupies the deep ravines and attains the height of from 120 to 150 feet and from 1 to 2 feet in diameter; the trunk is as straight as an arrow; the lower branches decumbent; the branches above are numerous, short and thickly set, forming a long tapering pyramid or spire, which gives to the tree that peculiar appearance, which is not seen in any other kinds of the Pinus tribe. When standing far apart and clear from the surrounding trees, the lower branches frequently reach the ground and not a portion of the trunk is seen from the base to the top.

'Along the summit of the central ridges and about the highest peaks, in the most exposed and coldest places imaginable, where no other pine makes its appearance, it stands the severity of the climate without the slightest perceptible injury, growing in slaty rubbish, which, to all appearances, is incapable of supporting vegetation. In such situations it becomes stunted and bushy.... Douglas was mistaken in saying that this fir does not occur below 6000 feet elevation; on the contrary it is found as low as 3000 feet, where it meets *Sequoia sempervirens*.'

This was a useful acquisition, but the plant with which Lobb's name is chiefly associated is the giant redwood, long known as *Wellingtonia*, but now *Sequoiadendron giganteum*.[1]

[1] Unfortunately a Herr Meissnen had already used the name *Wellingtonia* for a different plant before Lindley published his name. It was in 1853 that Lobb was

An amusing taxonomic row broke out when Lindley christened the new plant *Wellingtonia* 'after the greatest of modern heroes'. The American botanists were quite clear that if a plant was to be named after the greatest of modern heroes, it should be known as *Washingtonia californica*. A Mr Alexander Taylor, writing in the *California Farmer*, let fly at Lindley in no uncertain terms. 'He says it ought to be called *Wellingtonia gigantea* and then goes on to call it so and actually describes it as such; thus making the first assumption of a name, which, with most European and English readers, will cleave to it, unless we enter our vigilant and vigorous protest. And, in the name of California, I shall assume to do so; for a more preposterous piece of cockneyfied nonsense never filtered through the brain down into the fingers through the ink of the pen of any denizen of the commercial Babylon of the modern world.

'Without detracting one iota from the claims and character of the great Duke of Wellington . . . let us ask what right his admiring countrymen . . . have for flying off to California to fasten his name and glory to the most wonderful specimen of the living spreading presence of the great Creative Author of all things, who planted this vegetable pyramid as a memento of his handiwork, when the Sierra Nevada was lifted from the volcanic centres of our planet, and emerged from a primaeval ocean which laved its bases.'

Lobb's first expedition lasted from 1849 until 1853. He returned again in 1854 and continued to collect for Veitch until his contract ended in 1857. He remained in California, sending back occasional collections of seeds until his sudden illness and death in 1863. Besides the *Abies bracteata* and the sequoiadendron Lobb sent back ample material of previously introduced, although rare, conifers that had been found to be satisfactory and, as we have seen, it is impossible to decide whether priority should be given to him or to Jeffrey for some *Abies* and *Thuja* species. Wherever Lobb travelled you could rely on his sooner or later discovering a curious relative of the yew. From California came *Torreya californica*, known as the California nutmeg. This can scarcely be termed a well-known garden plant, although that fine plantsman the late W. J. Bean thought that it had been under-rated. Veitch also speaks of him as being the first to send back seed of 'that fine fir, *Juniperus californicus*'. This, now called *J. occidentalis*, may be a fine fir, but it has made no impact in horticulture.

There were a large number of excellent garden plants that Lobb did introduce. *Rhododendron occidentale*, a fine late-flowering azalea, is not often seen today as a species, but as the main parent of the Occidentale

told of the Calaveras Grove and he sent back both young plants and seeds and the tree was planted quite extensively. Previously it is said that a Mr J. D. Matthew had sent back some seeds, but it is not known whether they germinated or not.

azaleas its influence is still potent. It is, also, a fine plant in its own right, which should be grown more often. On the other hand Lobb's other rhododendron introduction, *R. californicum* (syn. *R.macrophyllum*) is seen very rarely and is barely distinct from *R. catawbiense*. The deep yellow *Fremontodendron californicum* requires a sheltered wall in most gardens but has always been popular in such positions. He sent back a number of fine ceanothus, some of which, namely *C. lobbianus* and *C. veitchianus*, are thought to be natural hybrids and have not been found in the wild since Lobb sent seeds back. There is also a mysterious *C. floribundus*, which is thought to be a particularly good form of *C. dentatus*. He also introduced *C. papillosus* and the lesser known *C. velutinus*. Among other shrubs the attractive *Leucothoë davisiae* has maintained a place in cultivation, while the floribund but scentless *Philadelphus californicus* is now rare, although present in some hybrids.

Lobb sent back a number of herbaceous plants, of which few have persisted in cultivation apart from the scarlet *Delphinium nudicaule*. One would like to know what happened to *Dicentra chrysantha*, a tall, yellow-flowered dicentra, which looks an admirable plant in contemporary illustrations. Among annual plants the fine *Phacelia whitlavia* and *P. grandiflora* seem to have recently dropped out of the seed lists, but should be re-introduced as they are both good showy plants.

Benedict Roezl, who collected plants in enormous numbers, was frequently dashing through California from 1869 onwards and he introduced a number of California lilies, such as *Lilium humboldtii*, *L. roezlii* and *L. parvum*. I am not sure whether he should be credited with *L. pardalinum*, which has proved much the best of these for British gardens, the others proving extremely tricky.

In spite of various lilies, fritillaries, lewisias and other alpines which have often only been introduced quite recently, the bulk of the plants of western North America had been introduced by the time of Lobb's death in 1863. The annuals had an immediate effect and the herbaceous plants did not take long to follow. The shrubs naturally took longer to make an impact, but some of them quickly became immensely popular. The great trees were extensively planted, but it was naturally many years before their true virtues could be appreciated. Some throve, others proved difficult; some flourished in the north, others in the south and some, among which I regret to say we must include *Abies bracteata*, have proved generally unsatisfactory, although there are some exceptions. All these facts took many years to establish and for quite some time the planting of California trees was a hazardous experiment.

CHAPTER VIII

South America

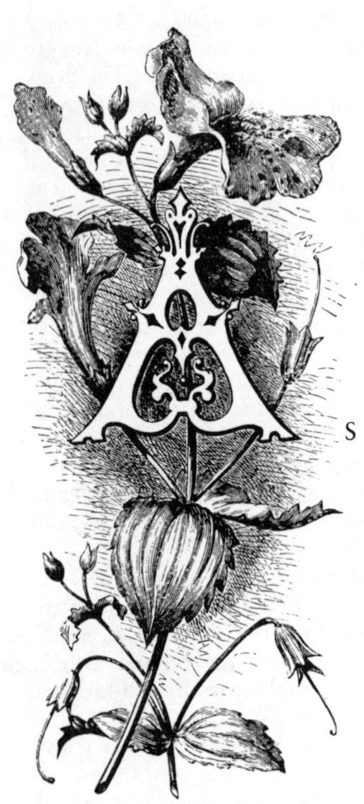

AS regards the start of plant collection, we have been able to proceed more or less in chronological order, but now we have to deal with simultaneity. By the eighteen-twenties plants were coming in from western North America, from the Himalayas and from the Andes more or less together and although the chapters have to be written in succession it should be borne in mind that the results tended to be presented to the gardener at the same time.

During the eighteenth century access to the Spanish and Portuguese possessions in South America was extremely difficult. We have seen how Joseph Banks was refused permission to land at Rio when accompanying Captain Cook and at the end of the century Humboldt was delighted at being given exceptional permission to explore in New Spain and Mexico. Also towards the end of the century both Spain and Portugal initiated work on the Floras of their American possessions. The *Flora of Brazil* by Padre Velloss has had to wait until our century to be published, while the expedition of Ruiz, Pavon and Dombey to Peru and Chile was only completely published many years after its completion.

In spite of this inaccessibility a number of South American plants did filter through to cultivation as the eighteenth century progressed. Most seem to have been obtained by the nursery of Kennedy and Lee. It is thought that they may have originally been introduced to Spain and then brought over here by Casimir Gomez Ortega. He was interested in the introduction of new plants and, indeed, wrote a book on the best methods of transporting plants both by sea and by land. He was a friend of both Joseph Banks and of Dr Fothergill and in 1777 was elected a member of the Royal Society. It seems to have been he, rather than Cavanilles who obtained the credit, who so improved the Madrid Botanic Garden. We know he introduced the first dahlia and the first zinnia to Britain and he may have been responsible for Lee obtaining *Alstromeria pelegrina* in 1753, *Aristotelia macqui* (syn. *A. chilensis*) in 1773, *Buddleia globosa* in 1774 and in 1776 another alstromeria, called at the time *A. ligtu*, but now thought to have been another species. The 1753 alstromeria may well have been due to Baron Alstromer himself, who certainly brought back specimens about that time, but the later sendings may well have been gifts from Ortega. On the other hand it is possible that they had some correspondent in either Chile or in Peru.

While on his voyage with Vancouver, Archibald Menzies, the surgeon, was entertained at a banquet at Santiago in Chile and he pocketed some nuts that were being served as dessert. He brought them back to Kew, they were sown and germinated and proved to be the Monkey Puzzle, *Araucaria araucana*. For a long time these plants were the only ones in Europe and it was one of the main objects of later collectors in Chile.

In Mexico some vestiges of the Maya gardening tradition lingered on and the dahlia was already fairly well developed. It does not seem to have reached Spain before 1789, but its real development dates from 1804 when Humboldt sent seeds of many varieties to Paris. By 1806 fifty-five varieties had been isolated and the first fully double form appeared in 1808. Ten years later it had become one of the most popular of garden plants and by 1840 nurserymen were growing over 1000 named doubles and anemone-centred. There may have been sendings subsequent to Humboldt's, but if so we know nothing of their provenance.

Another popular Mexican plant, *Zinnia elegans*, was received from Ortega in England in 1796, but it would seem that it was not a very attractive form and little notice was taken of it. More attractive forms, which one suspects were Mexican cultivars, were received in 1818 and again in 1829. According to Paxton it was in Italy that they were extensively bred and the results of these Italian plants became available to British gardens in the eighteen-thirties, since when the popularity of the zinnia has not waned.

Many Mexican plants were sent back by amateurs. In 1822 one of these sent back the gaudy and popular *Salvia splendens*, while in 1838 almost every post seems to have brought seed of the blue *S. patens*. This was also brought back by the Horticultural Society's collector, Theodor

Hartweg, whom we met in the preceding chapter. He also brought back the main parent of the garden fuchsia, *F. fulgens*, and seeds of the beautiful but tender Mexican pines, *Pinus montezumae* and *P. ayacahuite*.

So far as hardy plants were concerned it was in the south of the continent that most could be expected and as the Napoleonic wars ended Chile, Peru and Argentina threw off their allegiance to Spain, while in Brazil Portugal so far relaxed their closed door policy that Banks was able to arrange for Cunningham and Bowie to make an expedition in 1814. Even so their movements were somewhat limited; it took them a considerable time to obtain permission to visit Sao Paulo.

Further south there was ample opportunity for commercial men to establish what they hoped would prove profitable businesses in the newly independent countries and the British were among the first to arrive. The rich members of these countries were far too grand to worry about how they obtained their wealth, while the poorer inhabitants lacked both capital and technical know-how. A number of these businessmen seem to have made a hobby of botany and made considerable collections.

Nowadays John Miers is remembered as a botanist, but when he went to Chile in 1819 it was 'to erect a very extensive train of machinery . . . for refining, rolling, and manufacturing copper into sheathing.' This enterprise failed, but it induced Miers to write his entertaining and informative *Travels in Chile and La Plata*, which was published in 1826 and which gives a splendid picture of what it was like to travel in those parts at that time. Here, for example, is his description of the post-houses, at which all travellers had to stay on their journey from Argentina to Chile.

'It is a large hut, built of rough crooked stakes stuck into the ground; cross-pieces are lashed to the uprights with strips of hide; twigs of bushes or reeds are wattled in between the cross pieces and tied with strips of hide. The frame thus composed is daubed over on both sides with mud, laid on with the hands. The roof is framed in the manner of the sides . . . the ridge of the roof is supported by two poles inside of the hut and is thatched with grass. . . . There was neither chair, table, nor bed in this house of accommodation; these things . . . are rarely to be found in the post-houses; the only means of keeping off the bare ground is a kind of bedstead formed of four short stakes driven into the ground and four crossed sticks lashed with strips of hide as a frame from which a bullock's hide is stretched. Very few of these places are possessed of a door, but a hide is provided to keep out the weather. Another hut made in the same manner, often not plastered with mud . . . is commonly attached to these residences and is used for cooking. I need hardly say that these huts have no windows. Some, however, of the post houses are divided into two rooms, one of which is the shop or drinking room, the other the sleeping place; a square hole may be observed under the eaves of some of them, made to admit light and air....

'Miserable as they are, they afford some shelter to the traveller in a stormy weather, although it frequently happens that they are not impervious to rain, which falls in heavy showers during the winter and in thunder storms in the summer season.... The greatest objection, at least to Europeans, in these dreary receptacles is the incredible number of fleas, bugs and even still more disgusting vermin. The fleas breed in the very earth. This is no exaggeration, for, however many years one of these places may have been unoccupied, there does not appear the least diminution of these vermin. There is no exception; every hut is alike, whether it be inhabited or not. They are never swept out, nor is any filth removed; the ashes of the occasional fires made in them remain from year to year.'

In spite of these unattractive staging posts, most people seem to have preferred the overland route from Argentina to Chile to the necessity of rounding Cape Horn. There seem, in the eighteen-twenties, to have been a number of people in Chile who were nominally engaged in commerce, but who managed to collect and send back seeds. Miers himself only collected botanical specimens, but he detected several new genera and the first that he found he named *Placea*. This was in honour of Francis Place, who may have been Miers's partner in the copper-sheathing enterprise, but who remains a shadowy figure. It is fairly sure that he was not the Francis Place who organised the Corresponding Societies and agitated for the Reform Bill, but whether he visited Chile himself or simply organised the importation of seeds and plants still requires elucidation. The fruits of his sendings appeared in the Botanical publications of the day, usually having been grown by John Walker of Arnos Grove. At one moment Lindley, in his *Botanical Register*, notes that he sends back very little that is not worth growing and, of the plants attributed to him, the majority have persisted in cultivation. These include two popular annuals, *Schizanthus pinnatus*, the main ancestor of our modern schizanthus, and that odd crucifer *Schizopetalon walkeri*; two of the most used calceolarias, *C. corymbosa* and *C. integrifolia*; *Eccremocarpus scaber* and *Oenothera acaulis* and two important varieties of *Fuchsia magellanica*, known as *conica* and *gracilis*. In the early nineteen-hundreds a Frenchman who was writing notes on the history of various garden flowers was working on the fuchsia and said that *F. magellanica gracilis* was sent by Alexander Cruckshank to Francis Place, which rather suggests that Place was simply acting as an agent for amateurs in South America. Unfortunately no evidence is provided for this statement, which is repeated in the latest issue of Bean's *Trees and Shrubs Hardy in the British Isles*. It seems odd that anyone should go to the trouble of getting people to send him seeds from South America if he had no intention of growing them himself, but all Place's sendings were illustrated from plants grown by others, so it seems more probable that he himself sent the seeds back from Chile.

Thanks to Miers we know more about Dr John Gillies. According to him Gillies arrived at Mendoza on the Chile-Argentine frontier about 1820. Miers writes 'Doctor Gillies, an English physician, who has been four years resident in this town, describes the climate ... as superior to any other. He was compelled to leave England from a severe pulmonary affection [sic], which had gone to such an extent that his friends scarcely expected he would ever reach the shores of South America alive.' Once established at Mendoza, the tuberculosis seems to have cleared up rapidly and 'the rapid improvements that have taken place in Mendoza during the last few years are in great measure due to the indefatigable exertions of Dr Gillies, who has applied himself incessantly to the amelioration of the people.' Among his activities were a school for girls 'upon the Lancasterian system' and 'he obtained the co-operation of the natives in forming a sort of literary society ... among the young men of the town ... and books for a public library were collected from Buenos Ayres.' Not surprisingly perhaps 'Improvement and liberal notions were propagated so fast ... as to alarm the older bigoted people and the clergy and serious measures were had recourse to, to suppress these useful institutions, and they were all abolished ... fortunately, however, the girls' school was overlooked.... A counter-revolution had taken place ... before the beginning of 1825 and Dr Gillies was then actively employed in his former useful and meritorious labours—the re-establishment of the society, the library and the schools.'

Mendoza lies in the Cordillera and, according to Miers, 'To a botanist no treat can be greater than a journey through the Cordillera ... the trees and shrubs are all evergreens, infinite in variety, rich in foliage, beautiful in flower and mostly peculiar to Chile; while the herbaceous plants and flowers are rich, various, beautiful and novel. Gillies botanised enthusiastically, although he was more concerned with obtaining specimens than sending back seeds. For example he first observed that popular little bulb *Ipheion (Triteleia, Brodiaea) uniflorum*, but left it to a later collector, John Tweedie, to introduce. He does seem to have introduced *Salpiglossis sinuata*, four calceolarias and three schizanthus, *S. grahamii, S. hookerianus* and *S. retusus*, as well as other plants that have not persisted in cultivation. Both he and Place are credited with the scarlet *Verbena peruviana melindroides*, a plant on which all travellers commented, so that the probability of sendings being duplicated must be recognised. Gillies also sent back the tall purple *V. rigida* (syn. *V. venosa*).

Alexander Cruckshank was botanising in Peru from 1825 until 1856, but he only seems to have sent plants back until about 1830. It may well be to him that we owe the first sendings of the Southern Beeches, *Nothofagus antarctica* and *N. betuloides*, which arrived in 1830, but do not seem to have long survived. Cruckshank wrote about his travels and about the climate and provinces of Chile and Peru. Thus we learn that the araucaria 'is only found in the interior of the Indian country, south of the Biobio'. Since this district was regarded as dangerous for Europeans to visit, it explains why it should not have been much introduced. It is true that in 1824 the Horticultural Society's collector James McRae visited Chile and obtained a quantity of araucaria seeds, but the plant still remained very scarce. Apart from a leucocoryne, the rest of McRae's sendings were singularly dreary.

Cruckshank ends his observations on the climate of Chile with some notes on their cultivation in Britain and these are still relevant.

'From the peculiarities of the climate in the various districts both of Peru and Chile, the greater part of the indigenous plants flourish at a season and under circumstances peculiarly favourable to their cultivation in Britain and other parts of the north of Europe... In illustration of this I may mention that *Palavia rhombifolia* and *Loasa hispida*, which inhabit the low country near Lima, succeeded perfectly in the open air at the garden of the Horticultural Society during the wet and boisterous summer of the present year, 1830....

'In cultivating Chilean and Peruvian plants, the climate and progress of vegetation on the coast of the middle provinces of Chile may serve as a guide to their treatment, and it may be as well to take a short review of the leading phenomena. The rainy season ... begins in May and continues till October; the heaviest rains are in June and July. After a few days of rain, there is an interval of fine weather ... and the quantity that falls during the season is small, varying from 12 to 16 inches. In summer the atmosphere is excessively arid and there is little or no dew.... During the latter part of the summer vegetation is almost dormant, and scarcely a plant of any kind is to be seen in flower; but in a very few weeks after the first rains, every part of the country is clothed with verdure. By the end of July many plants are in bloom, and a rapid succession of species continue to put forth their blossoms for several months, and the hills are adorned with many beautiful species of alstromeria, calceolaria, tropaeolum, hippeastrum, schizanthus, oxalis, sisyrinchium and other interesting genera. After the end of November few of these remain in flower.

'The principal objection to the climate of Britain as regards the habits of these plants is excessive humidity, rather than any defect of temperature; and to this circumstance the attention of those who are interested in their cultivation should be chiefly directed. From the hilly nature of the country they inhabit and the moderate rains, the soil retains little moisture during the season they are in flower, and, while they are seeding, the ground is perfectly dry and hard.'

Besides ornamentals Cruckshank sent to the Horticultural Society a Peruvian potato, renowned for its flavour, but a shy bearer even in Peru. In Britain it flowered and even set seed, but failed to produce any tubers. A Chilean tomato proved equally unsuccessful. Few of his new ornamentals have persisted in cultivation, but the scarlet *Geum chiloense* is still a fovourite herbaceous plant and two of his calceolarias, *C. integrifolia angustifolia* and *C. purpurea* were the most important parents of the bedding and of the greenhouse calceolaria. *Escallonia rubra* seems to have been the first of these popular shrubs to be available to gardeners. Why that showy mallow relative *Palaua (Palavia) rhombifolia* should have dropped out of cultivation is not easy to understand, except that all annuals seem to be unfashionable at the moment. One can sometimes obtain *Lupinus cruckshankii* (also known as *L. mutabilis cruckshankii*) a very large annual lupin, which makes a rather striking plant.

Between 1825 and 1830 the survey ship *Adventure* was around the coasts of Chile and the Admiralty had included in the crew under Captain King (who had befriended Allan Cunningham in Australia), the botanist James Anderson. He augmented his salary by sending seeds to the Clapton Nursery of Hugh Low and Son and he seems to have had a good eye for a commercial plant. The list of his introductions is not long, but almost every one has persisted in cultivation. It includes *Alstromeria aurantiaca, Berberis buxifolia* and *B. empetrifolia, Libertia formosa, Solanum crispum, Tropaeolum tricolorum* and *Habranthus andersonii*.

It was also Anderson who encouraged Hugh Cuming to show an interest in plants. Cuming had been born in 1791, but went to Chile in 1819 and started some unidentified business, which was sufficiently successful for him to have built himself a boat, which he used to sail along the coast to enable him to collect the sea shells on which he was becoming expert. According to Loudon the meeting between Cuming and Anderson tood place in 1830, but this must be wrong as Cuming's first sendings date from 1826 and he left Chile in 1831. Many of his introductions have dropped out of cultivation, but one may still see *Azara dentata, Colletia infausta, Escallonia pulverulenta*, a very tender species, a compact form of *Schizanthus pinnatus*, which has proved important in the breeding of the modern hybrids, and the popular *Verbena laciniata*. His most popular introduction seems to have been the Bridal Wreath, *Francoa racemosa*, but at the time the very variable annual *Collomia biflora* was extensively grown.

Another of Cuming's companions was Thomas Bridges. He had a passion for exploration and field botany and, eventually, he was able to find some patrons who would finance him to Chile in return for natural products of South America. Bridges arrived at Valparaiso in 1828 and, rather oddly, started a brewery, which was meant to carry him over until he could make a living from his collections. Among his original patrons was a famous plantsman, Robert Barclay, 'to whom birds and plants, both of considerable interest were sent.' The Rev. G. Reading Leathes, of whom nothing seems to be known, was also sent seeds, while seeds and insects were sent to Robert Bevan, who lived at Rougham in Yorkshire. This last person sent his seeds to the nurseryman Thomas Knight, who owned the Exotic Nursery at Chelsea, and it was by this means that many of Bridges' sendings got early into cultivation. The number of new species introduced by him does not seem to have been very large, but he may well have been responsible for a large sending of araucaria seeds in 1839, which the firm of Youell was advertising in 1843 as four-year-old plants. *Azara petiolaris* (syn. *A. gilliesii*), presumably first discovered by Dr Gillies, was introduced to cultivation by Bridges and he also sent back what appears to be a very attractive white schizanthus, *S. candida*. *Lobelia bridgesii* and *Mutisia latifolia* were said to have been sent back by Bridges and Cuming. Bridges' most notable discovery, the giant water-lily, *Victoria amazonica*, did not take place until 1845 and, naturally, not in Chile. Although he brought back seeds, none were raised successfully and its introduction to cultivation was due to Robert Schomburgk.

Although Bridges was working spasmodically during the decade, the eighteen-thirties saw a slackening of plant collection from the Andes and it might be worthwhile pausing to see how rapidly the plants got into cultivation. Here is an advertisement from the *Floricultural Cabinet* of 1835, listing the seed novelties of Messrs Warner, Seaman and Warner. It includes 4 alstromerias, 2 calandrinias, 2 calecolaria species as well as 'mixed perennial varieties', both the francoas, which had only been introduced in 1830 and 1831, *Lupinus mutabilis* and its variety *cruckshankii, Mimulus variegatus* no less than six cultivars of salpiglossis, as well as 'mixed varieties', *Schizanthus hookeri*, and *S. retusus*, and *Tropaeolum pentaphyllum* make up the South American plants.

Three years later the same firm, having apparently disposed of Mr Seaman in the interval, were able to offer as many as 13 alstromerias (of which two were bomareas), 4 calandrinnias, *Collomia bicolor, Schizopetalon walkeri*, as many as 7 schizanthus, although only 5 of these would seem to be genuine species, the remainder being colour variants, and the popular *Tropaeolum tricolorum* had been added. It would seem that already the hybridists had so bedevilled the calceolarias that they are only offered as mixed shrubby, or as mixed herbaceous, varieties. There is one significant innovation, 'petunias, mixed hybrids, 20 splendid varieties.' There is one rather odd omission. Not a single verbena is offered.

Both the petunias and the verbenas would have been due to the activities of James Tweedie, who had been born as long ago as 1775. He was a trained gardener and eventually became the head gardener at the Edinburgh Botanic Garden. He then set himself up as a landscape gardener and it was in pursuit of this trade that he left for Buenos Aires in 1825, when he was fifty years old. Once arrived in the Argentine he does not seem to have persisted for long at his original trade, but set up a store in Buenos Aires, which could be run by his family when he was away on botanical excursions. As far as we know these did not start before 1832, when he travelled up the Uruguay and along the coast to Rio, when he was accompanied by the British Envoy to Brazil, the Honourable H. S. Fox. From this expedition came the brilliant scarlet *Verbena phlogiflora* (syn. *V. tweediana*). He may have been encouraged in his activities by our minister at Buenos Aires, H. J. Mandeville, who is credited with himself introducing the fragrant Argentine jasmine, *Mandevilla suaveolens*. After travelling north Tweedie went south to Patagonia, but his first trip there ended in disaster and it was not until 1845, in his seventieth year, that he made a successful expedition there. We have his accounts of journeys to Tucuman at the foot of the Andes and to the Sierra de Tandil, some 300 miles from Buenos Aires, which they seem to have covered in five days.

The main recipients of his sendings were botanic gardens and a full record has survived for the Glasnevin garden at Dublin. The first dates from 1834, his first expedition. There is nothing in 1835, but in 1836 'A tin box of South American seeds from Mr Tweedie, collected by him in the pampas of Buenos Ayres on the way to the Cordilleras'. There were also sixty growing plants in this sending. This must refer to his journey to Tucuman, which one would have thought from his own account had proved very disappointing. Almost the only plants he mentions are 'a very beautiful kind of *Digitalis*' as well as 'a curious *Eryngium*, smelling strongly like Angelica and a species of *Eupatorium* with fine tufts of peach-coloured flowers.' He also mentions 'the beautiful little *Nierembergia gracilis*.' Apparently from this trip came that showy, but stinging, half-hardy annual *Blumenbachia lateritia*, which is still to be found in the more recondite seed lists.

In 1837 Glasnevin received 'A box of plants and another of seeds by the Barque *Standard* from Mr Tweedie of Buenos Ayres: epiphytes and about 30 species of Cactus from South Brazil, in pretty good condition.' In 1838 Tweedie sent '100 papers of seeds and a box of roots' and much the same happened in 1839, although the roots arrived in bad condition. Nothing happened in 1840, but to compensate there were three sendings in 1841. One was, rather bafflingly, a 'small box of seeds of *Araucaria araucana*, which do not appear very fresh.' Where did these come from? Did

Tweedie visit Chile or was there a plant cultivated in Buenos Aires setting good seed? In the same January the garden received a package containing 71 species of seeds, while towards the end of the year came 15 kinds of living plants, but, alas, 'mostly came in bad order'. The sendings came yearly until 1845 and then there is a seven-year silence. However seeds were received in 1852 and Tweedie seems to have celebrated his eightieth birthday with renewed activity, sending in 1855 in all 135 packets of seeds, while the next year they received '100 kinds of seeds and 10 kinds of grapes.' His last sending was in the following year.

It is not surprising that the number of plants credited to Tweedie is very large, although few of the names mean much to us today. The tree tomato, *Cyphomandra betacea*, a popular fruiting plant in Australia and New Zealand, was received from him and the Cruel Plant, *Araujia sericofera* is planted fairly extensively in warmer climes. The brilliant blue *Pharbitis learii* is too tender for Britain, outside the greenhouse, but is extensively planted in the Mediterranean, where it makes a very showy, if rather too vigorous, climber. Another plant frequently seen in such places is *Bignonia unguis-cati*, with attractive yellow flowers; this was long known as *B. tweediana*. The plant named after him, *Tweedia coerulea*, is one of the most attractive of greenhouse plants. On the other hand the charm of *Boussingaultia baselloides* lies mainly in its luxuriance of growth and its persistence in cultivation is rather surprising.

Tweedie cannot have sent the first *Petunia violacea*, which had arrived by 1830, but he may well have sent numerous variants as the breeding of our modern petunia dates from the later eighteen-thirties. Although his contribution to the petunia may be doubtful, there can be no question of his sendings being responsible for the verbena. This is generally reckoned to be bred from four species, and of these four Tweedie introduced three, *V. incisa, V. platensis* and *V. phlogiflora*. Finally it is to Tweedie that we owe the Pampas Grass, *Cortaderia selloana*, which so impressed gardeners with its massive plumes and vigorous growth. As we have noted it was he who actually introduced *Ipheion uniflorum*.

We must now return to Chile and at length to a professional collector, whom we have already met in California, William Lobb. There were two members of this Cornish family who worked for Messrs Veitch: William who collected in America and Thomas who collected in eastern Asia, which accounts for the epithet *lobbii* being applied to plants of widely separated provenance. William had been born at Perran-ar-Worthal in 1809 and was sent by Veitch to South America in 1840. He went first to Brazil and thence to Chile by the overland route from Buenos Aires, when he was able to visit the more southerly parts, which had been regarded as dangerous in earlier years. Lobb returned to England in 1844 and then made a second expedition in the following year, returning finally in 1848.

During this second expedition he also visited Peru. In Paxton and Lindley's *Flower Garden* for 1851 there is printed Lobb's account of part of this second expedition, which is very vividly written.

'I visited a great part of Chiloe, most of the islands of the archipelago and the coast of Patagonia for about 140 miles. I went up the Corcocobado, Caylin, Alman, Comau, Reloncavi and other places on the coast, frequently making excursions from the level of the sea to the lines of perpetual snow. These bays generally run to the base of the central ridge of the Andes, and the rivers take their rise much further back in the interior. The whole country from the Andes to the sea is formed of a succession of ridges of mountains rising gradually ... to the central ridge....

'Ascending the Andes of Comau I observed from the water to a considerable elevation the forest is composed of a variety of trees and a sort of cane, so thickly matted together that it formed an almost impenetrable jungle. Further up, among the melting snows, vegetation becomes so much stunted in growth, that trees seen below 100 feet high and 8 feet in diameter, only attain the height of 6 inches.

'On reaching the summit no vegetation exists ... nothing but scattered barren rocks, which appear to rise amongst the snow, which is 30 feet in depth and frozen so hard, that on walking over it, the foot makes but a slight impression...

'A little below this elevation the scenery is also singular and grand. Rocky precipices stand like perpendicular walls from 200 to 300 feet in height, over which roll the waters from the melting snows, which appear to the eyes like lines of silver. Sometimes these waters rush down with such force that rocks of many tons weight are precipitated to the depth of 2000 feet. In the forest below everything appears calm and tranquil; scarcely the sound of an animal is heard; sometimes a few butterflies and beetles meet the eye, but not a human being is seen. On the sandy tracts near the rivers, the lion or puma is frequently to be met with; but this animal is perfectly harmless if not attacked.'

Lobb seems to have been fascinated by relatives of the yew and never failed to find some examples and in the southern Andes he found *Saxegothaea conspicua* and *Podocarpus nubigensa* 'which are beautiful evergreen trees and ... afford excellent timber.' Lobb also introduced other conifers, two libocedrus, *L.* (now *Austrocedrus*) *chilensis*, which had previously been sent by Bridges to Hugh Low in 1847 and *L. uvifera*, which has not proved very stable in cultivation in Britain. On the other hand *Fitzroya cupressoides* (syn. *patagonica*) has proved quite successful, although slow-growing.

A very large number of excellent garden ornaments were introduced by Lobb. After his visit the monkey puzzle was no longer hard to obtain and

Abutilon vitifolium, although Captain Cottingham had flowered it in Dublin in 1836, had never been easily obtainable. Now it became widespread.

Berberis darwinii, one of the most popular members of the genus, was introduced by Lobb, as was also another species, which is referred to as *B. lutea*. Could this plant have been the showy *B. chillanensis*? In any case it would appear to have been lost. We have already noted Anderson's introduction of the dwarf *B. empetrifolia*. About 1860 this seems to have become accidentally hybridised with *B. darwinii* in the nursery of Fisher and Holmes at Handsworth, near Sheffield. The resultant plant was *B.*x *stenophylla*, which is probably planted more extensively than any other berberis.

Colletia cruciata, a curious gorse-like plant that bears masses of fragrant, tubular, pale pink flowers in late autumn, is another of Lobb's sendings and so was *Desfontainea spinosa*, with its holly-like leaves and large tubular orange flowers. The Chilean Fire Bush, *Embothrium coccineum*, is among the most spectacular of garden shrubs although it seems to thrive best in the milder parts of the British Isles. *Escallonia rubra macrantha* is not only extensively planted in coastal districts, but is one of the main parents of the many hybrid escallonias which are offered. The glowing crimson Chinese lanterns of *Crinodendron hookerianum* are one of the most vivid of garden ornaments where it can be grown. It thrives in Eire and near the west coast of Scotland, but may well be damaged by cold winters elsewhere. The same may be said of *Eucryphia cordata*, but this again is magnificent where it can be grown. The scarlet-flowered *Mitraria coccinea* is yet another Lobb shrub. Among trees *Nothofagus obliqua* has proved generally hardy. The magnificent *Lapageria rosea* usually needs a cool greenhouse, but its relative *Philesia magellanica*, although tricky to establish, is more amenable. Three myrtles, *Myrtus chequen, M. luma* and *M. ugni* survive as wall plants in many gardens. Few people now grow the blue nasturtium *Tropaeolum azureum*, which Miers had detected as early as 1819, but the flame flower *Tropaeolum speciosum* is yet another reminder of what we owe to the energies of William Lobb. We should also, perhaps, pay tribute to the enterprise of the Veitch nursery. By no means all the results were immediately profitable. Among Lobb's sendings were the seed of a boraginous shrub, *Cordia decandra*. Veitch received the seed in 1849, but had to wait twenty-six years, until 1875, before seeing the flowers.

In any case they were so well pleased with the result of their original investments, that in 1859 they decided to send a collector again to Chile and Peru. This was Richard Pearce, who, in 1859, signed a three-year contract to go to these parts as 'a collector of plants, seeds, land-shells and other objects of Natural History'. He returned again in 1863 with a further three-year contract. His instructions were to collect further material of Lobb's most successful introductions as well as any other plants that he considered might be profitable.

The most important of Pearce's introductions were among greenhouse plants; he introduced three of the four basic ancestors of the tuberous begonia and also the enormous brick-red *Hippeastrum leopoldii*, which has since been used in every facet of amaryllis breeding, sacrificing delicate colours and graceful shapes to enormous size.

Among his contributions to the garden pride of place must go to *Eucryphia glutinosa*, one of the most attractive of shrubs, both for its late flowers and for its autumn tints. The spicily scented *Azara microphylla* is an attractive wall-shrub and so is the coral-belled *Berberidopsis corallina*. The white-flowered, deciduous *Escallonia virgata* is easily the hardiest species in the U.K. and has been invaluable for the breeding of hardy hybrids which incorporate the red flowers of such species as *E. rubra*, with the greater tolerance of cold of *E. virgata*. Pearce also found and brought back the white form of the lapageria and, surprisingly, found a yew that had escaped Lobb, *Podocarpus andinus*, which was long known as *Prumnopitys elegans*.

After Pearce's visit we know little of collectors in Chile before this century, although the vivid *Tecophilaea cyanocrocus* was introduced in the eighteen-seventies. We know that Roezl was in the Peruvian Andes in 1872 and he may have dashed down to Chile.

In this century the expedition of Harold Comber in 1925 brought into cultivation some superb new berberis, including *B. linearifolia* and *B. montana* and that curious member of the potato family, that looks like a heather, *Fabiana violacea*.

There is a curious lack of any alpines among all these sendings during the nineteenth century. Admittedly it was not until the eighteen-sixties that alpines began to be extensively cultivated. As early as 1838 Hartweg had mentioned the scarlet gentians in the Bolivian Andes and many botanists had commented on the curious rosette-forming violets, that are such a feature of the Andes. In 1927 Clarence Elliott, who was a nurseryman specialising in alpines, visited the Andes, but even he does not seem to have introduced any Andean dwarfs. In 1972 Messrs Beckett, Cheese and Watson sent back ample material, not only of many plants that had previously been introduced and subsequently lost, but also of many alpines that had never been in cultivation hitherto. It remains to be seen how many can become established in cultivation. In 1860 Pearce had spoken of the 'numerous pretty rock plants' that 'meet one at every step'. With the loss of all the Veitch records we do not know whether he sent back seeds which failed to develop or whether he simply did not bother.

There is a violet among Lobb's sendings, but this, which he called *Viola pyrolaefolia*, is not rosulate.

I suppose the trouble is that in northern Europe, Chilean plants are barely hardy. During the mid-nineteenth century there was much hybridising done among the various alstromerias, but most succumbed during severe winters, while in Mediterranean regions the climate is, presumably, too dry. In any case there are no nineteenth century alstromeria hybrids surviving and the only species that is well established in gardens is *A. aurantiaca*. The Ligtu hybrids, in which the Brazilian *A. haemantha* plays a large part, date from this century and have proved successful.

Of the plants that are hardy few have been so extensively planted as *Berberis darwinii*, and its hybrid *B.* x *stenophylla* is even more widespread. The South American contribution to our gardens may not be so large numerically, but it is important, even disregarding such half-hardy plants as petunias, tropaeolums and verbenas.

CHAPTER IX

India

NO ONE would have expected Joseph Banks to fail to take advantage of the British conquest of India. In 1787 he sent out A. P. Hove, a Pole, to make a collection for Kew. At this time the East India Company were inimical to the idea and Hove was made to suffer so many delays that few, if indeed any, of his plants were received at Kew. More success attended Christopher Smith, who was appointed botanist to the Company and stationed at Calcutta. His collections were actually brought back to England by the gardener Peter Good, who was later to accompany Robert Brown to Australia. They were all greenhouse plants. The same can be said of the plants that were sent to Banks from 1793 onwards by William Roxburgh, who became the first Director of the Botanic Garden at Calcutta. This garden was to prove of immense importance both to British and to tropical gardens. For example in 1828 Professor Wenzel Bojer, who was botanising in Madagascar, discovered the Flamboyant, *Delonix regia*; a plant that would seem always to have been very rare. He sent seeds to the curator of the Mauritius Botanic Garden, Mr Telfair, who in turn sent seeds to Wallich at Calcutta, and it is from Calcutta that it was sent to every tropical city in the world. The Flamboyant is nearly extinct in Madagascar as a wild plant, but it exists in huge numbers in cultivation. Rather more curiously Calcutta was a useful half-way house in the early nineteenth century, between China and Britain. In the eighteen-twenties Reeves sent the Chinese *Artemisia lactiflora* to Calcutta, whence it was sent to England, arriving in 1828. The plant is still much grown as it bears tall plumes of white flowers in autumn, at a time when any flowers are welcome and it would seem odd that a plant that is perfectly hardy in Britain could have survived the tropical heat of Calcutta. Similarly many forms of *Rosa chinensis* were known as Bengal Roses, since they had come from China via Bengal, and the Chestnut Rose, *R. roxburghii*, another Chinese species, travelled first to Calcutta and thence to Britain.

Roxburgh sent plants not only to Kew but also to various keen private gardeners, but they were all greenhouse subjects and it was left to his assistant and eventual successor, Nathaniel Wallich, to explore and introduce plants from the Himalaya, which would prove hardy. Wallich was by birth a Dane and christened Nathan Wolff. He had joined the Danish East India Company as a doctor and had been captured in 1808 when hostilities broke out between the British and the Danes. He was soon released and appointed to assist Roxburgh at Calcutta. After three years his poor health, which dogged him throughout his career, enabled him to visit Mauritius while on sick leave and he must have established good relations with Telfair, the curator of the Botanic Garden on that island. After Roxburgh retired he was appointed temporary director of the Calcutta garden and in 1817 the appointment was confirmed on a permanent basis. Wallich was not to visit England until 1828, but he seems to have been impressed by the need to introduce hardy garden plants, with the result that, as one of his obituarists wrote, 'there was scarcely an English garden of magnitude, which was not much indebted to his liberality'.

Although Wallich did go on many expeditions himself—he visited Nepal in 1820 and in 1825 was in the Himalaya, reaching as far as Dehra Dun, he relied mainly on an army of helpers who collected on his behalf in the various districts of India to which their duties assigned them. His collectors included the farrier Moorcroft, the soldier Buchanan-Hamilton, Robert Blinkworth and even His Majesty's resident in Nepal, the Hon. Edward Gardner. It was in 1817 that Wallich sent to Banks seeds of the blood-red *Rhododendron arboreum*, which he had packed in brown sugar. Indeed the successful transport of material from India to Britain much exercised his mind and in 1829 he delivered a lecture on the subject to the Horticultural Society.

'The subject,' he stated, 'may be considered under the four following heads. 1. The preparing of plants for the voyage. 2. The packing them. 3. Their treatment during the voyage and 4. their management upon arrival.' With regard to the first point Wallich says it is essential to 'select plants already advanced in age with a strong root and a thick stem, and only such grafts as have already been established two or three years.' I think we should regard 'grafts' here as representing any form of asexual propagation. Wallich seems to have realised that during the voyage it was absolutely essential to secure the captain's interest and good will. This had not always been available as 'it had been the custom to make the chests very large and to crowd into such chests as many plants as they will hold; this practice has had, among others, this bad effect, that captains, however well-disposed at first to pay the plants every attention, have soon found these cases troublesome, unwieldy and unsightly.' Wallich recommended ideal dimensions of 3 feet long, 18 inches wide and 16 inches deep and that 'some attention should be paid to the neatness of the appearance of these cases, as captains are very unwilling to allow the deck to be occupied by unsightly objects'.

The roofs of these cases were to be 'glazed either with stout glass or with the Chinese oyster shell or with plates of thick talc'. 'Each plant should have a separate, square pot made of wood, of such a size that eight should be contained in each case; they should not fit too tightly together ... the pots should have 3 or 4 holes bored in their bottoms, but there should be no holes in the bottom of the chest, for it is at such apertures that rats on shipboard always commence their depredations . . Between the bottom of the pots and the case should be a layer, 3 inches deep, of broken glass and pebbles, which renders it impossible for vermin to establish themselves.' He also advised that the cases should have short legs to raise them slightly above the deck.

During the voyage Wallich recommended that the cases be opened whenever the weather was suitable. Unless the plants were under an awning, they should not be exposed to the tropical sun, but only in the evening and at night. The plants could be exposed to showers with good results, but during storms the cases should be kept closed and covered with canvas. The Captain should be asked to supply water at the average rate of a pint per day per plant, although the quantity should not be slavishly adhered to. During cool or wet weather very little water would be required, while during very hot dry weather more than a pint per day might be needed. Of this part should be used to keep the soil moist and part to moisten the aerial parts of the plant.

Once the plants had been received in England Wallich recommended that the plants should be well cleaned but kept in their square wooden pots until signs of fresh growth were noted, when they could be transferred to conventional pots.

In 1833–4 the Wardian case had triumphantly taken plants without loss from Britain to Australia and further plants from Australia to Britain and the next year Wallich seems to have adapted the case. The method was described in the *Gardener's Magazine* by Captain Gillies of the *Hibernia*. 'The plants were all intended for the greenhouse in England and, I presume, were of a delicate kind ... and, no doubt, well saturated with water previously to being put into the large outer box, which contained eight of these small ones.

'The large box was constructed in the usual way; that is a glazed roof about 2 foot high, the glass strong enough to resist the fall of a small rope or other light body. It was hermetically closed with the common *Chunam* (a sort of lime, used in India as cement . . .) of the country and was never opened during a voyage of five months. When we arrived in England, the plants were all in beautiful health, and had grown to the full height of the case, the leaves pressing against the glass.'

The original Wardian case was made entirely of glass, but Wallich's adaptation would be less liable to breakage, although the plants, being only lit from above, might tend to get drawn in transit. In 1836 the Duke of Devonshire sent John Gibson, his gardener, out to India to bring back *Amherstia nobilis*, recently discovered by Wallich, and to do some independent collecting; he was using Wardian cases throughout this successful expedition and they were used consistently from then on, even for the transport of plants over land. Joseph Hooker records the arrival of fruit trees in an ice ship from America, which were thawed out on arrival at Calcutta and planted up and put in Wardian cases for the long journey to the Himalayan foothills.

I have a tendency to regard all Indian plants introduced between 1818 and 1836 as being done through the instrumentality of Wallich, but this is not entirely true. Although Wallich was acquainted with *Clematis montana* and with *Anemone vitifolia*, it was Lady Amherst who collected and introduced these two favourites. Again, although Wallich had introduced the Deodar as early as 1822, there were very few plants around, as most of the seed sent proved non-viable and it was not generally available until Lewis Melville brought back a large number of young trees in 1831. There must also be many unrecorded introductions. In the 5th volume of Loudon's *Gardener's Magazine* it is recorded that the members of the Caledonian Horticultural Society received in 1829 a collection of seeds from Dr Govan, who was employed in a survey of the Himalayas. We have no idea what was sent, nor what plants were raised.

Wallich's introductions almost certainly include, among conifers, the deodar, *Abies spectabilis*, the attractive, pendulous *Picea smithiana*, *Pinus gerardiana* and *P. wallichiana* and probably *P. nepalensis*.

Particular importance attaches to the various colour forms of *Rhododendron arboreum*, to which can be added *R. campanulatum, R. barbatum,* and two dwarfs, *R. anthopogon* and *R. setosum*. Various Asiatic cotoneasters were received for the first time and greeted with enthusiasm. They included *C. frigidus*, with its massive heads of fruits, and the smaller *C. microphyllus* and *C. rotundifolius* (syn. *C. prostratus*). *Hypericum uralum*, with its large patulate flowers was the first of this section to arrive in gardens. *Spiraea bella* is an attractive shrub. That vigorous climber *Rosa brunonii* seems to have supplanted the true

Musk Rose, once it became generally available. Wallich also introduced the four-petalled *R. sericea* and the handsomely hepped *R. macrophylla*. It is not easy to identify with much certainty the various berberis species that were introduced. They were known then as *BB. aristata, asiatica* and *wallichiana*. Modern taxonomists regard the plants introduced as *B. aristata* to be, in fact, *B. glaucocarpa*, while Wallich's *B. wallichiana* turns out to be *B. hookeri.* No one seems to have cast doubts on *B. asiatica*.

Among herbaceous plants are *Tulipa stellata, Bergenia ligulata, Houttuynia cordata, Geranium lambertii, G. nepalense* and *G. wallichianum, Morina longifolia* and *Potentilla montana* (syn. *P. splendens*). I am only mentioning here plants that have persisted in our gardens; the full list is considerably longer.

In the eighteen-thirties Himalayan plants were also being received from the botanic garden at Saharanpur in the Punjab, whose superintendent, John Forbes Royle, was to write a flora of the Himalayas in 1832 and who employed Indians to collect Himalayan plants for him and sent material to the Horticultural Society. After he retired, his successor Hugh Falconer continued with this work and the results of their joint sendings are impressive. In 1837 *Abies pindrow* was at last successfully introduced, otherwise it is chiefly shrubs and herbaceous plants that came from this source. The shrubs include two more berberis, *B. coriaria* and *B. umbellata*, two deutzias, *D. corymbosa* and *D. staminea, Elaeagnus umbellata,* the large-flowered form, *affine*, of the common white jasmine, Job's Tears (*Leycesteria formosa*), a philadelphus which seems lost to cultivation as is probably *Spiraea vacciniifolia, Sorbaria tomentosa* was the first of the genus to get into cultivation and *Pyracantha crenulata* was the first of the Asiatic firethorns to be introduced. The handsome Himalayan lilac, *Syringa emodi*, also came from Saharanpur.

Among herbaceous plants they sent the easy and popular *Androsace lanuginosa, Anemone rivularis, Aquilegia fragrans, Bergenia ciliata,* the first codonopsis, *Cynoglossum grandiflorum*—they sent several species, but this is the only Indian hound's tongue to persist in cultivation—*Filipendula vestita*, a large meadow sweet, *Iris aurea* and *I. biglumis*, two important potentillas, *P. argyrophylla* and *P. nepalensis*, the ever-popular *Primula denticulata, Polygonum vacciniifolium*, that useful late-flowering rock plant, the orchid-like *Roscoea purpurea* and the curious *Salvia hians*. The most successful of their introductions must be the Policeman's Helmet, *Impatiens roylei*, which has become naturalised along many river banks.

Wallich did not retire before 1844, but for the last years of his life he was in poor health and did little in the way of introducing plants, apart from superintending the transport of collectors such as the Duke of

Devonshire's John Gibson, who collected in the Khasia hills in 1837, but, apart from the tender *Rhododendron formosum*, only brought back greenhouse plants, and the introduction of new plants became dependent on amateurs, so far as the Himalaya were concerned. A surprising number of these came from officers in the Indian Army. Thus the first nomocharis, *N. oxypetala,* was sent back by Lieutenant Strachey, the future Sir Richard and the father of Lytton and James. Major Vicary sent back the incarvillea relative *Amphicome arguta*, while Captain Munro, who later became the greatest authority on Indian grasses (and also was appointed General) sent back *Cyananthus lobatus*, *Primula munroi* and *P. involucrata*.

The most important of these botanically inclined military men was Edward Madden, who seems to have spent most of his leaves botanising in the Himalayas and sending his collections to Glasnevin Botanic Garden. His first sending arrived in 1841 and then, after a three-year gap, a succession of sendings between 1844 and 1850. Many of his expeditions Madden described in the *Asiatic Journal of Bengal* and since he was a writer of both wit and acumen his accounts are among the most enjoyable descriptions of plant collecting that have survived. Thus to give some idea of the Himalaya he writes: 'There is a bitter proverb that if you want to know the value of money, try to borrow some; so to realise the height of these mountains, you must walk up one of them.' Being Madden this leads him to an examination of Bishop Berkely's theory that things only exist as they are perceived in the mind and have no real existence, but concludes that 'the higher we mount in the atmosphere, the lower we fall in the region of metaphysics; and on the summits of the mountains will generally in practice be found pure materialists.' These flights of fancy are just embellishments to what are serious and valuable accounts of his expeditions. His practice is first to describe his day's journey, with details about the state of the paths, the geology and the landscape and any other notes that travellers might find useful. Thus, 'Puralee boasts a small bungalow of one room, which is cooler than a tent, but by no means so clean, being infested with almost all the insect plagues of Europe.' Here is his entry for 11 September 1847 on his way to the Shatool Pass.

'To Kala Koondar, 10 or 11 miles, which took us eight hours, being much delayed by the constant halts of the coolies, by my own rests and search for plants, and, after quitting the forest, by a very difficult path. The distances are indeed but approximations ... but Kala Koondar and the next two stages being "vox et praterea nihil" are not inserted on the maps. Soon after leaving Moojwar we passed the hamlet Jutwar, the last and highest (9200 feet) on the route. Brushwood and meadows succeed; the first formed by *Rosa sericea*, *Berberis brachybotrys* (with bright red fruit) and abundance of the beautiful yellow-flowered *Potentilla dubia*, while the pastures abound with the sessile flowered *Iris kamaonensis* ... The late Dr Hoffmeister showed me specimens of the above Potentilla, if they were not varieties of *P. atrosanguinea* ... in which some of the petals were yellow and some carmine. On quitting the meadows, the route enters and ascends steeply through a forest of *Picea smithiana, Pinus wallichiana*, *Abies pindrow* and *A. spectabilis*, *Quercus semicarpifolia*, *Taxus baccata*, *Ribes acuminatum*, the lemon-scented laurustinus (*Viburnum nervosus*), *Rosa sericea* etc.; none of the trees remarkable for size. .. We emerged from the forest at a spot called Bhoojkal, 11,700 feet above the sea and about 3 miles from Moojwar; the rest of the day's journey lies along the east or S.E. exposure of the mountains, destitute of trees but covered with a new and rich series of alpine plants... We encamped amidst heavy rain and hail from the north, which rendered the grass very cold and wet for our people and for ourselves too, having been compelled, for want of hands, to leave our charpees on the road to-day. In these difficult tracts a good tarpaulin under one's bedding is much more conveniently carried than a bedstead and excludes the damp almost equally well; where both are absent a very excellent substitute is a thick layer of pine or yew branches.

'The creeping juniper (*Juniperus squamata*) commences from 800 to 1,000 feet below Kala Koondar. The open pastures are covered with a profusion of alpine flowers, among which are the *Cyananthus lobatus*, the *Saussurea religiosa, Saxifraga diversifolia* (or a species very like it...) and (on rocks) *Saxifraga mucronulata, Sieversia (Geum) elata, Swertia caerulea* and several other species (one, a large plant with pale blue blossoms is probably Royle's *S. perfoliata*), the *Sphelia latifolia (sic)* of Don, *Polygonum molle* or *polystachyum, P. brunonis* and *P. vaccinniifolium* (the last on rocks, a very beautiful species), *Lonicera obovata, Senecio nigricans, Achillea millefolia,* a yellow tanacetum, *Osyris elatior, Sibbaldia procumbens, Filipendula vestita* (very like Meadow Sweet), several sedums, *Morina longifolia, Caltha himalaica, Delphinium vestitum, Aconitum heterophyllum, Phlomis bracteosa, Corydalis goveniana*, *Geranium wallichianum*, *Picrorhiza kurroo* and many more. *Rhododendron campanulatum* is common in the region of birch and above it is the much smaller *R. lepidotum* or *anthopogon*, with aromatic leaves smelling, when bruised, like a walnut. The capsules are in dense terminal clusters and the flowers are said to be red. *Gaultheria trichophylla* with its beautiful azure fleshy calyx abounds on the sunny banks. The above are so general in all the region above the forest on the snowy range that it will be needless to specify them on every occasion. The *Cyananthus lobatus* covers extensive tracts with its blue (occasionally white) periwinkle-like flowers; at and above Nooroo Bassa on the north side of the Roopin pass I found the seed ripe on the 20th September, while lower down the plant was still in full bloom. In the same way on the Changsheel Range, *Morina longifolia* was all ripe on the 25th of September, while on the 30th it was still in full flower on Huttoo. *Rhododendron arboreum* flowers in February and March at 7,000 feet and is not ripe till Christmas, but *R. campanulatum* and *anthopogon*, which flower in May, June and July at 12,000 feet are ripe by the end of October. A strange alchymy of nature this, to ripen her products first in the colder sites, but perhaps necessary to the existence of plants in these elevated spots, where, but for this provision, the early winter would prevent them ever coming to maturity.'

These last remarks seem obvious to us nowadays, but they were original observations in 1847. So indeed was the following about the high alpine flora. 'Nature where she cannot be useful seems determined to be ornamental, and converts these tracts where grain will not ripen into pastures and flower gardens, where thousands of butterflies and insects enjoy their brief existence. The utility of nature must not, indeed, be limited to man, for there is scarcely one of these plants the seeds of which do not support myriads of insects as well as many birds.'

There are one or two rather mysterious remarks in his writings. Several times he mentions a Sorbus 'the berries occasionally of a beautiful waxy white.' This sounds like *Sorbus cashmiriana*, which has only got into cultivation quite recently. Did Madden bring back seeds which failed to germinate? On 24 September Madden arrived at a village called Doodoo or Doodrah, where he noted 'The *Iris nepalensis* is plentiful here on the damp shady ground as *Iris decora* is on the sunny meadows below.' In all books of reference you will find that the *I. nepalensis* of David Don is a synonym of the *I. decora* of Wallich. What is overlooked is that there was an *I. nepalensis* of Wallich, which is one of the sterile hybrids lumped under *I. germanica.* It would seem probable, therefore, that the *I. nepalensis* on the damp shady ground was a bearded iris of some kind. It is not, however, likely that a sterile garden plant would be found so far from habitation and most probably the bearded iris was the fertile *I. kashmiriana*, an important species in iris breeding as the flowers are more often white than purple and the white colour proves to be dominant in hybrids. This, however, is supposition and it would be nice if someone could repeat Madden's expedition and see what does grow near Doodoo.

The number of new plants that are ascribed to Madden are comparatively few, but includes such plants as *Cardiocrinum giganteum, Lilium wallichianum, Abelia triflora, Cassiope fastigiata* and the purple-flowered *Thermopsis barbata*, now lost to cultivation but a plant that should obviously be re-introduced as soon as possible. We can gather from his narratives that he sent back seed of, among other plants, *Primula macrophylla* and *stuartii* and two meconopsis, of which one was *M.*

horridula. Did these fail to germinate or were they simply not recorded? We know too that he sent a berberis. 'The barberry at Nagkunda is a distinct species, which is now covered with the most profuse crop of fruit of a fine blue, with a bloom of pink or lilac colour. It makes excellent jam, and I have had the pleasure of seeing young plants raised in Dublin from seeds that had undergone the fiery ordeal.' Blue fruits with a pinkish bloom rather suggests *Berberis lycium*, but it is far from easy to identify these early sendings of Himalayan berberis with any certainty.

Although Madden's writings are immensely entertaining the most important work in the Himalaya was done by Joseph Hooker, between 1848 and 1850. Although he was partly working for them the East India Company according to Hooker himself 'snubbed me before I went out, refusing me assistance and official letters of introduction to India and even a passage out.' Earlier Humboldt, who wanted to explore the Himalaya, found the company equally obstructive and gave up the whole idea. Hooker was also employed by the Admiralty and could not be entirely neglected but the Company were not helpful.

Although he arrived in 1848, incidentally by taking ship to Egypt, crossing the Suez isthmus by horseback and then taking ship from the Red Sea to India, which gave a great saving of time which was increased when in the later eighteen-fifties a railway was built. It was not until 1849 that Hooker started for the Himalaya. On his journey he arrived at 'Pacheem bungalow, the most sinister-looking rest-house I ever saw, stuck on a little cleared spur of the mountain, surrounded by dark forests, overhanging a profound valley enveloped in mist and rain and hideous in architecture, being a miserable attempt to unite the Swiss cottage with the suburban Gothic; it combined a maximum of discomfort with a minimum of good looks and cheer.'

There have been very few plant collectors with Hooker's extensive knowledge, which was by no means confined to botany. Indeed Humboldt is the only figure with whom he can be compared, but there were fifty years between Humboldt's and Hooker's expeditions and the increase in scientific knowledge had been considerable. Hooker was able to survey and map the hitherto unmapped regions over which he passed; he was able to report on the geology and on any fossil vegetation that might come his way. He has left us some valuable precepts for this kind of exploration.

'The course generally pursued by Himalayan travellers is to march early in the morning and arrive at the camping-ground before, or by, noon, breakfasting before starting or en route. I never followed this plan, because it sacrificed the mornings, which were profitably spent in collecting; whereas if I set off early I was generally too tired with the day's march to employ in active pursuit the rest of the daylight.'

It would seem, indeed, as though the fear of fatigue making him unobservant was ever-present. On one day when he had ascended to 17,000 feet above sea level he noted: 'Lassitude, giddiness and headache came on as our exertions increased and took away the pleasure I should otherwise have felt. . . . Happily I had noted everything on the way up and left nothing intentionally to be done on returning. In making such excursions as this, it is above all things desirable to seize and book every object worth noticing on the way out: I always carried my notebook and pencil tied to my jacket pocket, and generally worked with them in my hand. It is impossible to observe too soon or too much: if the excursion is long, little is done on the way home; the bodily powers being mechanically exerted, the mind . . . can endure no train of thought, nor be brought to bear on a subject.'

At the end of 1849 Hooker and his companion Dr Hodgson were forcibly detained by the Dewan of the Rajah of Kashmir and for some time there were fears, exaggerated according to Hooker, for their lives, but the episode ended without bloodshed. Otherwise the expedition was fairly troublefree and delightful for the botanist. In the Sikkim highlands 'Rhododendrons occupied the most prominent place, clothing the mountain slopes with a deep green mantle glowing with bells of brilliant colours; of the eight or ten species growing here, every bush was loaded with as great a profusion of blossoms as are their northern congeners in our English gardens. Primroses were next, both in beauty and abundance; and they were accompanied by yellow cowslips three feet high, purple polyanthus and pink, large-flowered, dwarf kinds nestling in the rocks and an exquisitely beautiful blue miniature species, whose blossoms sparkled like sapphires on the turf. Gentians began to unfold their deep azure bells, aconites to rear their tall blue spikes and fritillaries to burst into flower. On the black rocks the gigantic rhubarb formed pale pyramidal towers a yard high, of inflated reflexed bracts that conceal the flowers and, overlapping one another like tiles, protect them from the wind and rain; a whorl of broad green leaves edged with red spreads on the ground at the base of the plants, contrasting in colour with the transparent bracts, which are yellow margined with pink. This is the handsomest herbaceous plant in Sikkim.' This handsome plant was *Rheum nobile*, which has proved very difficult in cultivation, unlike the 3-foot cowslip, *Primula sikkimensis*, one of the most popular of Hooker's introductions. It seems, however, not to have proved too easy to cultivate at first as, as late as 1869, a plant fetched the high figure of five shillings.

The most important of Hooker's introductions were 25 new species of rhododendrons, all of which he introduced. By no means all of these have been much cultivated; one only sees in specialist collections such plants as

RR. camelliaeflorum, obovatum, vaccinioides and *virgatum*. In the same way *RR. dalhousiae, edgeworthii, maddenii* and *pendulum*, although all except the last are popular garden plants, need cool greenhouse treatment in most parts of the British Isles. Slightly easier, but not possible in all parts, are the large-leaved *R. grande*, and *R. hodgsonii*. On the other hand the large-leaved *R. falconeri* succeeds in most gardens not too exposed to strong winds. Among the more important of his introductions were *RR. campylocarpum, ciliatum, cinnabarinum, lanatum, niveum* and *thomsonii*. He also introduced the large lily-flowered tender *R. griffithianum* (as *R. aucklandii*), but presumably not in a very good form as a later importation about 1867 at once caused great enthusiasm and it is after this importation that we find it being used increasingly in hybridisation. As with all new introductions there was a tendency to regard all these new rhododendrons as tender and to grow them in conservatories, away from districts such as Cornwall, but even so they got very rapidly into commerce. In 1856 a provincial nurseryman could offer nine of the newly introduced species and it was also not long before some, especially *R. thomsonii*, started to make their mark. The earliest hybrid using one of these new species would seem to be the still popular *Rhododendron* x *praecox (ciliatum* x *dauricum)*, bred by Isaac Davies in 1856. Of the larger flowered plants, 'Ascot Brilliant', a *thomsonii* hybrid, appeared in 1861, closely followed by 'Boddaertianum', 'Cynthia', which is claimed to be *catawbiense* x *griffithianum*, 'Sappho' with its huge purple blotch, the salmon 'Mrs R. S. Holford' and the very dark purple 'Old Port', to mention only such early hybrids as still survive in cultivation. It seems odd that there would seem to be no record of any *campylocarpum* hybrids, as one would have thought its soft yellow colour would have proved particularly attractive; possibly its rather small flowers militated against its use and also, the yellow would probably prove recessive in first generation crosses.

It was not only rhododendrons that Hooker collected; and, as he wrote to his father Sir William Hooker, the Director of Kew Gardens, 'it is no light work to be the pioneer of these fine things' as he had been having his fingers frozen as he collected seeds at a height of 13,000 feet. He also introduced at least four berberis, *concinna, virescens, insignis* and *wallichiana*; the last two are evergreen. *Sorbus thomsonii* and *S. hedlundii* both seem to have been regarded as forms of *S. cuspidata*, which had been introduced, presumably through Wallich, in 1820 and it is only comparatively recently that they have been accorded specific rank. The Himalayan Birch, *Betula utilis*, is often attractive, but the Himalayan larch has not proved a success. I suspect that we must also owe to him *Magnolia campbellii*. He describes the plant several times in his *Himalayan Journals* and it was illustrated in the *Botanical Magazine* in

1868. If Hooker sent back young plants about 1850 and they were grown in a cool greenhouse at Kew this would be about the right period to elapse. Others say that it was introduced about 1865, in which case it may well have come over with the improved form of *Rhododendron griffithianum*. Among Hooker's herbaceous introductions were yet another bergenia, *B. purpurascens*, a number of meconopsis, *M. nepalensis*, *M. paniculata* and *M. villosa* and possibly *M. simplicifolia*, the attractive *Astilbe rubra*, now rarely seen, and a number of primulas.

Inspired by Hooker's rhododendrons, the veteran American botanist Thomas Nuttall, who had inherited a property in Lancashire, determined to mount an expedition of his own and entrusted it to his nephew Jonas Booth, who was as ignorant of travel as of botany. He underwent a crash course at Kew and then left for India on 30 June 1849. On arriving at Calcutta he consulted the Director of the Botanic Garden, Dr Falconer, and was advised to visit Assam, where he could have the advice of the Commissioner, Major Jenkins, and the Government Apothecary, Charles Simons, both of whom collected plants and sent them to England on a free-lance basis. Most of their sendings were of greenhouse plants, principally orchids, but it is thought that Simons introduced the widely-grown *Cotoneaster simonsii*.

By the end of 1849 Booth was in that part of north-east Assam known as the Balipara Frontier Tract, which adjoins Bhutan. Bhutan itself was regarded as dangerous for foreigners; Hooker had written that he would not go there 'without 500 men in front of me and as many in the rear.' In contemporary publications Booth's introductions are invariably described as coming from Bhutan, but the late Frank Ludlow, who had himself collected in Bhutan and who made a study of Booth's expedition, doubts if he ever entered the country.

Owing to his inexperience Booth was still in Assam when the monsoons arrived and was almost bled to death when myriads of leeches emerged. Fortunately he survived without any serious illness. In the winter of 1850 to 1851 he was in the Darrang district, hoping to go north to Tibet, but was forced to give up. Later in 1851 he returned to England. After his uncle's death in 1859 he opened a nursery at Rainhill, near Prescott, presumably specialising in rhododendrons and Himalayan plants. In 1878 he left England and is never heard of again. Before 1859 Nuttall had been selling his surplus plants to Hendersons of St John's Wood in north-west London.

In 1862 Booth wrote an article for the *Gardener's Chronicle* on the culture of rhododendrons and quotes extensively from his journal, which one would like to think survives somewhere. He notes that grafted plants come into flower sooner than plants on their own roots, but that the latter make more luxuriant plants. He has a further note about culture, which is probably still apposite. 'Although in their native habitat they may be densely shaded and growing in glens, I think we should not give them a similar situation in this country, as the sun is much more powerful in their latitude, although at a high elevation, than in the alternatively wet and cold climate of England ... even in the case of wild plants shade and extreme moisture do not promote their flowering.' He then proceeds to quote from his journal to prove his point as:

'December 17, 1849. Country densely wooded ... large underwood trees of *R. grande* destitute of seed or flower buds ... came upon a dense thicket of *R. maddenii*. I was very much disappointed at not being able to discover a single seed pod.... Continued our ascent; mountain less densely wooded; came upon large thickets of *R. grande* and *R. maddenii*; seeds and flower buds abundant.' At the top of the mountain, where the large trees had ceased he found '*R. campylocarpum, R. keysii* and *hookeri* with leaves curled up like so many Havannah cigars and assuming a very winterly appearance' and he noted that at night the temperature fell to 7° F.

Although he introduced many new species of rhododendron, the bulk have proved somewhat tender. The enormous-flowered *R. nuttallii* and the handsome *R. lindleyi* are popular greenhouse plants, but the attractive yellow *R. boothii* is too tender for most parts of the British Isles. The same would seem to be the case of the magnificent red-flowered *R. hookeri*, which opens its flowers very early in the year, but it sounds from Booth's journal as though it should tolerate quite considerable cold. That curious member of the Cinnabarinum series, *R. keysii*, with its tubular orange, red-tipped flowers, clearly shows the relation between rhododendrons and heathers and has maintained itself in cultivation, although it is curious rather than attractive. On the other hand two members of the Irroratum series, the first to arrive in cultivation, *R. kendrickii* and *R. shepherdii* have always been rare and it is doubtful if *R. shepherdii* has ever been rediscovered. The same would seem to apply to *R. calophyllum*, of which only a dried flower and a single leaf exist and which may only be a form of *R. maddenii.* Of Booth's other new rhododendrons, *R. wallichii* is barely distinguished from *R. campanulatum, R. eximium* is very close to *R. falconeri* and *R. smithii* is surely only a form of *R. barbatum*.

Mention should perhaps be made of yet another collector in 1849, Thomas Lobb, but he was mainly collecting in Moulmain in Burma on his way to Malaysia. According to Veitch his sending of *Berberis wallichiana* arrived before Hooker's sending. He also sent back the showy but tender *Hypericum hookeranum*, the greenhouse *Rhododendron veitchianum* and the first of the Stamineum series to reach cultivation, *R. moulmainense*.

After this mass of collecting around 1850 we have no news of any systematic collecting in the Himalayas before this century, although plants were continually being sent back, mainly by people whose names are now lost. During this century both R.E. Cooper and Messrs Ludlow and Sheriff collected in Bhutan, while Kingdon-Ward visited Bhutan, Assam and the Himalaya Frontier tract and they all sent back interesting plants, few of which have established themselves to any large extent, although one should probably except *Lilium mackliniae* from Assam.

Principally owing to their splendid rhododendrons the influence of the Himalayan Flora on gardens and garden design has been very considerable. *Clematis montana* is one of the commonest of garden climbers and the graceful deodar has been extensively planted since it was introduced. Herbaceous borders are now not so popular as they used to be, but here the hybrids raised from the various Himalayan potentillas used to be regarded as essential. We still see vast numbers of *Primula denticulata*, while *P. sikkimensis* remains one of the easiest and most popular of Asiatic primulas. Indeed, with the exception of the plants of China we would be justified in saying that the Himalayas have had more influence on the inhabitants of British gardens than any comparable region.

CHAPTER X

Horticulture in the Early Nineteenth Century

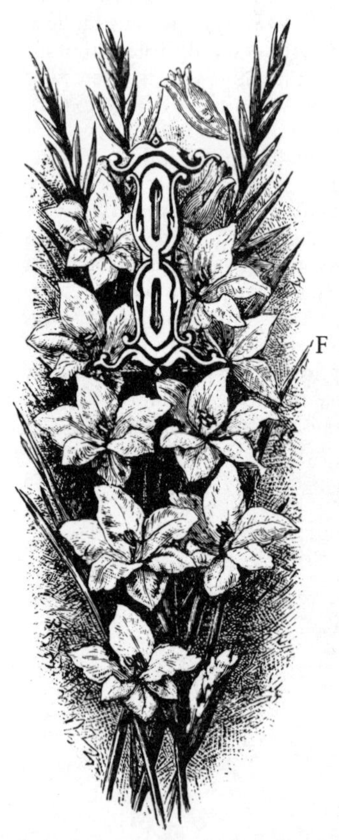

IF the reader is feeling rather breathless and surfeited after reading about so many introductions from so many parts of the world in so short a time he is in much the same state of mind as that of the gardeners. When Loudon started his *Gardener's Magazine* in 1826 he wrote in his introductory essay 'landscape gardening about a century ago was as much the fashion as horticulture is at present.' And the shift of interest from large landscapes to flori- and arboriculture was directly attributable to this enormous inflow of novelties. At first it does not seem to have been received with unmixed approval. In his *Encyclopaedia of Gardening* of 1824, we find Loudon writing:'It has been frequently observed that flower gardens have been on the decline for the last half century; and the cause of this appears to have been the influx of new plants during that period, by which gardeners have been induced, without due consideration, to be more solicitous about rarity and variety than well-disposed colours and quantity.' Loudon seems to be saying that the flower garden was at its best in the seventeen-seventies, when the bulk of the plants grown were either European or from eastern North America and when there were great numbers of cultivars of the florist's flowers; auriculas, carnations, tulips, hyacinths, Spanish iris, ranunculus and so on. I imagine that the employment of new plants, such as were available when Loudon was writing, must have brought more variety and less masses of the same plant into the flower garden, so that the overall effect may have been less brilliant. If this was so, it was not to remain in that condition for long, as we shall see.

The main trouble with this great surfeit of novelties is that it induced something akin to indigestion. There were just too many new plants for their worth to be properly evaluated and many were thrown out after an inadequate trial. Joseph Paxton was particularly concerned about this. In 1838 he wrote: 'There is a fashion in all things, and novelty as respects flowers is now a complete mania.' Throughout his writings he often complains that attractive subjects were being thrown out of gardens, simply because they were no longer to be regarded as novelties. Moreover he said that often plants were given incorrect treatment. 'It not unfrequently happens that when a plant is first introduced into this country it is cultivated at a much higher temperature than is really necessary for it.' We frequently find Paxton writing that a plant that had proved unsatisfactory in the stove would look much more ornamental in the cool greenhouse, or in the open air. 'It is much to be lamented that many persons who receive or purchase new plants ... cultivate them under the erroneous opinions before alluded to for one or perhaps two years, merely for the sake of their novelty, and then, without ever investigating their true habits, or enquiring what further purposes of ornament they may be made to supply, they are by degrees discarded and lost sight of.... Thus it is that plants which are in themselves truly beautiful and which may be made to answer various ornamental purposes, are either for want of attention (having lost their novelty) wholly annihilated, or are thrown out of large establishments as unworthy of notice, and rescued only from total destruction by the amateur or cottager; so that we consider that any person who exerts himself to ascertain the true habits of plants, or what purpose they may be applied to, does a signal service to the science of floriculture.'

Much the same could have been written in the nineteen-twenties and thirties, when the flood of new plants from the Sino-Himalaya resulted in many very desirable plants being lost to cultivation after a very short time.

Although it may have been deplorable that so many potentially ornamental plants never had their potentialities fully exploited, the increase in ornamentals arrived at much the same time as the industrial revolution and the rise of a prosperous middle class. Both the Duke of Marlborough and the Duke of Devonshire were keen gardeners, but many members of the aristocracy were becoming impoverished. In 1833 Loudon noted the decay of many large estates, but added: 'Let not this view of the decay of noblemen's gardens induce gardeners in want of places to despair. Every gardener who has seen much service knows that a situation under a rich tradesman, merchant, or small landed proprietor is productive of far more comfort to him than under a nobleman.... As the country goes on improving, the small places will gradually increase, and with them a taste for gardening and situations for first rate gardeners.' This was quite true, but the rich tradesman was liable to want to see something tangible for his outlay and after the table had been well supplied, he usually required a brilliant display of flowers. The emphasis tended to concentrate on display rather than on interesting plants or on artistic design, although there would, then as now, be numerous exceptions.

One way of making a brave display is by planting up beds with plants that have very brilliant colours and which will continue to flower over a period of months. By the mid-nineteenth century this form of gardening had become very popular and was known as the Bedding Craze. Since it was principally tender subjects, such as verbenas and geraniums, which formed the foundation for this form of gardening, it presupposed a number of hothouses. In 1845 the tax on sheet glass was repealed and greenhouses became available to people of moderate means and it was this that made ostentatious bedding so widespread. We are now so used to the idea that it seems hard to imagine it was ever a novelty, but for many reasons at one time it must have been. After all the hybrid verbenas were not bred before the late eighteen-thirties and the first really dwarf geranium, 'Tom Thumb' became commercially available in 1844. It rather looks as though this idea of brilliant bedding may have arisen in Ireland. In the first volume of the *Gardener's Magazine* (1826) it was noted that Mr Robson, the gardener at the Viceroy's residence at Phoenix Park 'has been in the habit of propagating in autumn, by cuttings, large quantities of the different free-growing sorts of Pelargoniums, Alonsoas and heliotropes etc., which he keeps in winter in frames and in spring plants out distinctly in separate beds throughout the flower garden, where they blow throughout the summer and autumn in great luxuriance.'

During this period there was a return to the formal geometric garden and it is a moot point, whether this was due to the appearance of plants suitable for planting up the beds in this sort of situation or whether the plants were bred to fill the need for suitable subjects for the geometric garden. By 1829 the modern bedding seems already well established. In his *Gardener's Magazine* for that year Loudon reproduced plans of two formal parterres in the garden of Robert Mangles, at Whitmore Lodge, Sunning Hill in Surrey. One had a central bed of *Salvia splendens*, and around this were grouped nine beds, of which five were planted with variegated-leaved scarlet geraniums, while between these were four beds of ivy-leaved geraniums, outside these were three larger beds planted with the Bath scarlet geranium, the Waterloo scarlet geranium and the Horseshoe geranium. These last were all fairly tall shrubs and must not be thought of as resembling the modern compact geraniums.

The second parterre had a central bed full of 'choice pelargoniums', surrounded by a number of beds planted alternately with standard roses and with *Calceolaria corymbosa*, a shrubby yellow-flowered species, both underplanted with mignonette. As time went on the choice of bedding plants became rather stereotyped, but in its early years a number of unusual subjects were tried, including, apparently, alstromerias, although how these touchy plants would survive lifting each autumn and being potted up is hard to contemplate. The sand verbena, *Abronia umbellata*, is nowadays regarded as a difficult subject, yet that was also used for bedding, while there were a large number of cultivars of *Anagallis linifolia*, that splendid Mediterranean pimpernel.

The eighteen-twenties and thirties were both given over to very many horticultural novelties. In 1829 Thomas Rivers of Sawbridgeworth described his winter garden. This was based mainly on evergreen shrubs and trees, which included laurustinus, Chinese privets (whatever they were; probably *Ligustrum lucidum*), hollies with variegated leaves and with yellow berries, phillyreas, *Danaë racemosa*, bay, butcher's broom, aucuba, the loquat, *Eriobotrya japonica*, and *Magnolia grandiflora*, as well as snowberry, firethorn and the red-flowered arbutus. During the autumn there were planted out a large selection of chrysanthemums (but this could not have been so very large in 1829), which, if covered with mats during frosty weather, would persist until Christmas. There were also *Sternbergia lutea* and the Christmas Rose. Mr Rivers conceded that January was rather a dull month but in February winter aconites and other spring bulbs paved the way for violets and primroses. The winter garden was unusual, but the idea persisted. We think of the eighteen-fifties as being the apogee of the Bedding Craze, yet in 1856 Saul, under his pseudonym of Eugene Delamere, returned to the subject of the winter garden as being 'very eligible for English villas'. His ideas are much the same as those of Tom Rivers, but to the berried shrubs he adds guelder rose, spindle tree, mountain ash and yew, all of which had long been available, as well as barberries evergreen and deciduous. He also adds to the flowering plants, the 'common pink and crimson China roses, which should be in beds, while there should be isolated plants of double gorse and dwarf almond. As borders to beds he recommends *Petasites alba* and *P. fragrans* and pulmonarias. He suggests a whole bed should be planted up with *Erica carnea*. Not only does he have the Christmas Rose, but also the 'green-flowered hellebore'. As spring advances he suggests many coloured primroses as well as japonica and a large selection of bulbs. It is interesting that so enterprising a planting scheme should have been recommended at a time when most garden historians would assure us that nothing existed save geraniums, calceolarias and lobelias.

We know remarkably little about early rock gardens. In the late eighteenth century Abercrombie noted that in some gardens they 'exhibited artificial rockwork, sometimes contiguous to some grotto, fountain, rural piece of water etc., and planted with a variety of saxatile plants or such as grow naturally on rocks and mountains', but from the writings of most eighteenth-and early nineteenth-century writers one gets the impression that the main point of the rock garden was the rocks themselves. In the eighteen-fifties we get Shirley Hibberd recommending the insertion of large rocks as objects of interest in themselves, a curious pre-echo of Japanese design. At the end of the eighteenth century William Beckford had an Alpine Garden at Fonthill, although we have no idea what it was like.

During the eighteen-thirties Lady Broughton made a famous rock garden at Hoole House, near Chester. This was a scale model of the mountains of Chamonix, with such features as the *mer de glace* represented by white marble chippings. In 1838 when describing the garden Loudon observed: 'The idea of imitating alpine scenery on a large scale is new in gardening. . . . In general artificial rockwork presents the appearance of a mere heap of stones, without any attempts at stratification, natural expression or appropriate character; but here we have the most marked expression of alpine character completely worked out.' Loudon had, however, a very telling point of criticism. 'In some places it appears mixed up with full-grown trees, which, being higher than the rockwork, have a tendency to destroy the illusion by deranging the scale of the rocks.' Hoole House was not the only rock garden that Loudon commented upon. There was also a remarkable one at Blenheim, of all unlikely places. This was intended to show outcrops of rocks, which Loudon refers to as 'scars' on the face of a steep bank. 'There is,' Loudon wrote, 'nothing particular in the disposition of the stones ... but the stairs, which pass obliquely through them from one scar to another, and thus connect different horizontal galleries, are very well managed. Each plant has a separate nidus with appropriate soil . . . among the plants are a number of rare alpine species in general mixture.'

One would like to know more about what plants were used in these early rock gardens. The catalogues of the time contain a very large selection of alpines, including such difficult plants as *Ranunculus glacialis* and *Gentiana ciliata*, but most writers on the subject seem to recommend growing the more difficult subjects in pots and in the shade. Thus in 1834 Thomas Rivers raised his alpines in this manner. 'On the north side of a hornbeam hedge is a raised platform, 3 feet wide, formed of two brick walls, each 18 inches high and 4 inches thick, with a hollow space between them 3 foot wide, filled with earth and paved with slates or tiles bedded in mortar. On the tiles are placed the pots, very close together, not plunged in summer; being shaded by the hedge and kept well watered they flourish admirably.... A hornbeam hedge is better than any other, for in summer there is plenty of shade; but in autumn and spring, as it loses the greater part of its foliage, it admits the sun and air. The worms, the greatest of all enemies to alpine plants in pots, are completely baffled and the plants seem to enjoy the trifling elevation, as if they were growing on their native rocks; besides which they are never removed to winter quarters, but stand here all the season, merely covered with fern about 9 inches thick, laid high in the centre of the platform, and over the fern a single covering of small Prussian mats.... They are the exact width of the platform: and from the fern being elevated in the middle and their close texture, all the heavy winter rains run off.... Keeping them from superabundant moisture is a great object; for frost, if it gets through the fern and mats, has no injurious effect if the mould in the pots is dry.'

It sounds an odd locality to grow Aretian androsaces and *Artemisia genipi*, but it presumably worked.

There were very large rock gardens at Syon Park and at Chatsworth, but here the object seems to have been to create romantic scenery and the enormous rocks were not regarded as a background for dwarf plants. This may have been the case with the rock garden at Woburn, which Loudon disliked. 'A rockwork has been formed ... made out of small loose stones; but we must not omit to state that such works, made out of such stones are not to our taste; this at Woburn is too much like a heap of small stones; and if the plants among these stones are not very constantly and carefully watched, the stones will soon be entirely covered by the plants and it will, by their luxuriance and confused intermixture, become like a heap of earth or rubbish covered by weeds. It wants rocky protuberances, large prominent masses of stone that will furnish features ... and make on every observer an impression.' Loudon goes on to recommend that 'where large masses or rock are not to be had, large conglomerations of small stones or brickbats should be formed by means of Roman cement'.

The habit of growing alpines in shade dates back at least to Philip Miller. Here he is in his famous *Gardener's Dictionary* giving directions for the cultivation of *Soldanella alpina*. 'They must have a shady situation, for if they are exposed to the sun they will not live.' Similarly *Saxifraga cotyledon* 'should be planted in a very dry soil and a shady situation', *S. oppositifolia* 'must have a shady situation and a moist soil'. And you will find the same insistence on shade for whatever alpine plant you look up. Since all the leading nurserymen grew alpines there must have been sufficient commercial demand to make it worth their while, but it seems hard to believe that they were all grown in pots. Indeed Loudon gives the planting at Hoole House, which was entirely of alpine plants in a large selection, so some people must have been growing alpines much as we do nowadays, before the revolution started by the firm of Backhouse in the eighteen sixties (see Chapter XIV).

To return to the adventurous gardeners of the early nineteenth century, one would have thought that if any garden was ageless it was the cottage garden, but although this may be so it does not seem as though it were so common as it became during the eighteen-twenties and thirties. Time and time again when Loudon is describing his peregrinations throughout England, he breaks off to congratulate some landowner on at last giving his cottagers gardens, with the clear inference that before this enlightened act the cottages had had no gardens. Very often surplus stock from the big house would be supplied to the cottagers. Loudon often comments with delight that so many cottage gardens contain the pink China rose, and it may well be owing to this fact that the old monthly rose has continued in cultivation, while such early roses as Hume's Blush and Parks's Yellow, which look much finer roses, have vanished. Once plants get into cottage gardens they tend to stay there and many eighteenth- and early nineteenth-century cultivars of popular plants owe their survival to this admirable trait. Moreover many of these gardens were already extremely attractive. One might think that this sentence was written in the eighteen-seventies by Robinson or one of his followers. 'Gardeners might find much instruction from an examination of cottage gardens, in many of which I have seen a degree of good taste that is not always found where there is more reason to expect it.' This was written in 1834, the author hiding his real name under the pseudonym of Calycanthus.

If there is one form of gardening that would seem to be the product of our century it would be the woodland garden which was created to house the various rhododendrons that were introduced by Wilson, Forrest and Ward, but here again the eighteen-thirties have forestalled us. Here is Bagshot Park in 1829. 'Rhododendrons and azaleas, indeed, abound in various parts of the garden, and, as they become too thick, are thinned out and distributed in the woods as substitutes for the laurels and other underwood now there. The surface soil of these woods being a soft black peat-like material, the rhododendrons have already sown themselves and in a few years will cover acres, as they already do at Caen Wood and at Fonthill. It seems to be part of the plan of management at Bagshot to distribute exotic trees over the margins of the native woods, and so, gradually, to give them a highly enriched and botanical character.' Nowadays of course these old woodland gardens have all too often become impenetrable thickets of *R. ponticum* and *R. luteum*, but that could not have been foreseen in the eighteen thirties and certainly rhododendrons and azaleas must have been preferable to cherry laurels.

Sir John Hill in his *Eden* (1757) is the only horticultural writer of the period I know who recommended selecting trees for their autumn tints, although many writers recommend plants with attractive fruits. It is hard to think of anyone in the early nineteenth century designing a planting such as that of Sheffield Park in Sussex, where autumn colouration seems to have been a principal objective. Nevertheless in 1834 Loudon noted at Claremont, the property of Leopold I of Belgium, 'About the end of October, when the foliage of the oaks has assumed all that variety of brown and red of which it is susceptible, and the elms their rich yellows, Claremont will be in the height of its autumnal beauty.' Evidently there was some regard for autumn tints. Loudon preferred Claremont at Christmastime, 'when the splendid hollies with their coral berries, bays, Portugal Laurels, Box, Laurustinus, Silver Firs, Cedars etc., and above all the undergrowth of common laurel, give it the appearance of a wood of evergreens.'

So far the gardens whose descriptions we have been reading could reappear at the present time without causing any comment, but there were others which were more peculiar. Loudon visited Cashiobury Park in 1825, although he only described it eleven years later. 'Roses and ornamental flowers are . . . disposed in masses. . . . Some are enclosed by basket work, others trail over rocks and fantastic stones; some of the rockeries have a margin of curious Derbyshire spar, and others are entirely of plum-pudding stone. There are groups of large shells, corals, corallines, madrepores, tuffa, lava, petrifactions, ammonites and different sorts of scoria, all curiously intermixed with flowers and plants. There is a picturesque aquarium, the sides of which are finely ornamented with rockwork and American evergreens. . . . The Chinese garden here is unique of its kind. It is not large, but contains a conservatory, a sort of low pagoda and other ornamental buildings, and a great quantity of valuable Chinese porcelain, of Chinese figures, monsters, mandarins, the god Joss, dragons etc., and paintings, fountains, goldfish, jets etc. In the conservatory are all the sorts of camellias that could be procured when it was planted; very large plants of green and black tea. . . . Among the hardy plants is a fine specimen of *Picea abies* 'Clanbrasiliana' above 20 years old and forming a tuft not above a foot high and a foot in diameter . . . such a dwarf is peculiarly appropriate in a Chinese garden.'

Indeed the early nineteenth century went in for a number of different sorts of garden architecture. Besides the Chinese garden Cashiobury also had a banqueting room and a Turkish pavilion, while Redleaf, near Penshurst, had a number of pastiche gardens. . . . Dutch, Italian etc., with appropriate buildings such as a Dutch billiards room and a Chinese dairy. As the century progressed there was less cause to introduce extraneous features into the garden, the number of possible plants was not only being increased by new introductions from all over the world, but, in addition, the nurserymen were producing new plants by creating hybrids and it is to this phenomenon we must now turn.

CHAPTER XI

Hybrids

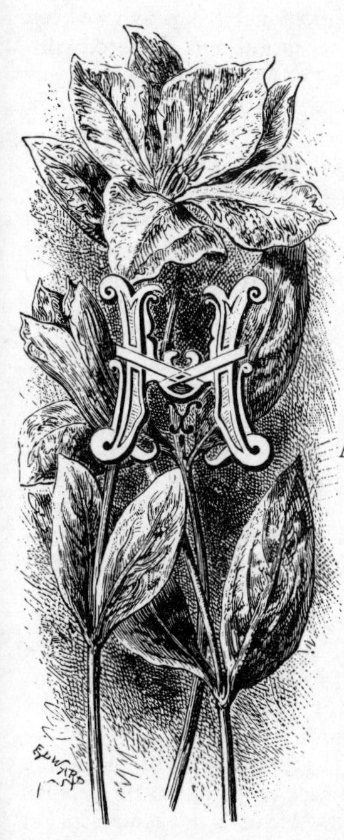

HARDLY had the eighteenth century begun than Dr Nehemiah Grew published his opinion that seeds were fertilised by what he termed the farina, and what we now call pollen, being deposited on the stigma. With some misgivings—to a religious man the act of creation might be considered blasphemous—Thomas Fairchild set about to prove this statement by putting the pollen of a carnation on to the stigma of a sweet william. The cross took successfully and about 1717 the first deliberately man-made hybrid flowered. Fairchild's mule, as it was called, had double red flowers. It resembled the sweet william in habit, but the flowers were somewhat larger. It flowered in August. With its double flowers it was sterile and had to be propagated by cuttings. Whether other growers copied Fairchild, or whether he grew on more than the one seedling is not clear, but in 1722 Fairchild sent to Bradley's *Monthly Register* lists of the plants in flower in his garden (at Hoxton) in the various months of the year. In May he notes the mule between the sweet william and carnation was in flower; in June there were two sorts of mules as there were also in July, although it is not clear whether they were the same as were in flower in June and it is not until August that we get to Fairchild's mule, although it would seem to have had the same parentage as the May-flowering hybrid.

There is indirect evidence of another dianthus hybrid. Miller in his *Dictionary* speaks of the old man's head pink, which seems to have been intermediate between the pink and the carnation and flowered continuously from July 'till the frost in autumn puts a stop to it'. This sounds rather like that putative ancestor of the perpetual carnation, the *Oeillet de Mahon*, which the late Montague Allwood suggested was a hybrid between the carnation and *Dianthus chinensis*, which sounds plausible, although it has never been proved. But even if it was the case we have no evidence that the cross was made deliberately. It is always possible, when large numbers of different species of the same genus are grown in proximity, for accidental hybrids to arise—indeed in the case of aquilegia it is difficult to prevent it but the significance of Fairchild's mule is that it was made deliberately.

Dr Grew's point was made, but gardeners seem to have taken little notice of the importance of Fairchild's work and it was not until later in the century in Germany that Dr Koelreuter started some serious work on the potentialities of raising hybrids, and he worked with vegetables. It was not until the early nineteenth century that gardeners started to work with flowers. This was due, almost entirely, to William Herbert (1778–1847), later Dean of Manchester. 'To the cultivators of ornamental plants', he wrote, 'the facility of raising hybrid varieties affords an endless source of interest and amusement. He sees, in the several species of each genus that he possesses, the materials with which he must work and he considers in what manner he can blend them to the best advantage, looking to the several gifts in which each excels; whether of hardiness to endure our seasons, of brilliancy in its colours, of delicacy in its markings, of fragrance or stature or profusion of blossom.'

It is clear that Herbert had realised the advantages of hybridisation in the creation of garden plants right at the outset of his career. He seems to have begun his work about 1808 and he also seems to have interested at least two nurserymen in the technique; Thomson of Mile End and Colvill at Chelsea. However, Robert Sweet was working at Colvill's nursery at the time that so many hippeastrum and pelargonium hybrids were being raised, and it was probably this well-known botanist-writer who actually did Colvill's work.

Herbert started work with two South African genera, *Erica* and *Gladiolus*. His gladiolus hybrids mainly used the rather small-flowered species and may well have looked like the Purbeck hybrids of Dr Barnard of our own day. The parentage of many of his hybrids were published and it is interesting to see that on occasion he used three species. Thus *G.* x *spofforthianus* was a cross between *G. blandus* and *G. cardinalis* (which is probably the foundation of our modern Nanus gladiolus rather than *G.* x *colvillii,* which was *cardinalis* x *tristis*). *G.* x *spofforthianus* was crossed with *G. tristis* to give *G.* x *herbertianus*. We find the same use of hybrids as parents in many of the early hippeastrum hybrids, which are now almost all lost. Incidentally *Hippeastrum* x *johnsonii flowered in* 1810, so may well have anticipated Herbert's work.

Mainly owing to their size and long life the most spectacular of the early hybrids occur in the genus *Rhododendron*. So far as I can make out, the first of these was 'Azaleoides', which was in commerce by 1819 and is said to be *R. nudiflorum* x *R. ponticum*. Since the plant is markedly fragrant, which neither of its parents are, it would seem likely that the given parentage is incorrect. The same parentage is given for 'Odoratum' which is still in cultivation. Since it flowers rather late it might seem more probable that the fragrant *R. viscosum* was the other parent rather than *R. nudiflorum*. At the same time Herbert produced 'Hybridum' which was *R. viscosum* x *R. maximum*, which might well prove to be a valuable late flowering shrub, but I doubt if it now survives. These azaleodendrons, as they were called, were attractive, but the real impetus to hybridisation came with the arrival of the first Himalayan rhododendrons, particularly the blood-red *R. arboreum*, which first flowered in the early eighteen-twenties in Britain. This was somewhat tender and so it was thought necessary to hybridise it with other more hardy rhododendrons in an attempt to get the glowing colour into the range of hardy plants. The first of these arboreum hybrids seem to have been raised at the Hampshire residence of the Earl of Caernarvon, Highclere, and the guiding spirit seems to have been a Mr Gowen, who would appear to have been a friend rather than an employee of the Earl. At some time someone had crossed *R. ponticum* with *R. catawbiense*, which seems rather a meaningless cross, but it was this hybrid that was selected as the seed parent for the first *arboreum* hybrid, known as 'Gowenianum' which was either made or first flowered in 1825. In the next year came 'Carnarvonianum' which had *catawbiense* as the seed parent, while the nurseryman, William Smith of Coombe Wood, who specialised in rhododendron hybridisation used *ponticum* as the seed parent and called his plant 'Smithii', which is unfortunate as there is an *R. smithii*, which is a form of *R. barbatum*. 'Altaclarense', the best-known of these early hybrids, has the same parentage as 'Gowenianum'.

In the *Botanical Magazine* for November 1830 Gowen gave a description of his methods in raising azalea hybrids. 'Lord Caernarvon had long been desirous of raising seedlings between the late-flowering and light coloured varieties. To effect this object I selected for mother plants *R. speciosa* ... and a late flowering variety called by some of the nurserymen *R. rubescens*, by others *R. autumnalis rubra*'—this sounds like a pink form of *R. viscosum*. 'The first mentioned are, in the climate of Highclere, and perhaps throughout England, very unproductive of pollen, rarely seeding when unassisted.' In another experiment '*R. speciosa* were dusted with the pollen of a late-flowering *R. luteum* for several successive mornings no care was taken to deprive the plants ... of their anthers, their deficiency in pollen having been ascertained. Many pods swelled, which were found to contain heavy seed; these were gathered at the first approach of winter, kept in a drawer for some weeks and sowed in the first week of January.' Gowen also used the pollen of *R. rubescens* on a fine form of *R. calendulaceum*, known as 'Triumphans'. 400 seedlings were raised from the first cross, of which 300 were close to *R. luteum*, although varying in colour from orange to palest cream, while 100 resembled *R. speciosa* in 'various tints of crimson and vivid pink or scarlet'. Gowen had had less hopes of the *calendulaceum-rubescens* cross, but found that 'they surpass them greatly in magnificence, following generally the type of *R. calendulaceum*, and are very late-flowering plants of many gradations of colour, from pale yellow to orange, salmon colour, pink and beautiful mixed tints; they produce large umbels with expanded corollas, are elegant in habit and hardly to be surpassed in loveliness.'

Of the various seedlings Gowen named thirty cultivars. It has always been thought that the first hybrid azalea was 'Mortieri' raised in Ghent in 1828, but it looks as though M. Mortier was only one of many people working in this field.

Indeed there seems to have been a general desire to hybridise the evergreen rhododendrons, although there were comparatively few species available to the hybridist. From North America came *R. catawbiense* and *R. maximum*, from the Near East, *R. ponticum* and *R. caucasicum*, and from Asia came *RR. arboreum, campanulatum, barbatum* and *chrysanthum*. *R. dauricum* was also available, but as lepidote rhododendrons such as *R. dauricum* or *R. lepidotum* will not hybridise with elepidotes, such as the other species mentioned, it was not of any use to the breeders. Nevertheless it was reported, both by Loudon and by Herbert, that Smith had crossed the Indian azalea with *R. dauricum* and *R. arboreum* with *R. dauricum*. It seems safe to say that neither of these two hybrids could have been made. What seems to have happened is that either Smith or his reporters said *R. dauricum* when they meant *R. caucasicum*. Smith's *arboreum-caucasicum* hybrid survives to this day as 'Venustum', while a similar cross raised by Waterer is known as 'Nobleanum'. One would like to know what the crosses between the Indian azalea and *R. caucasicum* looked like. One of Smith's ambitions was to produce a good yellow rhododendron. In theory he could have used *R. chrysanthum*, but this flowers so irregularly in cultivation that it is rarely available. There was in cultivation a pale yellow form of *R. caucasicum*, known as 'stramineum', and various yellow azaleas were available to make azaleodrendrons, but these tend to resemble the azalea rather than the rhododendron. Incidentally 'stramineum' was not available before 1835. In May 1847 the *Floricultural Cabinet*, considering Smith's latest hybrids, which they described as buff in colour stated: 'A true yellow-flowered rhododendron is still a desideratum.' Still, by 1856 a provincial nurseryman, William Rider of Moortown, near Leeds, was able to offer 'Aureum punctatum', described as primrose yellow and 'Aureum superbum' said to be 'one of the best yellows'. There was also 'Cupreum' which was deep copper-orange, edged with pink and with dark spotting, while 'Ornatum' was straw with deep yellow spots. 'Aureum superbum' was said to need greenhouse protection. This catalogue, which includes no hybrids raised from the Hooker introductions (although Rider was able to include eight of the newly introduced species) listed eighty cultivars. This included three with double flowers: one was 'Fastuosum plenum' which is still in cultivation, the others were *ponticum* 'Verbaneanum' and 'Speciosissimum'. The blood-red *arboreum* had been followed by forms with white and with pink flowers and the bulk of the hybrids were between these and *ponticum*, *catawbiense* and *caucasicum*. One does find the occasional reference to a *campanulatum* hybrid, but I know of only one description, which describes the flowers as 'French White'. Herbert employed *R. maximum* as a parent, and presumably other breeders did too, but we have few details, although one would have thought it would be useful with its late flowering. With the employment of the Hooker introductions the number of hybrids increased dramatically and by 1868 Van Houtte was offering 138 rhododendrons and 277 named azaleas.

The only other shrub to be extensively hybridised during the early nineteenth century was the rose, to which we have already referred in Chapter V.

There was also intense activity among herbaceous plants. In 1832 the Botanic Garden at Bury St Edmunds noted some odd seedlings from a plant they called *Delphinium grandiflorum chinense*. There were six distinct varieties: 1. White spotted with green. 2 and 3 had flowers of two different shades of light blue with green spots, 4 had a fine lilac flower, 5 had a flower of very brilliant blue spotted with purple, while 6 was semi-double, blue spotted with purple. Loudon's assistant editor, John Denson, added a note to the descriptions saying that the plant commonly grown in gardens as *D. grandiflorum*, fl. pl. 'can be no form or variation of the *D. grandiflorum* . . . it is unlike in stature, in foliage, in the size and form of its flowers and in its general greater robustness.' Denson wondered to what species it should be assigned, but it sounds like a modern *elatum* hybrid. The nurseryman Wood at Huntingdon had raised a plant which had a height 'nearly double that of the old variety, and branched, laxer racemes, so that it is altogether a more showy, airy, graceful plant.'

Henry Turner, who had written the original note about the Bury St Edmunds's plants added that he had been told by a respectable nurseryman that he had raised delphiniums of all colours, including 'a fine yellow' and wondered whether anyone had seen this. There was no reply to this query, but in his 1839 Supplement to the *Hortus Britannicus* Loudon listed some delphinium hybrids, one of which raised by John Cree, one of the best nurserymen of the day, was called 'Rubrum' and had reddish-pink flowers. In 1785 Dr Pitcairn had presented Kew with a plant of the Siberian *D. puniceum* and it is, I suppose, possible that this plant, which seems quite unknown nowadays, had persisted in cultivation to give this reddish hybrid. Besides Cree the nurseryman Pope, of Handsworth, was also hybridising delphiniums.

The bearded iris hybrids were at first raised almost exclusively on the Continent and we know remarkably little about them. They seem to have been bred entirely from two species, *I. pallida* and *I. variegata*. There had existed in the wild natural hybrids between these two species, which at that time were thought to have specific rank and were called *II. amoena, plicata, squalens* and *sambucina* and which were brought into cultivation, so that the early hybridists had two species and four hybrids with which to work. All the early work appears to have taken place on the Continent. The first record we have is of a Herr von Berg raising flag irises as a private hobby and the first commercial hybrids, raised by M. de Bure, a Parisian nurseryman, came on the market in 1822. His work was followed by another Frenchman, M. Jacques, one of whose seedlings, 'Aurea', was to prove the best of all yellow flags for nearly a century. Jacques' nursery was taken over by a M. Lemon, who had 100 named cultivars in his catalogue for 1840, and who continued to breed new cultivars until 1855. It seems improbable that no British nurserymen were raising their own hybrids, but I have been able to find any record during the early years of the century. In 1854 William Harrison was offering fifty different German Irises, but he does not go into any details. Towards the end of the century Sir Michael Foster obtained plants of bearded iris from the Near East which were much larger plants than the two original European species and which have since transformed the garden iris into much taller and more floriferous plants, while the introduction of other species and more selective breeding has increased the colour range. It should perhaps be mentioned that the true *Iris germanica* and the Orris root, *I. florentina*, are both sterile hybrids and cannot be used in breeding, although available for several centuries.

During the eighteen-thirties there was much hybridising done between perennial lobelias, the species used being *L. cardinalis* and *L. syphilitica* from North America and *L. fulgens* from Mexico. This resulted in a number of tall perennials, which were late flowering and which ranged in colour from blue to various mauves, purples and reds. As late as 1854 Harrison was offering twenty-nine named lobelias, which included two whites. Towards the end of the century they seem to have dropped from popularity, but some breeders are now remaking these early hybrids.

By the eighteen thirties it might seem as if plants were being thought of only in respect to their breeding value. When *Potentilla arguta* was brought into cultivation Loudon commented 'This in foliage and inflorescence is a fine plant, needing only the colour of *P. formosa* or *P. atrosanguinea* to render it very ornamental. It would be an eligible stock for Mr Dennis, or some other able cultivator to attempt the raising of hybrids from.' We seem to hear Lancelot Brown telling a landowner that his grounds have great capabilities, but the capability is now contained in a single new plant.

Sometimes the hybridists not only attempted but claimed success in crosses which are surely impossible. Mr Campbell, gardener to the Comte de Vandes, claimed to have pollinated the yellow *Digitalis grandiflora* with the gloxinia *Sinningia speciosa*. It seems improbable that a gesneriad would cross with a scrophulariad, although, oddly enough, both species have the same chromosome count. However, Loudon's assistant editor, John Denson, saw the resultant plant and wrote: 'The flowers of the hybrid differ from those of *D. grandiflora* in being slightly larger, more fleshy in texture and in having the yellow ground almost obliterated or covered over with a reddish one, the colour being now, perhaps, a buff-red one; the leaves are those of *D. grandiflora* much increased in size, and, I think, in pubescence, and perhaps in succulency.' (GM VIII, 478). This sounds exactly like the modern *D.* x *mertonensis*, which is *D. grandiflora* crossed with *D. purpurea*, the common wild foxglove, and this is surely what Campbell achieved.

There seem to have been few protests about this dilution of the wild species. It was apparently assumed that hybridity was a virtue in itself. John Lindley did raise his voice in the *Botanical Register* for 1835. He was particularly anxious about calceolarias, which were being hybridised with such ease that the true species were already difficult to obtain. Lindley castigated gardeners for their haste and unskilfulness in converting the fairest races of the vegetable world into unhealthy mongrel and debased varieties and he urged them 'to abandon a pursuit which has, as yet, led to few results which good taste can approve'. The warning was timely but Lindley was not the right man to utter it, as his opponents could quote him as having previously uttered such opinions as 'hybrid productions are undoubted cases of improvements resulting from skill'. In any case the main point was surely not the creation of hybrids, but the neglect and eventual disappearance of the true species, which in many cases gave as much loss as gain. We have been able to see this recently in the various *Schizanthus* species which were reintroduced from the Beckett, Cheese and Watson Andean expedition. The hybrids, which supplanted these species, are much easier to grow and come into flower more rapidly, while the seeds germinate readily; the wild species have far more grace of habit and more delicate flowers, but they are far less easy to grow, take longer and the seeds germinate irregularly.

Of course many hybrid strains were eventually lost to cultivation. In the twelfth volume of the *Gardener's Magazine*, Loudon gives a summary of the rose catalogue of Hooker of Brenchley. In this list are 5 sweet briar hybrids, 9 hybrids with *Rosa sempervirens*, 6 with *R. pendulina*, and no less than 22 with *R. bracteata*. These last one would like to see; by the time that Hibberd wrote *The Amateur's Rose Book* in 1874, he could mention only two *bracteata* hybrids and nowadays we can only put forward the ever-popular 'Mermaid'.

Another lost strain were the hybrid cowslips raised by Gibbs at Brompton. Loudon says that the hybrids 'were arranged in four divisions; oxlip cowslips, polyanthus cowslips, primrose cowslips and auricula cowslips, and the varieties under each division were numerous and very beautiful. We believe Mr Gibbs was the first that ever originated such varieties' (*GM* III, 126). He also seems to have been the last; one would like to have seen the auricula cowslips. Oddly they seem to have been frost tender, which may explain why they failed to survive.

During this period the most popular hybrid magnolia, *soulangiana*, appeared in 1826 in the garden of M. Soulange-Bodin at Fromont in France. This was not made deliberately, but was a chance seedling in which *M. denudata* had been fertilised by *M. liliiflora*. The nurseryman Cels seems to have obtained other seedlings from this cross and in the eighteen-thirties he distributed several named clones including 'Alexandrina' and 'Norbertii', both of which persist in cultivation. In 1829 Loudon recorded that Messrs Young of Epsom 'have bought the entire stock of *Magnolia soulangiana* from M. Soulange-Bodin for 500 guineas, in consequence of which that fine tree will soon be spread all over the country.' An earlier magnolia hybrid, *M.* x *thompsoniana*, regarded as a cross between *M. virginiana* and *M. tripetala*, had occurred in 1808 as a chance seedling among the stock of *M. virginiana* in the Mile End nursery of Thomson, whom we have already noted as one of the early rhododendron hybridists. There seems no reason to suppose that *M.* x *thompsoniana* (the 'P' in Thomson's name is due to Loudon, who named the hybrid) was deliberately created.

Although, as we have seen, bedding was in existence before most of the plants which were to be used in these beds had been bred, it was the breeding of petunias, verbenas and later zonal geraniums which gave the system such great popularity during the late forties and fifties.

The first of these hybrid strains to arise was the petunia. In 1823 the white *Petunia nyctaginiflora* had arrived in cultivation. This has large night-scented flowers and is an annual. In 1830 the red or violet-flowered *P. violacea* arrived. Although it is said to have been sent back by Tweedie, we have no record of him sending back seeds as early as 1830, although doubtless many later sendings came from this source. *P. viola cea* is a straggling perennial in the wild and has smaller flowers than the white species. The first recorded hybrid that I know of dates from 1834 and was called *P.* x *atkinsiana*, and this, I suppose, would be the correct botanical name for the whole hybrid strain. These early hybrids seem to have been very different from the reasonably compact modern plants. A writer in 1841 describes training a single plant over a circle 8 feet in diameter. By the later eighteen-forties the petunia as we know it today seems to have become established.

However, the great stand-by for the earlier massed beds was the verbena. This seems to have been principally bred from four wild species. The earliest was *Verbena incisa*, a moderately tall plant with scarlet flowers, which often have a white eye, and it had entered cultivation in 1824. This was presumably the species used by Henry Eckford in the eighteen-seventies to produce his 'auricula-eyed' strain, which is what we know nowadays. *V. peruviana*, native over much of southern South America, whence all the parents come, may be met with as *V. melindres* or as *V. chamaedrifolia*. It is a spreading plant with heads of brilliant scarlet flowers and it gave both the procumbent habit and its brilliant colour to many of the early hybrids, although it must have been a very brilliant plant in its own right. The introducer of these two species does not seem clearly known, but the last two were certainly due to Tweedie. *V. phlogiflora*, which was long known as *V. tweediana*, comes from Uruguay and southern Brazil and is a sub-shrub which is usually of a somewhat sprawling habit, but can have erect stems, which may be several feet long. It exists in numerous colour forms, which include blues and purples as well as reds and is obviously the source of the violet flowers in the hybrid strain. This came from Tweedie's 1834 expedition. The last to be received was *V. platensis*, met also as *V. teucrioides*, which Tweedie sent over in 1837. This is another sprawling plant, which tends to root as the stems elongate. The flowers are white or pale pink and are carried in an elongated raceme, different from the rather flat corymbs of the other ancestral species. Owing to their rapidity of growth it took only a short time after the hybrids had been made for the results to be seen and since they can be raised equally well from seed or from cuttings their propagation was rapid. By the eighteen-forties they were the most popular of all bedding plants and maintained their pre-eminence at least until the early years of this century.

As we have seen, hybridisation among various gladiolus species was among the pioneer work of the hybridists, but it was not until the late eighteen-thirties and early eighteen-forties that the ancestors of our modern tall gladiolus made its appearance. There would appear to have been three species used in raising these tall gladioli. *G. psittacinus* does not seem to have got into cultivation before 1830. It may have been a Bowie sending, but we have no record of that fact. The white-flowered *G. oppositiflorus* was sent, if Herbert is to be believed, by the unfortunate John Forbes, who died in 1823 on an expedition to Madagascar. *G. oppositiflorus* is South African, but could have been collected by Forbes en route. *G. cardinalis* is a smaller plant and was probably originally collected by Thunberg. In 1789 a famous gardener, Graeffer, obtained plants from Holland and they were received at Kew and other places. The first hybrid appeared at Ghent, is known as *G.* x *gandavensis* and does not seem to have got into commerce before 1842, although Herbert had mentioned it earlier. The parentage of *G.* x *gandavensis* was given by Herbert as *G. psittacinus* x *G. oppositiflorus*, while others give it the same parentage as the nearly contemporary hybrid, known as 'Brenchleyensis' which was *psittacinus* x *cardinalis*. These three species seem to have formed the basis of the race of tall gladioli which were bred and, so far as we know, no further species were introduced into the strain before 1878, when *G. purpureo-auratus* was added to give a violet colouration. Most of the later work was done in the eighteen-eighties in the U.S.A. when large-flowered and long-spiked species, such as *GG. saundersii, cruentus* and *quartinianus* gave long spikes and much larger flowers, as well as introducing more brilliant reds. The foundation species were very hard to cultivate in Europe, but the nurserymen J. L. Childs, and Kunderd and the amateur Dr van Fleet were able to grow them in the U.S.A. The modern gladiolus, indeed, is not much older than this century.

The Zonal geranium had been in cultivation since the end of the seventeenth century, but it was grown as a tall shrub. It is not clear exactly what species was being grown under the name *Pelargonium zonale*; the plant is described as having a conspicuous horseshoe mark on the leaves and this feature is not found in what is regarded as the true *P. zonale*, where the horseshoe is very faint. At some stage in the eighteenth century this plant, which might have been the plant now known as *P. frutetorum*, must have become hybridised, probably accidentally, with the brilliant *P. inquinans*. The earliest knowledge we have of the hybrid is a plant owned by Dr Fothergill, so in existence before 1780, which was known as 'Fothergillii' and in the early nineteenth century a number of different Horseshoe geraniums were available. We have already seen Robert Mangles using them for bedding work, but they were all tall plants. Dwarfer plants were produced in the so-called Unique strain, which hybridised the Regal pelargoniums, which were conservatory plants, with the dwarfer but small-flowered scented-leaved geraniums. These were attractive, but not very brilliant. Evidently what was required was a low growing plant with the flowers of the zonal geraniums. This seems to have arisen in the first place in the garden of R. Pigott, Esq. at Dullingham, near Newmarket. His gardener, Mr B. Wilson, took seeds from the tall shrubby 'Frogmore Scarlet', which was growing underplanted with a white ivy-leaved geranium, so the resultant offspring might have been a hybrid. The resultant seedling seemed to be a miserable little plant and was thrown on the rubbish heap, whence it was rescued by young Master Pigott, as being just the right size for his tiny garden. When the plant eventually flowered it was found to be compact but very floriferous and was brought back into the garden proper, propagated and distributed among Mr Pigott's friends, among whom was a Mr W. P. Ayres, who grew it in large quantities, eventually selling his stock to a geranium specialist nurseryman, Conway of Brompton. By 1844, when Conway was ready to put the plant on the market, London was flocking to see the dwarf General Tom Thumb, so the geranium was sold under the name 'Tom Thumb' and for long held a pre-eminent position among bedding geraniums, although a perusal of the literature does suggest that other dwarf zonals had appeared around this time. The history of 'Tom Thumb' was recorded in the *Gardener's Chronicle* for 13 October 1866.

Once the break had been made it was easy to breed further dwarf zonals and the colour range also increased. By 1860 Shirley Hibberd was writing: 'What a charming thing is "Amy Robsart", with its coral stems, ruby-tinted leaf and blossoms combining salmon and carmine.' Still he maintained that they still needed 'bright carmine, bright purple, and, if we could have it, true mauve.' There were a number of cultivars described as having purple flowers, but presumably the purple was not sufficiently bright.

By the mid-eighteen-fifties people seem to have been getting somewhat tired of the brilliant flowers of the geraniums and two breeders, Kinghorn and Peter Grieve, started to breed geraniums in which the leaves were brilliantly coloured. These were known at the time as Tricolors, and the leaves were variously marked with gold or with silver and with maroon. One of Grieve's plants 'Mrs Pollock' is still in cultivation to this day and the employment of geraniums as foliage rather than as flowering plants gave them an extended lease of life.

The last of the popular plants to be developed was the fuchsia. In the early years of the century the only species available seem to have been *F. coccinea* and *F. magellanica* and the dwarf *F. lycioides* of the Encliandra section. This was of no use in the hybridisation programme, although in

1839 there was illustrated a hybrid between an Encliandra, known as *reflexa*, and the tall *F. arborescens*, but this had evidently only curiosity value. Hybrids between *F. coccinea* and *F. magellanica* were made, but do not seem to have been markedly distinct. *F. fulgens* is said to have been received in 1830, but does not seem to have been commercially available before 1837. In 1839 the *Floricultural Cabinet* illustrated 'Chandleri', raised by the famous camellia nursery from *F. fulgens* and *F. magellanica* 'Globosa' and in the note to this they say that workers in the field get the best results if *fulgens* is used as the pollen parent. Indeed almost all modern fuchsias come from this *fulgens-magellanica* cross. In the late eighteen-thirties an albino form of *F. magellanica* was received. It was called 'Rosea-alba' but is presumably the plant now called *molinae*. This was used to produce fuchsias with white sepals, of which the small-flowered 'Venus Victrix' is the best known, although it does not seem to have been the only one. In 1842 not only was this illustrated, but also a cultivar called 'Enchantress', which looks like a modern white-sepalled hybrid. Other species were introduced to cultivation and employed in hybrids, but the most famous is a mystery. In 1855 Mr Story brought out four cultivars with red sepals and white corollas. In the *Florist* of that year we read 'There is no record of the parentage of these varieties . . . and Mr Story, after a severe illness, has just passed away. It has been stated that he used pollen from a species with an almost white corolla, flowers of which he obtained from Mr Veitch . . . and that the species died after flowering.' I imagine the basic truth is correct, although since Lucombe and Pince also produced white-corollaed hybrids about this time, it may have been they rather than Veitch who had the mysterious white-corollaed species.

The fuchsia became a popular plant, but the flowers got larger and larger and in 1870 John Walsh uttered a significant protest. 'The fuchsia has suffered a terrible degradation within the past few years, for almost every addition to the lists of new sorts has been an addition to the family of monsters of hideous mien. The corollas have expanded more and more, until what was once like a cup, a goblet or a Rhine wine glass, has become at last a flat disc or a miniature washing tub, a shameful mockery of all our pretensions. . . . As for some of the doubles, they may resemble the tassels of window blinds, but they are an outrage upon the ideal of a perfect fuchsia. . . . It is a dispiriting reflexion on public taste that a plant so renowned for grace . . . has become in the hands of certain florists a very type of deformity.'

Here, rather early in its history, we find the almost universal history of garden hybrids. Size in itself is regarded as a desirable goal and the flowers get larger and larger, until some perceptive onlooker points out that they have lost grace and any sense of proportion between the size of the plant and the size of the flower. Why this always has to happen is odd, but we can see it in the rose, the gladiolus, the dahlia and the rhododendron. It takes a long time for hybridists to learn that size is not, in itself, a virtue.

CHAPTER XII

China II

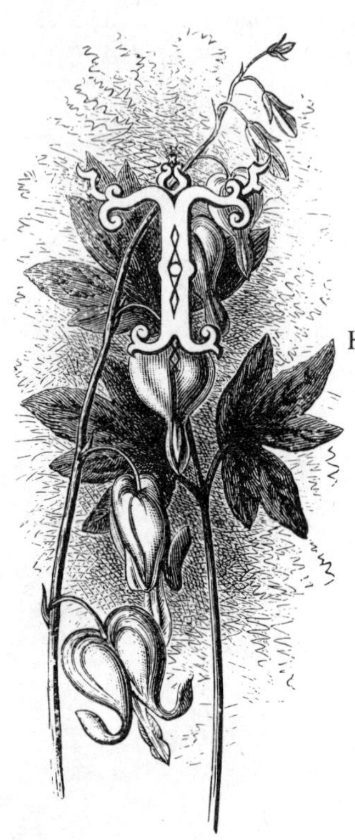

HE horticultural exploration of China falls conveniently into three sections. The first lasted from the earliest importations until 1842, when Europeans were confined to Canton and Macao. The second from 1842 until 1860, when Europeans were allowed to visit the ports of Canton, Amoy, Foochow, Ningpo and Shanghai and from these ports were allowed to travel within a day's journey, which was reckoned at 30 miles, into the interior. After 1860 the whole of mainland China was, theoretically, open to foreigners, although they were, as we shall see, somewhat tardy in taking advantage of the opportunities.

Europeans had chafed increasingly under the humiliation of being confined to Macao with a yearly visit to Canton and Britain took advantage of her wealth and military strength, but, regrettably under the unfortunate pretext of freedom to sell opium (which at that time could be freely purchased in any shop in Britain as Coleridge and De Quincy testify) to make war upon the Chinese to improve their trading position. The Opium War lasted from 1840 to 1842, at the end of which Britain had acquired Hong Kong as well as the right of access to the ports listed above. No sooner was peace declared than the veteran John Reeves suggested to the Horticultural Society that they should send out a collector and this they decided to do.

We have said that these parts of China were available to collectors from 1842 until 1860, but the horticultural exploration of China during this period was entirely the work of one man. No one else seems to have thought it worth while to send out a collector.

This man was the superintendent of the greenhouses at the Society's gardens at Chiswick. In 1842 he was thirty years old and his name was Robert Fortune. He was of Scottish descent, like so many of the great plant collectors, and he had been trained at the Royal Botanic Garden at Edinburgh. In 1842 the Society was going through its usual cycle of economic depression and they could only offer Fortune the same salary that Banks's collectors had received fifty years or so ago, £100 per annum. Even in those days they had inflation and the sum was worth far less then than it had been in the days of Masson and Kerr.

In spite of the success that John Gibson had had in bringing plants from India in 1837 and a small-scale, but impressive experiment in sending plants to, and bringing back plants from, Australia in the same year, it would seem that the Wardian case was still not entirely accepted. Fortune was instructed to take out three of these cases planted up with European plants 'for the purpose 1st, of making presents to those who may be useful to you, and, 2nd, of watching the effect upon the plants of the various circumstances to which they may be exposed during the voyage.' In the event they proved very successful and Fortune lost singularly few plants of the great number that he sent back.

Whenever the Society sent out a collector they supplied him with a formidable list of instructions and Fortune was no exception. All the living plants he obtained were the property of the Society and he had also to furnish them with herbarium specimens. He could, if he wished, collect further specimens (which would have been saleable at the modest rate of £2 per 100 specimens), but 'it is to be understood, however, that the Society is not to incur any expense in forming your private collections and that they are to be altogether subservient to the claims of the Society on your time.' So far as plants were concerned, Fortune was given a free hand, but, interestingly enough, the Society emphasised: 'in all cases you will bear in mind that hardy plants are of the first importance and that the value of the plants diminishes as the heat required to cultivate them is increased. Aquatics, *Orchidaceae* or plants producing very handsome flowers are the only exceptions to this rule.' After this sensible statement it is odd to find the Society listing among desiderata, 'the Nepenthes, which are different from those in cultivation.... *Biophytum sensitivum* and *Lycopodium cernuum*.' In fact there are no Chinese pitcher plants and neither the biophytum nor the lycopodium are at all showy, although they would both require warm greenhouse temperatures and, in point of fact, are pantropical in distribution and could be collected anywhere. Besides these greenhouse plants, Fortune was told to look out for 'The peaches of Pekin, cultivated in the Emperor's garden and weighing 2 lb.'

Since Pekin was inaccessible it is far from clear how Fortune was meant to obtain these plants. He was also to look out for 'Peonies with blue flowers, the existence of which is, however, doubtful' and 'Camellias with yellow flowers.'

Fortune collected in China from the end of 1842 until the end of 1845. He returned in 1848 to collect tea plants for the East India Company and take the plants to start tea plantations in India. This expedition lasted until 1851 and the plants collected on this expedition were sent to Messrs Standish and Noble. He returned to China again at the end of 1852 and left again in early 1856, this time sending the plants to Glendinning of Chiswick. He returned to China yet again in 1858, collecting tea plants for the government of the U.S.A. It is not clear whether he remained until 1860, when he was able to visit Japan and Pekin, and again sent his plants to Standish and Noble, or whether he had returned to England during the interval. He did not return after 1860.

Unlike many plant collectors Fortune was visiting a country with a very long gardening tradition and it could be assumed that most of the attractive local plants would have already been brought into cultivation. Some writers suggest that Fortune did nothing else except visit nursery gardens, but a reading of his writings will soon correct this impression. For example, 'The slow progress which we necessarily made suited my purposes exactly and enabled me to explore the botanical riches of the country with convenience and ease. I used to rise at break of day and spend the morning inspecting the hills and valleys.... Breakfast over I generally went on shore again, accompanied by my men, who carried the seeds, plants or flowers we might discover during our rambles.' And again in the Bohea hills 'I met with one or two new plants which deserve particular notice. One of them was a very beautiful species of Hydrangea; another was a species of Spiraea with red flowers ... a fine species of Abelia was also met with on the Fokien side of the mountains, which will probably be a favourite in English gardens.... I dug up from time to time living plants of all these species and took them on with me. Many a time I thought I should be obliged to leave them behind me, for the Chinamen could not see the propriety of being burdened with what they considered weeds and of no value.' But in many cases the wild and the cultivated plants were the same. Later in the passage describing his collecting methods he adds: 'during these rambles I met with many plants growing wild on the hills which I had never seen before except in gardens.'

If you consult an atlas you will see that the Bohea Hills are considerably more than 30 miles from any treaty port and you may well wonder how Fortune managed to make so long an excursion into the interior. The explanation seems barely credible; Fortune had attached a false pigtail to his head, was wearing Chinese clothes and giving himself out as a

Chinaman from beyond the Great Wall. In such a vast country as China it could be assumed that many racial types could be observed, but even so it seems unlikely that Fortune with his blue eyes and Scottish countenance could have really been taken for a Mongolian and one gets the impression that the inhabitants of the interior were not particularly interested in his nationality and just extended the normal Chinese courtesy to strangers. It was, it is true, part of the folklore that all Europeans had red hair, which was a feature that did not grace Fortune. He had first undertaken this hazardous course during his first expedition, when he was particularly anxious to visit Soochow, which was said to be the great place for tree peonies and nurseries in general. In this case his Chinese garb was somewhat improvised and he had considerable qualms while making the forbidden journey, but it was successfully accomplished, although he found that Shanghai was just as satisfactory as Soochow for nursery plants. His later trips to the tea districts were more thoroughly prepared and he had even learned some Chinese by then. By and large Fortune got on well with the Chinese and it is interesting to notice how, in his various books, his attitude changes from the conventional 'all foreigners are by definition inferior' to a genuine liking and respect. Only on his first visit does he record any instance of animosity directed against himself. He was, it is true, attacked by pirates, whom he put to flight with a fowling piece, but the pirates were not attacking him as a European, they were indeed attacking a Chinese junk and were discomforted to find a hostile European on board.

'Take things coolly and never lose your temper should be the motto of everyone who attempts to travel in China. This is always the best plan, for, if you allow things to take their course, ten to one you will get out of a dilemma ... but if you attempt to interfere you will probably make matters worse.' This excellent advice comes from his second book describing his 'Journey to the Tea Countries'. From this same book comes a description of how he packed his plants in the interior. They 'were carefully packed with their roots in damp moss and the whole package was then covered with oil paper. The latter precaution was taken to screen them from the sun and also from the prying eyes of the Chinese, who, although they did not seem to show any great jealousy on the point, yet might have annoyed us with impertinent questions.' Since Fortune was collecting plants to establish a tea industry in India, which would take away the Chinese monopoly, one can well appreciate that questions might have proved embarrassing. A tea industry was established in India but after the Mutiny of 1857 the East India Company was wound up and the British Government took control of India. The tea plantations were neglected and when the industry was restarted it was with the native Assam tea, not the Chinese plants. Since botanists tend now to think that the Chinese plants were originally imported from Assam, it would seem that Fortune's exertions were not strictly necessary.

For his first journey Fortune still had to make the long trip round South Africa. He left Canton on 22 December 1845 and did not arrive in England until 6 May 1846, a journey lasting 4½ months. For his subsequent journeys he travelled by the 'overland route.' This meant taking ship to Alexandria, travelling overland by an extremely rough route to Suez and then taking further ship to China. The time saved was considerable, but damage might well be caused during the overland section. In 1857 there was opened the rail link between the two Egyptian ports and after that there were fewer breakages, while in 1869 the Suez Canal was opened. When sending plants back Fortune used to divide his collections into three or four parts, putting them on different ships, so that if one met with disaster, the others would still get through. On his first voyage he had 250 plants that he was managing himself and of these 215 arrived safely in England. The Wardian cases had conclusively proved their worth. On his second voyage Fortune was able to extend their range of usefulness. He had vast quantities of seed of the tea plants, but he knew that, like other oily seeds, they tend to lose their viability fairly rapidly. He therefore sowed them in the Wardian cases when loading them in the ships. Most had germinated by the time the ship reached Calcutta and it was clear that other seeds with a short life could be treated in this way.

Fortune wrote a rather measured prose, with a certain pawky humour that seems to indicate his Scottish origin. Thus he noted at the town of Shaou-hing-Foo: 'I saw many ornamental gates in the town erected to the memory of virtuous women, who, judging from the number of these structures, must have been unusually numerous in the place.' Occasionally he indulges in rather broader jokes as when he delightedly recalls that the seedsman A-Ching, who found the letter R difficult, told him that he preserved his seeds in 'burnt lice'. Only once does his grammar and his prose suffer to describe some of the excitement of a plant collector's life. On the island of Koo-lung-su he had met with an enthusiastic amateur, Captain Hall. '"I have good news for you" said he one morning, when I met him. "Come with me and I will show you the most beautiful plant on the island. I have just discovered it".... What could it be? Was it new? Would it produce perfect seeds, or could young plants be procured to send home? were questions which rapidly suggested themselves. It is only the enthusiastic botanical collector who can form an idea of the amount of excitement and pleasure there is, when one fancies he is on the eve of finding a new and beautiful flower.' This is really the only passage in which he lets the veil drop and it seems rather a pity that Captain Hall's plant was only the beautiful but well-known wisteria. Usually he is far more in control. Here is the discovery of *Rhododendron fortunei* in 1854. 'In a romantic glen through which we passed on our journey I came upon a remarkably fine looking rhododendron. A species of the genus (*R. championai*) had been discovered on the Hong Kong hills, but none had previously been met with to the northward, although the azalea is one of the most common plants on the mountains of Chekiang. I therefore looked upon the present discovery as a great acquisition, and, as the plants were covered with ripe seeds I was able to obtain a good supply to send home. All the Chinese in that part of the country agreed in stating that the flowers . . . are large and beautiful, but as all rhododendrons have this character, it is impossible to predict what this one will turn out to be, until we have the opportunity of seeing its flowers.' As can be gathered from this passage, Fortune was not one to let any opportunity escape him, yet there are one or two odd omissions in his collections. One plant he records as finding on the Bohea hills he calls *Hamamelis chinensis*. Presumably this was *H. mollis*. Since Fortune was there in the summer he could not have seen the flowers, but it seems curious that he did not collect seeds. Possibly he did and they failed to germinate. On two occasions he mentions a maple, called *fung-tze* by the Chinese, which had blood-red leaves in the autumn, but he does not seem to have bothered with that. Like most collectors of those days he had an especial fondness for conifers, yet he does not seem to have bothered with *Pinus tabulaeformis* (syn. *P. sinensis*), although he also frequently mentions it. Among the plants he found on the Bohea hills was, as we have noted, a hydrangea. Fortune says that it arrived in Europe, yet there is no hydrangea listed among his introductions, so it must subsequently have been lost.

The list of new plants that Fortune did introduce in his seventeen years is very large and included many winter-flowering shrubs. The winter jasmine is the best-known of these, but two loniceras, *L. fragrantissima* and *L. standishii* are fragrant, although not showy. *Mahonia japonica* must surely be one of the best of all winter-flowering shrubs, but the smaller, autumn-flowering *M. fortunei* has proved somewhat tender in Great Britain.

Victorian gardeners rather enjoyed growing unsuitable plants, so that the hardy palm, *Trachycarpus fortunei*, was immediately popular, although few plants look so out of place in British gardens as palms. Previously Siebold had obtained a few plants from Japan, but it was Fortune's large sendings that made the plant widespread. Equally exotic-looking were some hardy bamboos, *Phyllostachys viridi-glaucescens* and *Sasa tessellata*. It seems hard to realise that before Fortune's voyages there were no forsythias in European gardens. (In 1833 a few plants of *F. suspensa* had been brought from Japan, but do not seem to have got into general cultivation.) Fortune introduced both *F. suspensa* and *F. viridissima*, while among other shrubs was *Weigela florida*, which caused an enormous sensation, *Prunus triloba* and *P. glandulosa* 'Sinensis,' and the Pearl bush, *Exochorda racemosa*. Fortune also introduced the Chinese Snowball tree, *Viburnum plicatum*, as well as the huge flowered but tender *V. macrocephalum*. Apart from *Rhododendron fortunei*, Fortune also sent back the azaleas, *R. farrerae, R. obtusum* and *R. ovatum*. Skimmias were not known before Fortune's sendings of *S. japonica* and *S. reevesiana*. We do not see *Clematis lanuginosa* nowadays, but it is the main parent of all the later-flowering large-flowered clematis, such as x *jackmanii*. Privets are not usually grown for ornament, yet the late-flowering *Ligustrum sinense* is probably the showiest of its genus. Among other shrubs are the enchanting but fiendish *Daphne genkwa*, its easier yellow relative, *Edgworthia papyrifera*, the showy *Indigofera decora, Ilex cornuta* and the Chinese Fringe Tree, *Chionanthus retusus.* Among climbing plants the favourite must be the white form of *Wisteria sinensis. Trachelospermum jasminoides* usually needs a cool greenhouse but *Akebia quinata*, although it is shy of producing its showy fruits in the British climate, is hardy enough and attractive with its vivid green quinate leaves.

Few of Fortune's trees have met with much success in Britain, although they may be found in climes with hotter summers and colder winters. Fortune thought very highly of the Chinese Judas Tree, *Cercis chinensis*, but this has never been a success in cultivation. The Golden Larch, *Pseudolarix amabilis*, thrives in northern Italy, but is rare in Britain, *Pinus bungeana* with its white trunk finds our winters far too mild. *Platycarya strobilacea* was originally named *Fortunaea* in his honour, but is somewhat tender for our climate, although successful elsewhere. The Funeral Cypress, *Cupressus funebris*, is one of the loveliest of trees, but too tender for us. The Plum Yew, *Cephalotaxus fortunei*, persists in cultivation, but is rather rare, while his two oaks, *Quercus myrsinifolia* and *Q. variabilis*, the last plant he introduced, are very rarely seen. Indeed the only tree that has been generally successful is the cryptomeria.

It was not only woody plants that Fortune sent back. We owe to him the bleeding heart, *Dicentra spectabilis*, the Japanese anemone and the pompon chrysanthemum. He also introduced a gentian, *Gentiana scabra fortunei*, but this has proved very difficult to keep.

Among cultivated plants pride of place must go to the thirty cultivars of the tree peony that Fortune was able to introduce, and fortunately we still have some descriptions of what they were like. We should bear in mind that previously there had only been white, deep pink and paler pink moutans in cultivation and whatever variants could be raised. Many of Fortune's introductions were in dark purple shades, that had not been seen before. For example 'Colonel Malcolm' was described in Van Houtte's catalogue in 1874 as 'bright violet, slightly edged with lilac', 'Osiris' was 'very deep purple', while 'Picta' offered the bizarre combination of 'deep violet purple and amaranth'. There were also much brighter reds; 'Robert Fortune' was 'bright scarlet', while 'Vivid' was 'bright orange scarlet'. Most of Fortune's plants were fully or semi-double and one would have liked to have seen 'Ida', described as 'milk-white, large and full'. All these old Chinese plants now seem lost to European gardens, although one cannot see that they have been replaced by any improvements.

Fortune also brought back numerous cultivars of *Camellia sasanqua*, but these have all gone and we do not even have any descriptions of them. On the other hand the double form of *C. reticulata*, now known as 'Robert Fortune' is still in cultivation, although less frequently seen than 'Captain Rawes'. We do not hear of any cultivars of *Paeonia albiflora*, which seems an odd omission. Among *Prunus*, Fortune brought back several double peaches, including one with striped flowers, which was much appreciated in Victorian days, but which now seems to have vanished from the catalogues. Among other *Prunus* were the tight double pink flowers of *P. triloba* and both double pink and double white forms of *P. glandulosa*. Fortune did not bring back many roses, but one is known as 'Fortune's Double Yellow', as 'Pseudindica', as 'Beauty of Glazenwood' and as 'Gold of Ophir', the multiplicity of names giving ample evidence of its popularity. This is a climber with yellow flowers with a coppery flush, which rather suggests that *Rosa foetida* must have been brought to China and got into their rose breeding; a feat that M. Pernet-Ducher found extremely difficult at the start of this century. The white-flowered x *fortuniana*, said to be a hybrid between *R. laevigata* and *R. banksiae*, is of little use in Great Britain, but survives in warmer climes. Presumably we must also thank Fortune for the form of *R. chinensis*, known as 'Mutabilis', in which the flowers change colour as they age. Fortune mentions it several times in his writings, so it is improbable that he failed to bring it home, although we do not hear much about it until the eighteen-eighties. Like so many of Fortune's plants, it seems to have been more popular on the Continent than in Great Britain. Indeed a number of his introductions are on the borderline of hardiness and have thrived better further south than the British Isles, but even so enough indispensable plants are left to give him one of the highest positions among those who transformed gardens with their introductions.

CHAPTER XIII *Japan*

IFFICULT though it was, before 1843, for foreigners to get plants from China, it was well-nigh impossible for them to get plants from Japan. The only Europeans permitted to trade were the Dutch East India Company and they were confined on the tiny island of Deshima, just off the port of Nagasaki. They were allowed from time to time into the port and once a year the senior members of the company made a journey to the capital, Yedo (now known as Tokyo) to give presents to the Emperor, but they were firmly confined to their travelling carriages, known as norimons, and had no chance to do any botanising. The Chinese were also allowed to trade with the Japanese, so that Japanese plants reached Europe via Canton.

In 1672 Engelbert Kaempfer published a book about Japan entitled *Amoenitates Exoticae* and this contained a section on the Japanese flora, but otherwise nothing was known of this until Karl Pehr Thunberg arrived at Deshima in 1775. He was employed as surgeon by the Dutch company, but he had been a pupil of Linnaeus and was an enthusiastic if somewhat careless botanist. He was also retained by Professor Burmann and some Dutch horticulturists to collect plants and seeds for the Medical Garden in Amsterdam and for private subscribers. He had been in South Africa with Masson and had sent back collections from there. To start with, Thunberg found the confinement on Deshima as frustrating as might be expected. His sole chance of botanising was in sifting through the fodder that was delivered for the livestock on Deshima. Later his skill in performing operations for cataract enabled him to get permission to make small excursions beyond Nagasaki. Naturally he was not allowed to do this on his own and he was accompanied by a sizeable retinue of police guards and interpreters. Thunberg soon got on good terms with the interpreters and they helped him in his collections, which tended to be of exsiccata, rather than of seeds or living plants. Thunberg accompanied the embassy to Yedo in 1776, expressing great dissatisfaction because the fields were so well-tended that he could find no weeds. Normally the travellers, as we have said, were kept in their norimons, but they had to alight while crossing the steeper parts of the Fakone mountains and Thunberg hurried on ahead in order to collect plants while the others caught up. In Yedo he made friends with some of the more influential Japanese scientists and they seem to have arranged for him to have been given a certain amount of freedom. On the way back he was even allowed to visit a nursery garden, where he purchased several cultivars of *Acer palmatum*, as well as *Cycas revoluta*. One imagines that he also got hold of the variegated *Aucuba japonica*, which Kew received from Graeffer in 1783. Graeffer was evidently friendly either with Thunberg or with one of his consignees and seems to have got quite a few plants in this way. The different maples do not seem to have arrived safely in Amsterdam. In 1784 Thunberg published a *Flora Japonica*, which is an unsatisfactory production, but, when one considers under what circumstances it had had to be produced, it is remarkable that it could be produced at all. Even so some of the attributions are rather odd. One can see some excuse for Thunberg assuming that the Hortensia hydrangea was a *Viburnum*, but why did he imagine that *Mahonia japonica* was a holly? Among the Japanese irises will be noted *I. graminea*, a European species in which the flowers are lower than the leaves. Thunberg later decided that this attribution was wrong and renamed the plant *Iris ensata*. The plant is the wild form of the well-known kaempferi iris and one must mistrust anyone who thought even momentarily that this could be conspecific with *I. graminea*.

In 1826 Philipp von Siebold arrived in Deshima as surgeon to the Company. Profiting from Thunberg's experience he had become a specialist in cataract operations and his services were in such demand that he was able to travel comparatively freely. He was born in Bavaria, in Wurzburg, but he was rather Prussian in his behaviour, seeming to many people to be arrogant and dictatorial, but against this he was a first-rate scientist and was later to publish excellent works on both the flora and fauna of Japan. He was also an ethnologist and he learned the language to the extent that he was able to acquire a Japanese mistress, whose name was Sonogi. He was also able to train a number of Japanese assistants, who were to send him seeds after he was forced to leave Japan.

In his studies he had obtained maps not only of the main Japanese islands, but also of the outlying Kuriles and Liu-Kius. Thunberg seems to have got his Japanese map with no trouble, but the officials were outraged by Siebold's behaviour and he was imprisoned in December 1828 and his maps were confiscated. Fortunately Siebold had managed to make copies. Siebold was kept in prison for a year and then banished from Japan. He left in January 1830 with 500 plants, in what were said to be 250 species, although doubtless many of these were only cultivars. He opened a nursery in Ghent in 1830, but this was just at the time when Belgium was fighting Holland for its independence and during the hostilities his plants were pilfered and he was only able to recover eighty plants. With these as a nucleus he started his famous nursery at Leiden, which had, at first, a monopoly of Japanese plants, Siebold having arranged that all plants received from Japan should be sent to him. Further materials were sent him by some of his Japanese friends and pupils and by some of his successors as surgeon to the Dutch company, most notably H. Buerger and, after 1840, Jaques Perot. After 1847 Siebold theoretically lost his monopoly, but the nursery continued to flourish and specialise in Japanese plants.

After 1854 the ban on the admission of foreigners to Japan was gradually modified and in 1858 Siebold was given permission to return to Japan. He went to Nagasaki in 1859 and lived on the outskirts, where Fortune called on him in 1860. In this year he was invited to Tokyo to act as adviser to the Japanese Privy Councillor with regard to smoothing foreign relations, introducing European sciences and other matters that were not clearly defined. For some reason his activities thoroughly alarmed the Dutch authorities. First they tried to persuade him to resign; then they tried to persuade the Japanese to dismiss him, but neither of these ploys worked. The Dutch then suggested a diplomatic appointment for Siebold and invited him to Batavia to discuss it. Once they had succeeded in getting Siebold away from Japan, they took good care to prevent him returning. Siebold returned in disgust to Europe, severed all connections with the ungrateful Dutch and retired to his native Bavaria, where he died in 1866. Siebold was active in Japan for only a short time, from 1826 to 1828 and from 1859 to 1861, yet his impact was out of all proportion to the short time that he was able to work in Japan. The *Flora Japonica*, which he undertook with J. G. Zuccarini was, unfortunately, never completed. The first volume appeared between 1835 and 1842. A second volume, based on notes left by the two authors appeared after their deaths, in 1875. Basically the diagnoses and taxonomy were entrusted to Zuccarini, while Siebold wrote the background information with regard to habitats, uses and other details. These descriptions are full of charm and give us a rather different picture of Siebold from the popular one of a somewhat unscrupulous money-grubber and place seeker. Here he is, for example, on *Lilium callosum*.

'This lily, which Thunberg mistook for our *L. pomponium*, grows in Japan in mountainous open country, especially on volcanic slopes, from 500 to 2000 feet above the sea. Usually it is found in company with *Dolichos hirsuta, Smilax pseudo-china*, various species of *Veronica, Lespedeza, Erianthus, Anthisteria* and other upland grasses. In the wild it is a slender plant, not more than 2 or 3 feet high; on the other hand in their gardens, where it is cultivated along with other species of *Lilium*, it becomes taller and stouter. In the autumn the bulbs, like those of *L. tigrinum*, which is also wild in Japan, are harvested and are eaten either boiled or roasted. They are very nourishing, floury, with a sweet agreeable taste.'

About *Cornus kousa* he writes: 'The Japanese name is jama boosi. Boosi means 'mountains', so the plant can be expected to be found at considerable heights. I myself have only found it in the mountains of Kyushu and Nippon at heights of from 2–4000 feet. My worthy friend the Japanese naturalist Wudagawa Joan, a doctor at Yedo, has found it in the mountains of Hako at a height of 6000 feet and in other high regions in the north. When it was brought down . . . to Deshima it failed to grow well, because it was too southerly and too low.'

It is not possible to distinguish between plants actually collected by Siebold and those that he obtained from other sources, but the number of Japanese plants that got into cultivation through the Leiden nurseries is very large indeed. It is interesting to note that at a time when horticulturalists were concentrating on the showiest of plants, Siebold was introducing many plants of quiet charm. For example the first of his plants to be illustrated in England was *Asarum thunbergii* (under the confusing alias of *Heterotropa asaroides*), which has a very strange flower, but one that is not at all showy. In this same line may be reckoned five species of *Epimedium, Stachyurus praecox, Corylopsis spicata* and *C. pauciflora*. He was probably personally responsible for the introduction of three hostas, *H. albomarginata, H. plantaginea* and *H. sieboldiana*. This genus, which was known in the later nineteenth century as *Funkia*, was not new; one species, *H. ventricosa*, had been introduced in 1790, but Siebold's plants appear to have made a considerable impression and they were grown for the sake of their bold foliage, rather than for their mauve flowers. Among other plants which first passed through Siebold's hands must be classed a number of plants grown in Japanese gardens, such as the kaempferi irises, a number of Hortensia hydrangeas, forms of *Lilium speciosum* and *L.* x *maculatum*, cultivars of *Clematis patens* and the double form of *C. florida*, which bears his name, 'Sieboldii'. There were also a few of the double cherries of Japan, which, strangely, do not seem to have made much impression on European gardeners at this time; they appeared more attracted to the various forms of *Acer japonicum* and *A. palmatum*. The long-racemed form of *Wisteria floribunda* was immediately popular. A variegated *Lonicera japonica* is credited to him, but this is probably not the popular 'Aureo-reticulata' which was subsequently introduced by Fortune, although there was some overlapping with Fortune in the eighteen-sixties.

Among species Siebold is credited with a number of conifers, *Abies firma, Cephalotaxus harringtonia* and *C. h. drupacea*, some cryptomeria cultivars, *Pinus densiflora* and *P. thunbergii* and some variegated forms of *Thuja orientalis*. During the period that Siebold was in Holland there was increasing interest among gardeners in bold foliage and Siebold's introductions of *Paulownia tomentosa* and *Fatsia japonica* were primarily prized for their foliage. Among other Siebold introductions which are still popular in gardens may be listed, *Cercidiphyllum japonicum, Deutzia gracilis* and *D. scabra*, *Euonymus japonicus* cultivars and forms of *E. radicans*. The introduction of *Hamamelis japonica* can now be seen as of great importance, but we do not find much contemporary acclaim for this delightful winter-flowering shrub. More interest was shown in the various *Malus* spp. which he obtained. These included *M. floribunda, M. prunifolia rinkii* and *M. toringo*. The introduction of *Osmanthus aquifolius* is a further example of Siebold's eye for a good plant that is not particularly showy. Among other introductions we should mention cursorily, *Raphiolepis umbellata* (syn. *R. japonica*), *Rhodotypos kerrioides* (syn. *R. scandens*), *Skimmia japonica*, three spiraeas, *Pterostyrax corymbosa* (erroneously in commerce as the more popular *C. hispida*, not introduced until the late eighteen-seventies), and *Weigela coraeenses*. There was also a variegated form of *Viburnum plicatum tomentosum*, which is now lost. For thirty years Siebold was like Wallich, doing comparatively little collecting himself, but through whom the new plants were distributed.

By 1860 a number of Japanese ports were open to British nationals and in that year both John Gould Veitch and Robert Fortune arrived. Veitch was collecting for the Veitch nursery, while Fortune sent his plants to Standish and Noble. Veitch arrived first on 20 July and he left again at the end of November, during which time he collected as thoroughly as he could. He found that at Tokyo his movements were very circumscribed and he had to rely on Japanese friends in that district to do any collecting. In August he complained that there were scarcely any wild plants in flower, and also that no seeds were ripe. However, 'I have been occupied in rambling over the hills ... and looking into all the gardens I can gain access to in the town. The people are excessively civil, and in no instance have I met with the least hindrance; on the contrary every one gives me any plant I take a fancy to, and seem pleased to do it.... The Japanese are great lovers of flowers and shrubs and I find quantities of plants grown in their gardens, which I never see growing wild, nor can I ascertain where they are to be had in a wild state. Endless varieties of plants can therefore be had in the towns themselves, and others I can procure from the natives as I go on.'

In September Veitch was given the temporary appointment of Botanist to Her Britannic Majesty's Legation at Tokyo, to enable him to accompany the ambassador to the top of Fuji-Yama. Veitch wrote a long piece enumerating all the plants he noted, which is interesting, but too long for inclusion here. It can be found in the 1860 volume of the *Gardener's Chronicle*. Considering his short stay Veitch travelled over a lot of Japan, including a three-day visit to Hakodate on the northern island of Yezo (Hokkaido). Apart from the splendid *Lilium auratum*, which was also sent back by Fortune, and a number of ferns, most of Veitch's successful introductions were conifers. He did collect seed of *Magnolia salicifolia*, but it failed to germinate. He does seem to have brought back the very dark purple form of *Magnolia liliiflora*. He also brought back numerous cultivars of *Primula sieboldii*, which were brought into commerce as cultivars of *P. cortusoides*. Among his conifers were both the type and various cultivars of *Chamaecyparis obtusa* and of *C. pisifera*. The charming form of cryptomeria known as 'Elegans' was one of his happier sendings and one of his most important was the Japanese larch. He is credited with two abies, three piceas and two pinus, as well as *Sciadopitys verticillata, Thujopsis dolabrata* and *Tsuga diversifolia*. He introduced *Zelkova serrata*, an attractive tree, but not one that has been very successful in cultivation. The plant that really obtained an instant success was the Virginia creeper, *Parthenocissus tricuspidata*, long known as *Ampelopsis veitchii*, which at one time seemed to be growing on every other house in Great Britain, as it appeared to be immune to most forms of atmospheric pollution. The true Virginia creeper had been in cultivation for over a century, but never seems to have been quite as popular as Veitch's plant was to become.

Veitch had arrived in July 1860 and in October Fortune disembarked at Nagasaki, when he at once called on Siebold. He remained in Japan for three months, but returned for a further three-month period in April, in order to see the spring flowers. For his first visit he had the assistance of the amiable Ambassador, Mr Alcock. Unfortunately he was absent in 1861 and his second-in-command was a particularly tiresome stickler for protocol and etiquette and far from assisting Fortune, actively hindered him. For his pains he is immortalised as a pompous fool in Fortune's *Yedo and Pekin*. Fortune does not seem to have been unduly impressed by Japanese gardens. At one moment he visited 'a large pleasure garden, which seems a favourite resort with the good people of Yedo.... The most curious objects in this garden were imitation ladies made up out of the flowers of the chrysanthemum. Thousands of flowers were used for this purpose, and, as these artificial beauties smiled upon the visitors out of little alcoves and summer houses, the effect was oftentimes startling.'

Fortune visited as many nursery gardens as he could and made a remarkable discovery. 'The most remarkable feature in the nurseries . . . is the large number of plants with variegated leaves. It is only a very few years since our taste in Europe led us to take an interest in and admire those curious freaks of nature called variegated plants. For anything I know to the contrary the Japanese have been cultivating this taste for a thousand years. The result is that they have in cultivation in a variegated state almost all the ornamental plants of the country and many of these are strikingly handsome. Here is a list of a few to give some idea of the extent and number of these extraordinary productions: Pines, Junipers, Chamaecyparis, Podocarpus, Illicium, *Pieris japonica*, Eurya, Elaeagnus, *Pittosporum tobira*, Euonymus (yellow), Fatsia, Laurus, Ginkgo. . . . Then there is a variegated orchid! a variegated palm! a variegated Camellia and even the tea plant is represented in this "happy family". The beautiful *Sciadopitys verticillata*, which is no doubt one of the finest conifers in Asia, has produced a variety with golden-striped leaves. All these things, and many more, are now on the wide ocean on the way to Europe, where we propose to establish them in a new home.'

Among these variegated plants must have been *Acer rufinerve albolimbatum*, which Standish and Noble were able to offer in 1869, ten years before the type was introduced.

The introduction which most pleased Fortune himself was a male plant of *Aucuba japonica*. The variegated female had been around since 1783, but it had not been realised that the plant not only had attractive leaves, but that it could also bear handsome red fruits. Fortune did not find it particularly easy to obtain a male plant, but he eventually succeeded.

Another important Fortune introduction was a number of the large ragged Japanese chrysanthemums, known in the trade, and not unfairly, as 'mops'. The British were used to the very formal incurved varieties and at first they thought that these Japanese flowers, however large they might be, were far too unkempt and rustic. There was, however, one nurseryman who had faith in them. This was John Salter, of the Versailles nursery at Hammersmith, who specialised in plants that were initially unpopular and which later acquired popularity. It is to him that we owe the modern pansies. During most of the 19th century the pansy was a show flower, which had to confirm to rigid rules and the so-called 'Fancy' pansies were thrown out and sold to Continental nurserymen. Salter brought them back into favour. He also specialised in plants with variegated leaves long before these became fashionable and he grew the Japanese chrysanthemums, until they too eventually acquired popularity.

Both Veitch and Fortune seem to have had their failures. We have seen how Veitch failed with *Magnolia salicifolia* and a similar failure seems to have attended Fortune with *Primula japonica*. He writes enthusiastically about it and advisedly, since it was the first crimson verticillate primula to become known, but it does not seem to have got into cultivation before 1871, so it looks as though his plants failed to survive. A plant that so entranced Fortune that he kept it by him to accompany himself was the variegated form of *Saxifraga stolonifera*, known as 'Tricolor'. To Fortune must also be credited *Rhododendron metternichii*, various garden forms of *Clematis patens* and *C. florida*; a double white, thought to be a form of *C. florida*, known under the name 'Fortunei', was an important parent in the early clematis hybrids. In his list of his Japanese introductions Fortune is somewhat vague on occasion. He speaks of 'Many Acers' without going into details, and of '*Lilium auratum* and other species' in an equally vague manner. It seems odd that he should have had to travel as far as Japan to find the variegated lily-of-the-valley.

Both Fortune and Veitch had spent only a short time in Japan, but in the same year, 1860, there arrived the Russian botanist Carl Maximowicz, who remained for three years. He acquired a number of Japanese helpers, of whom Chonosuke Sugawa, who appears in many specific epithets as *tchonoskii*, is the best known. He was born in 1841 and survived until 1925. He was able to visit northern Kiushiu for Maximowicz. Maximowicz's movements, like those of all Europeans, were still circumscribed. He stayed for over a year at Hakodate on Hakkaido, but his movements were theoretically confined to a radius of 20 miles from this port, which meant that most of Hokkaido remained unbotanised. As a result of Maximowicz's enterprise the Japanese Flora became fairly well represented in herbaria, but we know far less about the plants he introduced. These went to Regel at the St Petersburg Botanic Garden. He seems to have introduced a number of plants, but the only one that seems to have been generally distributed was a particularly fine form of *Rosa rugosa*, a plant that was not a novelty, having been in cultivation since about 1770.

There was yet another collector active in 1860 and this was an American, Dr George Hall. Among the plants he sent to the States were *Magnolia kobus* and *M. stellata* and the sterile form of *Hydrangea paniculata*, as well as the fine form of *Lonicera japonica* known as 'Halliana'. Many of his plants remained for some time in cultivation in the States, before they arrived in Europe, while, in the meantime, Japanese nurserymen had realised that they could build up a good export trade in plants and so many Japanese plants arrived in cultivation both in Europe and in America, via Japanese nurserymen. The opening of the Suez Canal in 1869 had shortened the journey considerably. Still Hokkaido remained unbotanised and in 1877 Veitch sent the 26-year-old Charles Maries to Japan to collect for his nursery. By now there was no restriction on movement in Hokkaido and Maries spent much of his time in the neighbourhood of Sapporo.

'We left our horses at a woodcutter's hut, about 1000 feet up the mountain; my object being to see what species of firs were forming the distinct black band round the top; but my object was not to be fulfilled today, for I found after I had ascended 2100 feet that it was perfectly impossible to get up that way. I therefore returned leisurely and I came upon two fine junipers; one was *Juniperus japonica*, the other in the way of *J. rigida*, but creeping along the ground.' I would interpolate here that the name *J. japonica* has been give to forms of *J. chinensis* and it is not clear what plant is meant here; the prostrate juniper was *J. rigida nipponica*. 'I also found magnificent specimens of a deciduous Magnolia, with flowers as large as those of *M. grandiflora* and deliciously scented; in fact in some of the vallies we crossed the scent was quite overpowering. A beautiful Styrax abounded everywhere and masses of pink and reddish rhododendrons. Large Umbelliferae, some of them 15 feet high, spread out their heads over the confused masses of Actinidia, Glossocomia and Artemisia.'

This trip was being made in July. The black band of firs turned out to be a new species, later named *Abies mariesii*; the magnolia must have been *M. hypoleuca* (syn. *M. obovata*), but it is doubtful whether Maries succeeded in introducing this. As we learn, there were some disasters on his trip. He wrote in September 1877: 'Seed collecting has now begun. Almost every day I am on the mountains gathering cones of the various firs and pines grown here. I have to do it all myself with the help of my boy. It is impossible to hire a man now; everybody is at the fisheries. The gathering of fir cones is rather a difficult undertaking; many of the trees we climb are 150 feet high. We generally saw off the top of an Abies, as it is dangerous to trust one's weight on the slender top where all the cones grow. On September 28th I had finished my seed gathering, so packed up my collections and prepared to send them to Hakodate.... The ship set sail with ... a basket containing 100 small bags of conifer seeds. The following morning a messenger came telling us the ship was wrecked. I rode off immediately and found she was ashore about 15 miles down the coast.... My box of seeds was taken out, put into a boat and the boat almost immediately turned over and my box went to the bottom.... I consulted my boy what to do about the seeds and the Japanese volunteered to help me get more. We started to the mountains at once, just in time to catch the falling cones. We procured about 50 lb of seeds.'

After this near-disaster Maries left for China and Taiwan, not returning until late in 1878 to collect further conifers, and again in 1879. He returned to England in 1880. Among his introductions he is probably best known for the plants that bear his name: *Platycodon grandiflorum* 'Mariesii' and *Viburnum plicatum tomentosum* 'Mariesii' but he introduced many other good plants, which included no fewer than 8 maples, of which *Acer nikoense* and *A. rufinerve* are probably the best known. Among other of his introductions may be mentioned the Japanese horse chestnut, *Aesculus turbinata, Abies mariesii, A. sachalinensis* and *veitchii*, the popular variegated *Actinidia kolomikta, Elaeagnus macrophylla, Enkianthus campanulatus*, the first of the lacecap hydrangeas, *H. macrophylla* 'Mariesii', *Rhododendron dilatatum, R. oldhamii* and *R. tchonoskii Schizophragma hydrangeoides*, a very popular climber, *Stephanandra incisa, Styrax obassia* and *Viburnum dilatatum*, as well as other plants that have not persisted in cultivation.

After Maries the most important collector of Japanese wild plants was Professor Sargent of the Arnold Arboretum, who was in Japan in 1893. The list of his introductions is long, but few of his plants have entered generally into cultivation, although exception should be made for various *Malus* species, including *M. sargentii* and *M. tchonoskii*. In 1893 he met Sir J. H. Veitch who was travelling around much of the world and collecting plants in a somewhat dilettante manner. However, he did observe the Japanese cherries and arranged for a collection to be sent him by a Japanese nurseryman. According to his own account they all proved useless save one; this was the deep pink cherry, which was long known as 'James H. Veitch' but which is now sold as 'Fugenzo', and it would seem that it was this plant that started the large double Japanese cherries on their popularity as garden plants. Nowadays when we think of Japanese plants it is of the cherries that we think first, but this seems quite a recent development. As early as 1822 the name *Prunus serrulata* was given to a double white cherry, which arrived from Canton, and subsequently Siebold is said to have introduced some cultivars of which only the pink semi-double 'Takasago' can be credited to him with any certainty. In 1914 Sargent sent Wilson to Japan to study the cherries and bring back a selection, while other forms had been introduced from time to time. For example 'Kanzan', a rather fastigiate tree and the best-seller among these plants, was in cultivation about 1910, although it does not seem to be known who introduced it or the greeny-yellow 'Ukon' which arrived at the same time and which is unusually coloured for a prunus. The definitive collection of these cherries was made by Captain Collingwood Ingram in 1927 and we must be grateful to him for distributing propagating material to the nursery trade. He was even able to collect cultivars which the Japanese had thought were lost and now there are 48 different cultivars available in the nursery catalogues.

The main result from Wilson's visit in 1914 was not cherries, but the azaleas grown at Kurume on the island of Kiushiu. These are low growing shrubs that so cover themselves with flowers that leaves and twigs become invisible. Wilson brought back fifty different forms and most of these have persisted in cultivation, although they are on the borderline of hardiness in the U.K.

Towards the end of the last century there was a tendency among some landowners to have a Japanese garden, often created by Japanese gardeners. They tended to be rather stereotyped with a bridge over a lake, a stone lantern, a bronze crane, and plantings of Japanese maples, kaempferi irises and the long-racemed *Wisteria floribunda* 'Macrobotrys' (syn. *W.f. multijuga*). They were always regarded as an exotic pastiche and had no effect on garden design in general. Even so the influence of Japanese plants on garden design has been considerable and plants such as some of the cherries, *Malus tchonoskii* and some ornamental crabapples have also been used to beautify our streets.

One aspect which has not yet been mentioned and which includes plants both from Fortune's Chinese collections and from various Japanese plants is the use made of hardy bamboos. They are not planted very extensively nowadays, but at the end of the nineteenth and the start of this century, they were planted largely, being regarded as handsome, exotic, easily grown and having possible commercial value. They are, indeed, all these things, but they are extremely difficult to keep under control and very hard to remove if you decide they are not wanted. They are quite capable of making the part of the garden in which they are planted impenetrable, if they decide to thrive. They will go for decades without flowering, but once they do flower they are liable to die and it is this curious feature of their life cycle which has cleared so many gardens of bamboo jungles.

CHAPTER XIV

Foliage and Alpines

THE creation of so many hybrids that would flower continuously over a long period had encouraged the massing of flowers in beds and gardens had tended to return to the geometric patterns that had persisted from the Tudor knot gardens to the eighteenth century, but in the meantime an essential feature had changed. The formal gardens of earlier times had been designed to be seen from the house and at those times one lived on the *piano nobile*, our modern first floor, and so the owner was able to look down on his patterns and perceive them as a whole. In Britain in the nineteenth century one lived on the ground floor, so, if one wished to construct a geometric garden one had also to construct a terrace, so that it would still be possible to look down and perceive the geometric patterns. This was possible with very grand houses, but gardening was being increasingly pursued by the prosperous rising middle class and they had neither the money nor the space to indulge in such luxuries as terraces. The formal geometric garden tended to disappear and its place was taken by a less formal arrangement of flower beds and the interest tended to become fragmented. One looked at each bed rather than at the general ensemble.

Few, if indeed any, of us nowadays can remember Victorian bedding and the Edwardian municipal gardening would seem to have preserved all the bad features, while eliminating so many of its virtues. For example in 1860, although the scarlet geranium (in this case 'Crystal Palace

Scarlet') was much in evidence, they also used among geraniums, the white 'Madame Vaucher', the salmon 'Henry de Beaudot' and ''Christina' with its full habit and large trusses of deep rosy pink.' Among petunias the recommended plant was 'Holland's Petunia Queen', which had large bright rose flowers with a white throat, although there was a huge range of colours available. Another popular subject was the new Tom Thumb nasturtiums and here the recommended cultivar was 'Triomphe de Hyris' which had flowers described as 'large canary yellow with dark spots'.

In this same year of 1860 Shirley Hibberd criticised the bedding displays at Kew and at the Crystal Palace. This latter, he maintained, had far too many calceolarias, although 'The edgings of the beds being of Mangles's variegated geraniums save the calceolarias from being utterly obnoxious and do something towards robbing the mixture of scarlet and yellow of the vulgarity inherent in it.' It would seem, however, that bad habits persisted. In 1870 we find him writing: 'The once fashionable, but always vulgar, repetition of scarlet, yellow and blue has given place to softened shadings and gentle transitions; to the use of leaves as well as flowers; to the larger adoption of half tints and secondary shades—which are at all times more pleasing than violent contrasts.' Even in 1860 there was 'the use of leaves as well as flowers'. Hibberd notes a bed which contained a central circle of snow-in-summer (*Cerastium tomentosum*) around which was a broad band of blue lobelia and around this a further edging of the cerastium, as giving 'an effect as remarkable as it is delightful for its grace and chastity'. Nor was cerastium the only foliage used. Hibberd praised another bed consisting of variegated geranium interplanted with the crimson-leaved *Chenopodium purpurascens* (syn. *C. atriplicis*), while at Kew they were using the almost black-leaved *Perilla frutescens nankinensis*. 'But', Hibberd continues, 'the range of subjects for bedding enlarges rapidly. A vast number of our choicest stove plants prove as adaptable to our outdoor climate as did the *Aucuba japonica*.... All the new begonias with their grandeur of form and their splendid tones of bronze and silver and Tyrian dye grow in the open air as thriftily as burdocks and keep over winter in cool houses as easily as geraniums.... We may yet see *Caladium chantini* in circular beds.'

This passage is interesting as showing that British gardeners had started to use tropical foliage plants—the 'new begonias' were the first forms and hybrids of *Begonia rex*—at about the same time as M. Barillet in Paris in the Parc Monceau was making the 'subtropical garden' with which his name was associated. During the late eighteen-sixties and early eighteen-seventies this was particularly finely exhibited at Battersea Park, where it was under the direction of John Gibson, the same Gibson who had gone to India for the Duke of Devonshire in 1836 and pioneered the se of the Wardian case. Here the emphasis was particularly on large eaves, which resulted in the cultivation of many plants that are never een nowadays. Who, for example, has recently seen *Montanoa* (known t that time as *Uhdea*) *bipinnatifida* with leaves from 60 to 100 cm long r *Wigandia caracasana* with leaves 'of a sombre green, boldly veined nd undulated, measuring two to three feet in length and breadth'. These eaves also had stinging hairs, which cannot have made them popular vith gardeners.

It may well be that the start of this fascination for bold foliage was roused by the work of the retired French consul-general at Valparaiso, M. Anneé. On his retirement in 1846, even if not slightly before, he had tarted work in hybridising cannas. In 1869 a M. E. Chaté published a ook entitled 'Le Canna' in which he gives the parentage of these early ybrids, although it is fair to point out that the names he gives are not asy to identify. It is, however, clear that the object of Anneé's breeding rogramme was the creation of plants with very large, bold, leaves, while lowers were not regarded as ornamental as such. This changed in 1856 with the introduction of the tall, scarlet-flowered *C. warscewiczii* (it eems a pity that anyone with so unpronounceable a name as Warscew-cz should have been so outstanding a collector) and Anneé used this as well as the handsome *C. iridiflora* to breed cannas with attractive flowers n addition to their foliage. Around this time he also distributed his stock among various nurserymen including Chaté and Crozy of Lyon. Indeed, n spite of the fact that the work was done by Anneé, these early hybrids were known as Crozy hybrids. In any case it is doubtful if any of these early hybrids survive. The modern bedding canna derives from some of these early hybrids crossed with the American *C. flaccida* and were bred at Naples in the eighteen-eighties by Herr Sprenger.

Huge leaves were one form of attraction, another were coloured leaves and among perennials it was the various forms of *Begonia rex*, which, as we have seen, first became popular and these have retained their popularity to this day, when they, like so many other products of the eighteen sixties and seventies, are used as houseplants. Although Charles Simons discovered it in Assam in the eighteen-forties it does not seem to have reached cultivation much before 1858 when the nursery of Charles Linden distributed plants. However, by 1866 a Mr W.B.B., writing in the *Floral World*, said that there were available 'about sixty varieties of nearly equal merit'. W.B.B. thought that it was these begonias which had given the idea of subtropical bedding.

In the eighteen-fifties the brilliant-leaved caladiums had been introduced from South America. Nowadays they are regarded as rather difficult plants to keep going successfully, but *C. bicolor* 'Chantinii' was recommended to amateurs as being of the easiest culture.

A dark purple-leaved coleus had also reached cultivation at the end of the eighteen-fifties, but there was not much variation available until after J. G. Veitch's introductions.

In 1865, J. G. Veitch, whom we have already met in Japan, went to Australia and thence to various South Sea islands, which included Tonga, Fiji, the New Hebrides and the Solomons. He did not spend very long at any one place and was unable to go far from the ports as the natives were not always friendly and as Veitch observed: 'one may most unintentionally offend a prejudice and excite their anger', but in spite of this he brought back a large number of very attractive foliage plants including eight different cultivars of *Cordyline terminalis* and thirteen different crotons, both of which derive their popularity from these introductions. The cordylines were particularly attractive, but they were to be considerably improved by a freelance hybridist, a Mr Bausé, who was retained at different times by various nurserymen and who would seem to be responsible for most of our modern cultivars of this attractive plant. Veitch also brought back some new coleus, the spider tree, *Dizygotheca elegantissima*, the variegated *Oplismenus imbecilis*, the variegated *Pandanus veitchii*, while in 1860 he had brought back *Aglaonema commutatum* from the Philippines. It would not be exaggerating too much to say that a large number of our modern houseplants derive from this Veitch expedition.

The subtropical garden was one reaction against the glare of the massed bedding plants, but this glare was being considerably reduced by the introduction of plants with white or silver leaves, most notably *Centaurea gymnocarpa*, *C. ragusina* and *C. rutifolia*, as well as various artemisias and *Senecio cineraria*.

It was not only in the flower beds that an interest in foliage manifested itself. Although ferns had been grown in gardens since the earliest records it was only in the eighteen-fifties that the fern garden became an essential feature of the demesne. It was understandable that there should have been some reaction against the massed bands of the salvias and geraniums, but it could have manifested itself in other ways. What seems to have given the original impetus was the discovery of various wild plants that differed from those more usually seen. Some had many extra pinnules; some bore crested fronds; others were depauperate, with very small pinnules, while others were simply monstrous, as in the hart's-tongues with divided leaves. Suddenly the English, and even more the Welsh, countryside was filled with gardeners and nurserymen looking for aberrant ferns. These were slow to propagate and expensive to purchase. In 1866 Sim of Foot's Cray, who, together with Stansfield of Todmorden, had more or less cornered the fern market, was offering eighty-two different forms of the hart's-tongue fern *(phyllitis scolopendrium)* and to urchase one each of these would cost £38 17*s* 6*d*. In 1876 J. Smith, who ad been curator at Kew and who specialised in ferns, noted that tansfield was listing nearly 500 abnormal forms of British ferns in his atalogue. The original discoveries could only be propagated by division, ut spores from these abnormal forms were likely to produce further bnormal forms in their turn, so that the fern craze eventually wore itself ut by the multiplication of sorts. Even so ferns continued to be grown, as ey would happily clothe parts of the garden that might be damp or adly lit, where few other subjects could thrive. After 1918 the interest in rns waned, but it is just starting to reappear nowadays.

In the eighteenth century the rock gardens seem to have been largely lanted with ferns, but as the nineteenth century progressed the rock arden tended to become the alpine garden. We have already observed ne alpine garden at Hoole House, but this seems to have been exceponal and the alpine garden, as we know it today, seems to have been rincipally the creation of the nursery of Backhouse at York. In 1859 they onstructed a famous rock garden. William Robinson described it in 866 thus: 'Nearly 500 tons of millstone grit were employed in the ormation, and the whole looks like the facsimile of a choicely-selected it of Wales or Cumberland. By making the huge slabs and banks urround a little bit of water, every sort of aspect or nook that could be esired for a plant is at hand, and thus plants the most diverse in character re accommodated within a few feet of each other: under the shade of the reat stones by the water, New Zealand filmy ferns; a few feet higher up, atives of Arctic Europe; and on the top, in the full sun and free air, the hoicest gems of temperate parts of Europe and America.' Although obinson conceded that no other nurseryman could have undertaken the xpense or had the requisite cultural knowledge, the investment cannot ave proved unprofitable, as in the eighteen-sixties, at a time when most istorians would tell you that bedding was the only interest of gardeners, ackhouse started issuing catalogues solely of alpine subjects. These were refaced by cultural notes of the greatest interest and as valid today as hen they were originally written.

There were, at least, two other reasons for the increase in interest in lpines. The first was quite simply the improved rail service. Once it was ossible to leave London one day and arrive in Switzerland the next, it as much easier to visit the alps and many gardeners would bring back lants of the superlative alpine display. The interest seems to have been so reat that in 1869 the *Floral World* published an article by a Mrs T. W. Vebb, describing the methods by which she collected, looked after and nally established alpine plants.

There is, unfortunately, an element of snobbishness in gardening. I lways have a suspicion that one reason why the great landscape-gardeners tended to ignore flowers was that they were grown to a larg extent by the bourgeoisie and the aristocrats wanted something differen The large rock garden was expensive. It was not that the rocks co much—Backhouse in 1867 mentions a price of nine shillings a ton— was the transport and the subsequent building that came expensiv Many members of the middle class could not afford this and tended t make their rockery out of burrs, lumps of calcined bricks, which no on can make attractive. Victorians liked to spend money ostentatiously an a large rock garden became a perfectly acceptable status symbol. It wa also extremely colourful and regarded as being in excellent taste. A ma of blue lobelias could be produced by anyone; a mass of *Gentiana vern* might not look so different at a distance, but it was very much harder t achieve. I do not want to overstress the social implications of the earli alpine gardens, but they should be borne in mind. On the other hand the brought into cultivation a number of entrancing plants, that previous had been restricted to culture in pots. They continued in popularity unt 1914, made a temporary return between the wars, and are now only see in large public institutions such as botanic gardens. They are too exper sive and require too much labour for most of us nowadays, althoug alpines are still being grown as much as ever on raised beds and peat bed It is only the 'choicely-selected bit of Wales or Cumberland' that ha vanished.

CHAPTER XV

China III and the Sino-Himalaya

AS we have seen, it was theoretically possible after 1860 for Europeans to travel anywhere in China, but few seem to have availed themselves of the possibility. The sole exception known to me is a Frenchman sent out by his government in 1863. This was Gabriel Eugene Simon, an agronomist, who managed to reach Hupeh and Szechuan. His main interests were agricultural, but he does seem to have collected some. There is a sizeable list of plants introduced by him, but it is far from easy to relate the names to any used nowadays. We do know that he introduced the handsome pinnate-leaved tree, *Cedrela sinensis*, a couple of *Philadelphus* species and the graceful, late-flowering *Ligustrum quihoui* (M. Quihou was superintendent at the Jardin des Plantes at the time). His best-known introduction, the Bamboo *Arundinaria simonii*, came not from China, but from Japan. *Populus simonii* is Chinese, but has not proved successful in cultivation.

The most probable reason for the reluctance of plant collectors to visit the interior was the xenophobia of the Chinese, which often resulted in a markedly hostile attitude. It was not until late 1878 that Charles Maries, who had been so successful in Japan, came to China to collect there and his biographer in *Hortus Veitchii* observed that 'With the natives of China Maries did not succeed so well as with the Japanese, he was not sufficiently gentle, and was often threatened and occasionally robbed of his baggage.'

We can get some idea as to what conditions were like for foreigners from A. E. Pratt's *To the Snows of Tibet through China*, referring to an expedition undertaken as late as 1888. Before he started he was staying at Chang-yang, which sounds an idyllic place in his description, with the countryside full of honeysuckle, pink azaleas and white fragrant rhododendrons. 'After residing for two months here, reports were constantly reaching me that the natives had convinced themselves that my stay would bring them bad luck. One day I found a disorderly crowd at my house, and heard that a big meeting was to be held the following day to consider what steps would be taken to remove me. Two days later I found notices pasted on the trees all round, to the effect that any native who was found to be collecting for me or assisting me in any way would be bambooed, and stating that I was bringing bad luck to the district. At the same time I was threatened that if I did not remove immediately, I should be tied to a tree and beaten.'

Mind you, Pratt, like, one feels, so many Europeans abroad, was somewhat insensitive. He travelled up the Yangtse in a houseboat, which he had had painted white, the colour of Chinese mourning, 'as I thought it would be cooler'. This ominous craft arrived at Kia-ting-fu just as the Civil Service examinations were due to begin, so it is not surprising, although regrettable, that Pratt and his crew were greeted with stone-throwing and general displeasure.

Even as recently as 1928 foreigners were liable to be blamed for any contretemps. In that year Joseph Rock had been botanising in the hitherto unexplored Konkaling range, but when he expected to return to collect seeds he was told that there had been unusually bad weather since his first visit, that the natives were convinced that he was to blame and that his safety could not be guaranteed if he returned.

Apart from Simon, the only expedition to collect plants seems to have been that of Maries in 1878 and again in 1879. In 1878 he was at Chinkiang and Kuikiang, while in 1879 he ascended the Yangtse as far as Ichang. He introduced a number of good plants, which included the most graceful of all the Manna Ashes, *Fraxinus mariesii*, that attractive form of *Lilium speciosum* known as *gloriosoides, Loropetalum chinense*, an albino *Daphne genkwa* and *Ligustrum strongylophyllum*, but probably his most important introductions were *Hamamelis mollis* and *Primula obconica*. The primula was immediately popular, but the witch hazel remained in Veitch's nursery at Coombe Wood unrecognised. It was taken to be a form of the well-known *H. japonica* and it was not until 1898 that it was recognised and Veitch started to propagate and distribute it.

Maries returned from Ichang, saying that so far as he could see there was nothing of interest in the interior of China. We now know that he was right on the edge of the most exciting flora in the world and he has been blamed for turning back when he did. I think this blame is unjustified. There had been little new in the approaches to Ichang and it would not have been easy to foresee the sudden change that would shortly have taken place, had he proceeded through the gorges.

In the meantime knowledge of the Chinese flora was being learned from an unexpected source. We have seen how, in the eighteenth century, most of the Chinese plants to arrive in cultivation were sent by the Jesuit advisers to the Emperor and during the nineteenth century it was the part-time interest of many Catholic missionaries, mainly Frenchmen, which made known the incredible richness of the Chinese flora. The first of these had a very wide knowledge of all forms of natural history. Père Armand David, indeed, was so outstanding a naturalist that he was relieved, unwillingly, of his missionary duties and instructed to collect animals and plants for the Museum of Natural History at Paris. It is to him that we owe our first knowledge of the Giant Panda and his name is perpetuated for botanists in the Handkerchief Tree, named in his honour, *Davidia*. From the floral point of view his most important trip was that to Mupin, which took place in 1868 to 1870. His journal for this has been published and a few extracts will give some idea of his application.

'March 15, 1869. I make a long excursion in the nearby hills, but do not find much of interest. At a height of about 2500 metres I see an Abies or an allied genus, of a species I have not seen before. Among other plants I collect a Primula with pale pink flowers and a Veratrum with white flowers, that grows abundantly....

'The ill-will of the Chinese follows us wherever we go. Today we are alarmed at a rumour that an important mandarin of the Chengtu government is attempting to persuade the princes of Mantzu to exterminate all the Christians established in their states.... I think these rumours are spread deliberately in the hopes that we will flee the neighbourhood.

'March 22. I hear the song of a new bird like that of the European nightingale, which is unknown in China. I find several flowering plants, a rhododendron with yellow flowers, a fragrant member of the *Liliaceae*, a mysosotis etc....

'April 8. My young man and I collect a good number of insects and a lot of new plants. I have my fifth species of *Viola* and my fourth *Primula*.

'April 15. The large rhododendrons are in flower and I can already detect at least 7 different species. Also in the middle of a damp forest I find a magnificent Magnolia with purplish flowers, but, as yet, no leaves.

'April 19. I make a trip down stream and collect several new plants.... I realise more and more just how rich the flora of this district is, but I fear that my preoccupation with zoology will not give me time to make a representative herbarium.'

In spite of his fears and in spite of losing many specimens when his boat capsized, David's herbarium was still large. His new plants were published in the eighteen-eighties by Franchet under the title *Plantae Davidianae*. David had also collected a number of young rhododendrons, which included *R. orbiculare*, but we hear no more of these, so they were either lost in the boating accident or perished en route back to France. On the other hand some of his seeds were successfully germinated, including that relative of the Almond, *Prunus davidiana* and the hyacinth-like herbaceous *Clematis heracleifolia davidiana*.

David's herbarium was significant, because it was the first, but it was nothing like so extensive as that of the man he encouraged to continue his work. This was Père Delavay, who, between 1881 and 1888 sent to Paris over 200,000 specimens, covering over 4000 species, 1500 of which were unknown to science at that time. Maybe there were more, for fifty years after his death some of his sendings were still at the museum, unopened. Delavay also sent back seeds, but those sent to the Jardin des Plantes did not seem to do well. Later he followed the example of some of his colleagues, such as Père Farges and Père Soulié, and sent his seeds to the firm of Vilmorin, which was more successful than the Jardin des Plantes. It was Farges who sent back the first seeds of the davidia, although out of the thirty-seven he sent only one germinated. Soulié seems to have been the first to send back seeds of a good form of *Buddleia variabilis*, the popular butterfly bush. Delavay was stationed in Yunnan, Farges, who did not start collecting until 1892, was in Szechuan, while Soulié from 1886 was at Tatsienlu on the Tibetan frontier, so that between them they covered a lot of China. Moreover there were other missionaries botanising at the same time, of whom Padre Giraldi is the best known. Between them many admirable plants got not only into cultivation, but since the recipient was Vilmorin, into commerce. Among these were such important plants as *Deutzia purpurascens, corymbosa* and *vilmoriniae, Incarvillea delavayi, Decaisnea fargesii, Paeonia lutea, Sorbus vilmorinii* and a number of useful rhododendrons, including *RR. adenopodum, augustinii, ciliicalyx, discolor, fictolacteum, irroratum, racemosum* and *yunnanense*. All these and other plants got into commerce in the eighteen-eighties.

At much the same time the Russians were also exploring in western China. Przewalski's most important expedition was between 1883 and 1885, while Potanin made two important sallies, the first between 1884 and 1886, and the second in 1893 to 1894. Plants collected on these expeditions were sent to the St Petersburg Botanic Garden and some of these were then distributed to other botanic gardens, including Kew. Przewalski introduced a number of attractive alliums, among them the blue *A. cyaneum*, that popular shrubby honeysuckle, *Lonicera syringantha*, the attractive but difficult *Gentiana kurroo* and the harebell poppy, *Meconopsis quintuplinervia*. Potanin's plants have made less impression on gardens, although they did include one of the best hardy bamboos, *Arundinaria nitida*, and one of the most brilliant of berrying shrubs, *Viburnum betulifolium*. Presumably this remained at St Petersburg, as it seems to have been thought of as one of Wilson's novelties in 1901.

So far the British have made a poor showing in the exploration of the Chinese flora, although Henry Hance, who was in China from 1852 until 1887, amassed a remarkable herbarium; however he himself seems seldom to have left Hong Kong and collected very little personally and never introduced a single plant. Far different was the case of Dr Augustine Henry, who had joined the China service first as a doctor and later as an inspector of Customs. In this capacity he was stationed at Ichang and finding time lying heavy on his hands he started to botanise and sent some specimens to Kew, asking if they were interested. This was in 1886. Kew were delighted and encouraged him to send more. In 1896 Henry was transferred to Mengtze in southern Yunnan and two years later to Szemao, where he remained until his return to England in 1900. By that time Kew had received herbarium specimens of 5000 species. Henry also introduced a very few plants, including the tall lily named *Lilium henryi* in his honour and the handsome *Hypericum beanii*, which is perhaps better known as *H. patulum henryi*.

In 1899 Sir J. H. Veitch engaged the young Ernest Wilson to go to China to collect the davidia for his famous nursery. Veitch is reported to have told Wilson, 'Stick to the one thing you are after and do not spend time and money wandering about. Probably almost every worth-while plant in China has now been introduced.' Glosses on this erroneous statement were to be heard at frequent intervals during the next decades and it may still be as untrue now as it was then. Wilson was instructed first of all to visit Henry and learn where the davidia might be found. It was not an easy journey. Wilson got as far as Hanoi in Indo-China and then had to proceed on foot. This was just before the Boxer riots, when China was in the grip of intense xenophobia. Wilson had to pass through Mengtze, where the troubles were particularly bad. He got as far as the village of Laokai in June 1899 and found himself unable to proceed further. As time went by and he was still marooned he became so discouraged that he wrote to Veitch and to Henry, warning them that he might have to call off the expedition. Finally in August he obtained an armed escort to Mengtze and from there it was comparatively easy to reach Szemao. Henry wrote to him with the reassuring news that the gang of highwaymen who used to practise on that road had all been captured. While at Szemao Wilson sent back various seeds including the huge yellow jasmine *Jasminum mesnyi* (syn. *J. primulinum*). After receiving his directions, Wilson returned to Hong Kong for the winter and in 1900 went to Ichang to set up his base camp. In point of fact Henry had only detected a single davidia in all his travels. This was at Ma-huang-po, ten days march from Ichang. Wilson arrived there on 25 April 1900 to find that this single tree had been cut down for firewood. His journey had been in vain. After some reflection Wilson decided to spend the remainder of 1900 collecting in Hupeh, where he was; and the next year to make the thousand-mile journey to David's original locality in Mupin. To his delighted surprise Wilson found a davidia on 19 May and during the season he found ten others, all in widely separated localities. Even more remarkably all eleven trees fruited abundantly. In 1901 Wilson was to discover 100 davidias, but they bore very few seeds and, indeed, he was never to find seeds so easy to collect again throughout all his travels in China.

These seeds were received at Coombe Wood, where the Veitch nursery was, in the spring of 1901 and were sown under varying conditions. 'Some,' Wilson recollected later, 'in strong heat, some in boxes and pots and placed in varying temperatures, others (and the larger quantity) out of doors in a prepared seed bed. Some were soaked in hot water, some in cold, others were filed down—in short, everything that a skilled and resourceful propagator could think of was put into operation. Weeks passed, months passed and nothing happened. When I reached England at the end of April 1902 not one seed had germinated and grave fears were expressed—failure almost anticipated. I made it my first business to examine the seeds. Those indoors under various conditions, save for being blackened, exhibited no apparent change and no signs of germination. Those in the seed bed outside had been subjected to the winter's frost, and, on digging out a few, signs of change were apparent.... All was well. In a month or so thousands had sprouted and from this bed an assistant and I potted up more than 13,000 plants, of which nearly every one grew. Of the seeds sown indoors scarcely a single one ever germinated.'

Wilson was rather put out to find that Farges had already introduced the plant, but since from the thirty-seven seeds Farges had sent Vilmorin only one had germinated, he need not have woried; the fact that the plant is widespread in cultivation is entirely due to Wilson. Incidentally the first of his seedlings flowered in 1911.

In all Wilson was to make four expeditions to western China, the first two for Veitch, the last two for the Arnold Arboretum, where Professor Sargent was in charge, although for these last two expeditions Wilson seems to have had a few private subscribers as well, among whom was that great gardener, but rather eccentric character Ellen Willmott, which will explain a number of plants with the epithet *willmottiae* among his sendings. Oddly enough his second Veitch expedition, from 1903 to 1905, was mainly in Szechuan in search of alpine plants. His main remit was to reintroduce the Lampshade Poppy, *Meconopsis integrifolia*. This had been introduced by Farges in 1895, but no seed had been set in cultivation and the plant had been lost. Wilson reintroduced this and other species, while he was also able to introduce a number of attractive and easily grown Candelabra primulas, which included such favourites as *P. cockburniana* and *P. pulverulenta*. However Wilson's main interest was in woody plants and in lilies and the more conspicuous fruits from his second expedition were that fine rose *Rosa moyesii*, with its ruby flowers and enormous scarlet heps and a large number of excellent rhododendrons. Wilson's third expedition lasted from 1907 to early 1909, during which time he detected *Lilium regale* and he returned in 1910 to make a further collection. This had to be broken off prematurely when Wilson broke his leg in a landslide. The tripod of his camera was used to supply makeshift splints, but as his assistants were applying these on a narrow road, a mule train arrived. The road had sheer precipices above and below, so it was impossible either to move Wilson or to deflect the mules. Wilson had to lie in the road with a broken leg, while fifty mules stepped over him. He was not touched, but it must have been a horrifying experience. The leg was eventually rather badly set by a medical missionary and when he eventually returned it was feared at one time that it would have to be amputated. Fortunately this was not necessary and Wilson walked with a limp for the rest of his life, although this did not prevent him making further expeditions to Taiwan and to Japan.

His original sendings to Veitch were just coming into maturity when Veitch decided to terminate the business. In 1914 the lease of the Coombe Wood nursery ran out and there were no young Veitches to carry on the famous nursery, so Sir J. H. Veitch auctioned off the contents of the Coombe Wood nursery. This was bad enough for the Wilson plants, but it was even worse for the plants that William Purdom had been collecting for Veitch between 1909 and 1912. Although he had sent back such popular plants as *Buddleia alternifolia, Clematis macropetala, C. tangutica* and *Viburnum farreri* (syn. *V. fragrans*), they must have been minute in 1914 and it was not until Purdom reintroduced them with Farrer in 1916 that they achieved their present popularity. Owing to the fascinating account that Farrer has left of this 1914 to 1916 expedition, he has received the credit to which Purdom was really entitled, although this was almost certainly not Farrer's intention.

The number of new plants that Wilson introduced reaches 1000, a quite fantastic amount, although, naturally enough, by no means all have established themselves in cultivation. Even so the number that have is so large that there can be very few gardens in temperate climes that do not contain at least one Wilson introduction. The list includes 9 acers, of which *A. griseum*, with its peeling bark and brilliant autumn colour is probably the best known, 9 berberis, including the berrying *B. prattii, B. polyantha* and *B. wilsonae*, 3 birches, the small white-flowered *Camellia cuspidata*, 5 clematis, among which *C. montana rubens* has proved extremely popular, 5 corylopsis, 9 cotoneasters, 5 deutzias, 2 dipelta, 3 hydrangeas, including the large-leaved *H. sargentiana*, the beauty bush *Kolkwitzia amabilis*, 7 loniceras, including *L. nitida* once extensively planted for hedging, 3 magnolias, of which *M. wilsonii* has proved extremely popular, 2 philadelphus, as many as 65 rhododendrons, 9 new roses including those giant climbers *R. filipes* and *R. helenae*, 17 rubus, few of which have persisted, *Salix magnifica, Schizophragma integrifolia*, 8 sorbus, including *S. hupehensis*, with its attractive light berries and glaucous leaves and the huge-leaved *S. sargentiana*, 3 spiraeas, 3 styrax, 3 tilias (lime) and 11 viburnum. He also introduced many herbaceous plants and lilies among which *Lilium regale* and *L. davidii willmottiae* have proved outstanding.

In 1904 a rich amateur A. K. Bulley decided to send out a collector to China with the object of obtaining alpines, in which Bulley was particularly interested. On the advice of Bayley Balfour at the Edinburgh Botanic Garden he decided on George Forrest. Forrest's original experience would have been enough to put most people off plant collecting for life. He was in the midst of an attack on all foreigners and most of his companions were killed. He himself escaped after appalling experiences, which included nearly dying from starvation. One would not have blamed Forrest for feeling embittered, but in point of fact he seems later to have established considerable rapport with the Yunnanese. During his first expedition he supervised the seed collecting himself, but later he seems to have trained a number of Chinese assistants, who could be sent out to districts that had been earlier visited when the plants were in flower, so that a lot of ground could be covered each season. Forrest returned home in 1905 and did not leave for China again until 1910. This time he was financed by a syndicate of private gardeners and botanical institutions and this pattern was to continue for the rest of his career. He made in all seven expeditions between 1907 and his death in 1932, during which time he was more often in China than outside. He ranged as far west as Burma and also went up to the Tibetan Frontier.

Among his subscribers were many who specialised in rhododendrons and they offered him a bonus for every species new to science that he introduced. This meant firstly that he tended to concentrate somewhat excessively on rhododendrons and secondly that a number of new species were created on quite insignificant differences; many of these new specific names have now either been discarded or reduced to varietal rank. In spite of this the number of new rhododendrons introduced by Forrest was still very large, including the scarlet *R. griersonianum,* which has been so extensively used in hybridising and the enormous-leaved *R. sinogrande*. A plant that he seems to have thought little of, but which is easily the most widely planted gentian, is *Gentiana sino-ornata*, which adds so attractive a touch of autumnal colour to any garden with acid soil. *Pieris formosa forrestii* with its crimson new growth and its panicles of lily-of-the-valley-like flowers has proved of the greatest popularity. *Jasminum polyanthum*, barely hardy enough out-doors in Britain, but popular here in cool greenhouses and outdoors in warmer climes with its profusion of pink-flushed white fragrant flowers in early spring, was only introduced from his last expedition in 1931. *Camellia saluenensis* is attractive enough in itself, but crossed with forms of *C. japonica* we have the race of Williamsii hybrids, which are tending to supplant the old japonica forms with their rather large heavy flowers. The Williamsii are lighter and more decorative as garden ornaments. Forrest also sent back great numbers of primulas, of which *P. malacoides*, although needing greenhouse treatment, has become an important subject for the pot plant trade. He also introduced many primulas that have persisted in gardens as well as even more which it has not proved possible to preserve. At his death Forrest was credited with the introduction of 309 new species of rhododendron and even though that total must now be considerably less, it is still an impressive total.

It was not only rhododendrons that Forrest sent back and there were very few departments of the garden that he did not enrich, although, as we shall shortly see, many of his introductions survived for only a very short time in cultivation.

A. K. Bulley, having lost Forrest to his private subscribers, financed a further expedition in 1911 led by Frank Kingdon-Ward, who, like Forrest, was later to be financed by private subscriptions. Kingdon-Ward had wider interests than Forrest and was as much an explorer as a plant collector. Unlike Forrest he personally collected the seeds of his plants, so that the amounts tended to be smaller, but the quality was often superior. This would be particularly the case in a genus like *Rhododendron*, which is very variable and in which the same species may show admirable forms, as well as many which may be unattractive. In addition Kingdon-Ward extended the collecting range from Yunnan to Burma, Tibet, Bhutan and Assam in the region known as the Sino-Himalaya, where the Himalaya of India go eastward to the ranges in Tali and Szechuan. Like Forrest, Ward was continually introducing new species, but, from the garden point of view, his most successful expedition was probably that of 1924 to 1925 through Bhutan into southern Tibet. From this trip came the most popular of the blue poppies, *Meconopsis betonicifolia* (syn. *M. baileyi*) and the giant cowslip *Primula florindae*, both plants that have remained popular in gardens since their introduction. The ranks of yellow rhododendrons were also notably increased by Ward's sendings. The attractive *Rhododendron wardii* was found on his first expedition and later he sent the large-leaved *R. macabeanum* and that attractive member of the Cinnabarinum series, *R. concatenans*.

In 1914 to 1915 Farrer and Purdom went to Kansu on the Chinese –Tibetan border, mainly to collect alpines. Owing to Farrer's delightful account of this expedition in the volumes *On the Eaves of the World* and the *Rainbow Bridge* this is the best-known of all plant hunting expeditions, but comparatively few plants were brought back that have established themselves in gardens, while of those that have, two seem to have arrived in error. The threepenny-bit rose, *Rosa farreri persetosa*, appeared as a rogue in seed of *R. multibracteata*, while the pale blue *Gentiana farreri* was thought to be lost, when seedlings of another gentian also produced *G. farreri*. Two of the most notable plants from this Kansu expedition had previously been introduced by Purdom, but no attention was paid to them until Farrer's vivid prose drew the attention of gardeners to them; these were *Buddleia alternifolia* and *Viburnum farreri*, known until recently as *V. fragrans*. Our alpine gardens still bear *Aster farreri, Geranium napuligerum* and *G. pylzowianum* and some others of his introductions, particularly alliums, but many of his introductions failed to persist. Even fewer came from his last expedition to Burma in 1919, when he was accompanied by Euan Cox. The plants on the Burmese mountains were very desirable, though few places have sufficient rainfall to enable them to thrive successfully in Europe. But although the expedition may have not been very rich in novelties, it gave rise to some of the best descriptions of the triumphs and disasters of a plant-collector's life that have ever been penned, as I hope this extract will show:

'And what is that we suddenly behold—some strange tone of purple surely, in one tiny spark of colour on the cliff of the gorge among the purples and lavenders of the Irids and the Harebell Poppy (*Meconopsis quintulpinervia*)? Through the tangle of Juniper and Rhododendron I wrestled and tore my way to the foot of the cliff and up through the tangle of their impending pendent branches I struggled from ledge to ledge until the treasure was within my grasp. And behold a little poppy of the rarest and most radiant charm, a poppy too, that was obviously new to the pages of the *Pflanzenreich*, with a stature of only six or seven inches, and ample tasselly blooms of many petals, held boldly horizontal, of finest Coan silkiness, in filmy iridescent shades of blue and violet, like little Catherine-wheels woven from the purple prisms of the rainbow

(*Meconopsis lepida*). The Dainty Poppy is the darling and Benjamin of her race. From that moment of rapture I saw her more and more beautiful, with several flowers pendulous up her stem, in the alpine lawns of Thundercrown; but only on the less sunny exposures and slopes of the fells . . . never in the open grass. . . .

'Such a discovery sweetens any climb with an ecstasy that hardly even the slaughterers of a new dead beast can rival, and which no less fortunate mortals can hope so much as to understand. Now, while the bearers toiled onwards up the ridge with their burdens, I myself descended glibly into the depth of the ghyll and ascended on its farther side, in complete forgetfulness of bumping heart ... until I came to the steep open banks and ledges of rock above. Along these I traversed in continual raptures, with ever increasing exhibitions of the Dainty Poppy, dancing amid fine herbage up and down the broken scarfs of little cliffs, amid Harebell Poppies and golden little stars of Bethlehem, and a bewildering enamel of Irids. . . . Who was it who told me, in so loud and authoritative a boom that it held all Vincent Square enthralled, that China was 'played out'? . . . . The disappointments of China on Thundercrown alone, are represented by seven Primulas, five Poppies, five Androsaces, together with such a lavishness of other makeweights as would make the reputation of any European heights for themselves alone. . . .

'For as soon as you have emerged from the ghyll and left almost the last lingering trace of coppice behind ... you emerge at length upon the full glory of the alpine turf, and the botanical exhaustion of China leaps plain to view, dappling the huge lawns so densely with jewels of every colour as far as the eye can see that one seems to be treading some sainted Cinquecento Paradise of Fra Angelico. . . .

'But Thundercrown, as the peasants of the valley had warned us, is a mountain of no easy temper, and soon he left us in no doubt that he was affronted at our intrusion. Grim wafts of icy wind drove down from the summit ... and the air of Thundercrown grew ever colder and colder towards us, till we were chilled to the bone and retired to the shelter of the tents. Having failed to dislodge us by these comparatively mild and civil hints, the mountain then lost his temper and began to cry with rage, in long icy flaws of rain that swept down in steady torrents, lashed into spattering special furies every now and then by violent gales and hysterical sobs of tempest. . . . And now at last the full anger of the mountain was roused to make itself heard. Thundercrown lifted up his voice and howled aloud in volleys of bellowing thunder, announcing to all his brothers and sisters of Tibet this outrage he was suffering, this microscopic intrusion he was powerless to repel. Awfully his utterance resounded from the crags and precipices, black in the darkness of the storm, except when the lightnings lit them in a ghastly glare and was gone. It was a grim welcome into regions notoriously haunted of demons.'

Tibet and Bhutan were also explored between 1933 and 1949 by Frank Ludlow and George Sherriff. They were the first collectors to send their gatherings back by air, so that they were often able to send plants as well as seed. Their most fruitful expedition seems to have been in 1936, but they continued to send back good plants at all times. The tall yellow tree peony, *Paeonia lutea ludlowii*, comes from their 1938 expedition, while their last trip produced the popular red-flowered *Euphorbia griffithii*.

There were still more collectors in western China during the period between the two wars and there was really far too much material for any institution or private gardener to assimilate. Owing to the enthusiasm of some gardeners most of the rhododendrons were grown on, although of the numerous sendings by Ludlow and Sherriff of *Rhododendron bulu* I cannot find any record of the plant having been raised. Other plants either got neglected or failed to survive. From his 1917 to 1919 expedition Forrest sent back *Sorbus filipes* with 'crimson flowers and red fruits', which sounds highly desirable, but which never seems to have been in cultivation. Indeed there are apparently a number of crimson-flowered sorbus in the Sino-Himalaya which have never been introduced to western gardens. Another Forrest sending, *Spiraea calcicola*, is said to be 'a very lovely shrub', but where is it? Forrest described *Anemone glaucifolia* as a 'glorious plant' with leaves 'densely coated with silvery down' and flowers ranging 'in colour from clearest blue to shades of purple'. This was at least raised and given a First Class Certificate by the R.H.S. in 1922, but seems to have been lost to cultivation shortly after.

Politics makes it unlikely that European collectors will be allowed in the Sino-Himalaya for some time, so it is to be hoped that the Chinese will re-introduce some of these lost treasures. Also from time to time we hear of exciting new discoveries from China. Plants of *Theopsis* are like a golden yellow camellia and new species of *styrax* have been discovered. The treasure chest of flowers is obviously far from empty.

CHAPTER XVI *Finale*

IN 1891 Vilmorin wrote an article in the *Revue Horticole*, which made known, for the first time, the work of Monsieur Marliac-Latour at Le Temple sur Lot. This was the first successful attempt to produce hardy hybrid water lilies. The tropical nymphaeas had been grown in greenhouses for most of the century and hybrids had first been raised in Germany about 1859, but it had not proved possible to produce worthwhile hybrids of hardy sorts. Most of the hardy water-lilies available were white-flowered and tended to produce an excess of leaves to very few flowers. It is true that pink-flowered forms of the European *N. alba* and of the North American *N. odorata* and *N. tuberosa* occurred from time to time, but no one seems to have paid much attention to these. It might seem that the impetus to Marliac's work came from the introduction, in 1881, of the Mexican *N. flava*, which had attractively mottled leaves, as well as yellow flowers, and was nearly hardy. By hybridising this with the hardy *N. tuberosa* Marliac was able to produce hardy yellow water lillies. He also produced pinks and deep reds, using not only the pink forms of various hardy nymphaeas, of which *N. odorata* seems to have been his favourite, but also pollen from the tropical *N. rubra*. At the same time Laydeker, who started as Marliac's foreman and ended as his son-in-law, was creating a parallel race of miniature water-lilies, in which the tiny *N. tetragona* or *N. pygmaea* were used. The technique of raising nymphaea hybrids is somewhat difficult and Marliac tended to be reticent, but a few American nurserymen were also able to raise some valuable hybrids, otherwise Marliac had the field to himself. He worked for some time to raise a hardy blue water-lily, but was unable to do so and this is still a desideratum.

These hybrid water-lilies could only be propagated by division, so that at first they were scarce and expensive, but in the course of time the price came down, with the result that everyone wished to have these new plants in their gardens. If they had no water already, ponds were constructed. In the eighteenth century great store was laid by the use of water in gardens, but this had been employed purely for its picturesque effect and there had never been any thought of employing the surface as a receptacle for floral display. By a happy coincidence soon after the water-lilies became easily available the Chinese candelabra primulas, which liked marshy conditions, came into commerce, so that the ponds could be surrounded by a marshy area. At the start of the nineteenth century flowers had been only an episode in the landscape, by the end only the lawn remained without flowers of some kind.

It is interesting to trace the number of plants that were available in catalogues at different periods and for this I have selected a number of varying dates. We might as well start with that of Messrs Loddiges for the year 1804. Loddiges of Hackney were eventually to become the best stocked nursery, probably in the world, but in 1804 it was a good nursery but not pre-eminent. We are here concerned only with hardy plants, but at this time Loddiges were listing some subjects that we now consider hardy, such as the yulan, *Magnolia denudata*, the monthly rose and the tree peony among the greenhouse plants, which also included a few alpines, such as *Antirrhinum molle*. It will be borne in mind that in 1804 there were as many parts of the globe which had yet to be visited by plant collectors, yet even then Loddiges was able to offer 487 shrubs and trees and 994 species of herbaceous plants. Apart from roses there were few cultivars, just the occasional double form of a plant with single flowers and, somewhat rarely, plants with variegated leaves.

For our second exemplar I would like to take the English catalogue of the Belgian firm of Van Houtte for 1868. This is not altogether a satisfactory exemplar, as the Indian and Japanese rhododendron species were in a separate list, which I have been unable to find, so it may well be that a further twenty items should be added to the shrub species. Otherwise this list has 264 species of trees and shrubs and 583 herbaceous species. On the other hand, although the number of species is less, the number of cultivars is large. There were, for example, among the shrubs 18 sorts of japonica, 19 named lilacs, 17 large flowered clematis, 138 rhododendron hybrids and the huge total of 277 named Ghent azaleas. In the same way among the herbaceous plants were 6 kaempferi iris (the germanicas were given a separate catalogue), 32 named delphiniums, 58 peonies, 32 potentillas, 82 named phlox and 120 named gladioli.

The breeding of large-flowered clematis, which only started in the eighteen-sixties, must have proceeded very rapidly. As we have seen Van Houtte only had seventeen in 1868, but six years later he was offering sixty. This 1874 list not only lists the huge total of 247 tree peonies, but various other cultivars for bedding use, including 43 pentstemons, 16 named forms of *Erythrina crista-galli* 'Compacta', 82 named coleus, 45 named lantanas and 31 cannas; these latter described entirely with respect to their leaves; the flowers are not mentioned.

My next catalogue is of herbaceous plants only and was issued by Forbes of Hawick in 1909. This gives a total of 1067 species and well reflects the interest in herbaceous plants at that period. Forbes also offered numbers of hybrids and cultivars. For example there were 108 named antirrhinums and new introductions cost as much as 3*s* 6*d* per plant. There were 86 named Michaelmas daisies, 41 show and 25 alpine auriculas, 159 delphiniums, 63 named gaillardias, 29 helianthemum, 9 named hellebore hybrids, 49 germanica irises, 41 named kaempferi irises, 14 lantanas, 7 perennial lobelia hybrids, 38 montbretias, 228 peonies, of which 41 were singles, 40 tree peonies, 290 named pansies, one of which, 'Lord Waveney' was said to be double, 195 named penstemons, a genus for which Forbes were famous, and no fewer than 413 named phlox. There were also 179 different pyrethrums, 88 of which were doubles; there were 39 double potentillas, 16 double primroses and four double polyanthus; one would like to know what happened to these last. There was evidently still considerable demand for bedding plants and Forbes had 19 calceolarias, including a white-flowered one and 27 named verbenas.

The 1914–18 war must have drastically reduced stocks, but in 1923 you could still get 31 Michaelmas daisies, 27 peonies, but only 21 phlox, but on the other hand there were now 53 germanica irises, 14 named lupins, while Forbes had only been able to offer five colour forms of *Lupinus polyphyllus*, but on the other hand you could get 12 named astilbes and 14 named Oriental poppies, neither of which had featured in 1909.

My shrub catalogue, that of Messrs Gauntlett of Chiddingfold, is undated, but I would imagine it dates from about 1923, although some of the illustrations are dated 1909. The list includes a number of Wilson plants and even one or two from Forrest. The firm made a speciality of bamboos, so that the number of Japanese plants is probably larger than might be expected in some other nurseries at that time. The list also includes a number of subjects said to be suitable for walls, but some of these are far from hardy even under such circumstances. Large rhododendrons were, apparently, listed separately, although a number of dwarf species are included and they also list eighty six-hybrids. By this time the number of large-flowered clematis hybrids had dropped to thirty-two. Gauntlett's list contains the surprising number of 1005 species. I think it might also be interesting to see where these plants all originated and this is done most easily in tabular form. Let us first look at the herbaceous plants.

	Loddiges 1804	Van Houtte 1869	Forbes 1909
From Europe	687	303	567
Near East and Caucasus	50	56	120
India	0	17	55
Far East	34	33	59
Japan	0	39	51
Eastern North America	214	88	143
Western North America	0	21	71
Central America	0	6	11
South America	8	13	41
South Africa	1	2	23
North Africa	0	1	3
New Zealand	0	3	22
Australia	0	0	1

I should emphasise perhaps that we are only dealing with hardy plants. Loddiges' catalogue in 1804 had no fewer than 827 different South African species in their greenhouse section.

Here now are the woody plants:

	Loddiges 1804	Van Houtte 1869	Gauntlett 1923
From Europe	234	60	145
Caucasus and near East	20	23	39
From India	0	18 (plus rhododendrons)	48
The Far East	31	71	284
Japan	0	71	137
Eastern North America	200	91	113
Western North America	0	31	55
Central America	0	0	9
South America	2	6	65
New Zealand	1	1	66
Australia	0	0	37
South Africa	0	0	6
Madeira and Canaries	0	0	5

Although I have shown no Japanese plants as being offered by Loddiges in 1804, there are two or three Japanese plants included among the thirty-one from China and the Far East. A survey of respectable nurseries in 1975 gave a total of 508 species of woody plants and 559 of herbaceous plants. As the number of species has been reduced the number of hybrids has risen. Thus our shrub catalogue was offering 205 rhododendron hybrids, quite apart from azaleas, while among the herbaceous plants no species of *Heuchera* were offered, but there were fourteen named hybrids and similarly no astilbe species were offered, but a choice of twenty hybrids. The choice is, therefore, rather wider than the smaller number of species might suggest. Another factor to be borne in mind is that nowadays nurseries tend to specialise more than they did formerly. Some nurseries confine themselves to bearded irises or to day-lilies or to rhododendrons and they will have longer lists than the general nurseryman at the present day. There are always the exceptional nurseries like Veitch at the end of the last century and Hillier in our day, but it is the less ambitious firms that we have been analysing.

It will have been noted that no regard has been paid to either annual or biennial plants, nor, unless they appeared among the herbaceous plants, to bulbous subjects, but they would probably not alter the general picture significantly. It seems odd that, apart from lilies, China, which has supplied so many subjects for the garden, can offer very little and one wonders if there is a dearth of bulbous subjects in China or whether there is yet another treasury awaiting collection. Travellers mention attractive lloydias in the mountains, but none have been successfully introduced and there are certainly many desirable terrestrial orchids that have so far resisted any attempt at cultivation.

In 1838 the Reverend Henry Hill opined that 'our island may be compared to a vase emerging from the ocean, in which the Sylvans of every region have set their favourite plants, and the Flora of every climate poured her choicest gifts, for the embellishment of the spot round which Neptune throws his fostering arms.' The sentiment is just but the application somewhat insular. Although one gets the impression that Britain was keener on gardening than other countries—we seem to have sent out more collectors—the interest in exotic plants was widespread in western Europe and only slightly later in the United States. There were famous nurseries in France, Belgium, Holland, Germany and Italy throughout the nineteenth century. There are few places nowadays where exotic plants are not to be found. Probably the most widespread globally is the Australian Blue Gum, *Eucalyptus globulus*, which was at one time thought to be prophylactic against malaria and has been planted wherever climatic conditions will allow, from the Mediterranean to the tropics. It is certainly effective in draining marshy ground, although it will also tolerate drought conditions. When one considers that the majority of plant introductions has occurred in the two centuries between 1736 and 1936, the rapid transformation of urban and garden landscapes is amazing. Moreover many plants that are not particularly widespread in nature have been preserved through cultivation. Thus the flamboyant, *Poinciana regia*, never seems to have been common in Madagascar and is now extremely rare, yet it is to be found making avenues in all tropical cities, while in temperate climes the same may be said of the horse chestnut, which is rare in the wild and confined to a few stands in the Balkans. One might have expected the maidenhair tree, *Ginkgo biloba*, to be as extinct as all the other ginkgo species are, but it was preserved by the Chinese and brought to Europe in 1754 and extensively planted there and later in the United States and it must now be reckoned a common tree. In much the same way the Monterey pine, *Pinus radiata*, is confined to a single population of rather poor specimens on the Monterey peninsula in California, but it is a common plant of forestry in many parts of the world. Moreover some plants have naturalised themselves in other parts of the world. The Indian hedychiums tend to be weeds in Jamaica, *Robinia pseudoacacia* is widespread in northern France, while the Australian *Acacia dealbata* is to be found apparently wild in Mediterranean France.

It is obvious that plant introductions must affect garden design, but the effects are not immediate. In the first place there is no guarantee that plants will behave in cultivation as they do in the wild. The Monterey pine, for example, gets much larger in cultivation. Again one can have only the vaguest ideas as to the shape and dimensions of mature trees. When Lobb introduced the wellingtonia in the early eighteen-fifties the plant was accompanied by drawings and by descriptions, which would have told the landscape gardener that he had a pyramidal evergreen in question. But he would have no idea as to how rapidly it would grow or how large it would become. At much the same time Fortune had brought the golden larch, *Pseudolarix amabilis*, from China. If the garden designer thought that this would take the place of the European larch in his plans he was mistaken. The plant thrives on the Continent, but is a poor doer in the British Isles and seldom makes a large specimen. Since the majority of shrubs and trees that Fortune introduced throve in Britain this failure of the golden larch could not have been foreseen. In any case the effect tends to be a matter of species rather than of design. The case may be rather different in the matter of the hybrid rhododendrons. At one time belts of evergreens were planted purely for their evergreen effect and few evergreens could show much in the way of flowers. Once the *Rhododendron arboreum* hybrids appeared, it was possible to have belts of evergreens which in due season transformed themselves into flower borders, so that evergreens came into parts of the garden that they would not previously have approached. Other features also began to be taken into consideration by designers. One can scarcely imagine Sheffield Park, which has been designed with a view to showing the most brilliant autumn colours, being planted up in the way it has been in either the eighteenth or the nineteenth century. Indeed there is a tendency to select trees and shrubs not only for their flowers, but also for their fruits or for brilliant leaf colour either in spring or in the autumn. This point of view seems to be fairly modern and mainly dates from the introduction of some of the Himalayan cotoneasters and the brilliant berries of some Chinese berberis. Even so in the eighteen-sixties we find Shirley Hibberd advising the planting of beds with berrying shrubs and underplanting with the wild arum, which would also bear berries at the appropriate season, so it would seem that there was always a tendency to use fruits ornamentally. Indeed we find this in the eighteenth century when yellow-fruited hollies and hawthorns were propagated, so there must always have been some appreciation of features other than flowers and the present tendency has simply emphasised this. Even so this tendency has brought into prominence some plants that in earlier days would have only been grown by specialists. We may instance *Malus tschonoskii* with silvery young leaves, which colour most brilliantly in the autumn, but whose flowers make very little impression; this is now even used as a street plant and from being a rare tree is becoming widespread.

It must also be realised that economics affect garden design as much as plant introductions. All the material is available for creating the great herbaceous borders of the late nineteenth and early twentieth centuries; it is the labour and the money to pay for such labour that is lacking, so the tendency is for more of the garden to be given over to shrubs and trees and less to herbaceous or alpine plants. Gardens are also getting smaller. Many of the great gardens of the past are preserved by the National Trust, but very few new large gardens are being created and the trend is towards small gardens that require no paid labour for upkeep. It is in these small gardens that the alpines and herbaceous plants are still abundantly grown. It is true that many plants were lost during the 1939–45 war, when nurserymen had to turn over most of their acreage to food production and it has not proved politically possible to reintroduce plants from the Far East. Even if it were possible inflation has made the price for mounting an expedition excessive, while mere novelty is not now sufficient to repay a nurseryman for large expenditure. To mount a plant-hunting expedition now means finding hundreds of subscribers, which makes the work of distribution at the end of the expedition yet a further charge on the time and temper of the collector. In spite of all this expeditions continue to be made and fascinating plants introduced, although most remain the preserve of specialist growers.

It is not easy to see what the future may hold, but it seems fairly certain that gardens will continue to exist. Logically the pleasure garden has no excuse for existence, but the charm of living plants seems to respond to some basic human need. If a garden is not available the house is filled with house plants and people even convert one room into what is termed a sun room, which the Victorians would have referred to as a conservatory. Indeed gardens appear to be a touchstone of civilisation. At a time when most of Australia was completely unexplored a botanic garden was started at Sydney, and one can think of no advanced civilisation where flowers do not appear to have played a part.

Index